CAREER GUIDE IN
Criminal Justice

Douglas Klutz
University of Alabama

New York   Oxford
OXFORD UNIVERSITY PRESS

Oxford University Press is a department of the University of Oxford. It furthers the University's objective of excellence in research, scholarship, and education by publishing worldwide. Oxford is a registered trade mark of Oxford University Press in the UK and certain other countries.

Published in the United States of America by Oxford University Press
198 Madison Avenue, New York, NY 10016, United States of America.

© 2019 by Oxford University Press

Library of Congress Cataloging-in-Publication Data

Names: Klutz, Douglas, author.
Title: Career guide in criminal justice / Douglas Klutz, University of
    Alabama.
Description: First edition. | New York : Oxford University Press, [2019] |
    Includes index.
Identifiers: LCCN 2018016492 (print) | LCCN 2018018429 (ebook) | ISBN
    9780190881313 (E-book) | ISBN 9780190881306 (pbk.)
Subjects: LCSH: Criminal justice, Administration of—Vocational
    guidance—United States. | Law enforcement—Vocational guidance—United
    States.
Classification: LCC HV9950 (ebook) | LCC HV9950 .K58 2019 (print) | DDC
    364.973023—dc23
LC record available at https://lccn.loc.gov/2018016492

9 8 7 6 5 4

Printed by Sheridan Books, Inc., United States of America

Brief Contents

Contents

CHAPTER 3   Intense Competition You Will Face 37

CHAPTER 9   Working in Law Enforcement–Public and Private Sectors   131

Preface

My goal in writing this textbook is to share insider knowledge about attaining a career in the criminal justice system. To date, I have created and facilitated over 1,000 unique internship opportunities for students with criminal justice-related agencies and companies. I have taught and advised over 10,000 students in my academic career. My former students have obtained careers in numerous areas in the CJ field including jobs in local, state, and federal law enforcement, the court system, the field of corrections, and the private sector. In terms of my teaching background, I have taught courses in Introduction to Criminal Justice, Criminology, Law and Society, Judicial Process, Law Enforcement, and Trials of the Century. Additionally, I have worked with students on independent research studies related to the field of criminal justice. I am also the Internship and Advising Director for the Criminal Justice Department at The University of Alabama. As Internship Director, I teach an internship course each semester as well. I have won multiple academic advising awards, including the "academic advisor of the year" at the University of Alabama. Over the past 4 years, I have been named by *RateMyProfessors.com* as one of the "Top 25 Professors in the Country," and in 2017–2018 was named #1 on their ranking list and also recognized in *Forbes* for this honor. *CriminalJusticePursuit.com* has named me as one of the top 5 student-rated criminal justice faculty members in the country. Prior to my career in higher education, I worked on a federally funded defense contract grant, and I also worked in loss prevention in the private sector.

This textbook provides a comprehensive career guide to getting hired and working in the field of criminal justice. It covers all facets of our criminal justice system including law enforcement opportunities in the private and public sectors, court systems, correctional systems (public and private), and community corrections, as well as careers in private investigations, the bond industry, forensic psychology, and many other criminal justice-related career paths. Special attention is given to building and developing real-world skill sets like networking and "soft skills," interview preparation, succeeding as a student in higher education, developing cover letters and résumés, ethics and professionalism in the field of criminal justice and discussing actual job descriptions and minimum qualifications for criminal justice careers. Another goal of this textbook is to correct many of the common misconceptions regarding applying and working in our criminal justice system. There is much misinformation out there that needs to be clarified largely due to the popularity of fictional television shows and movies related to the criminal justice system. This textbook separates the myths from reality and provides a practical real-world guide to obtaining careers in criminal justice.

Reading this textbook will make you a more competitive applicant by covering what you need to know for CJ jobs in the real world. My intent in writing this is to help save you time, money, and frustration, which negatively affects applicants who do not have knowledge of how to successfully apply to CJ positions. Over the years in my work experience I have seen what works and does not work for students and career professionals. You want to get on the right track as early as possible in your career. Thank you for taking the time to read this textbook, as I sincerely believe it will greatly assist you with your career and professional development. Be sure to also check out the companion website for this textbook at www.oup.com/us/klutz. This resource will provide you with additional career-development information and links to helpful career resources.

I would like to thank the following individuals for their time reviewing *Career Guide in Criminal Justice*:

Amanda Humphrey, Mount Mercy University
Alina Istrate, University of Central Oklahoma
Charles E. Wilson, University of Detroit Mercy
Frank E. Jones, New England College
Nicole Doctor, Ivy Tech Community College
Sarah Jakub, Bucks County Community College
Elizabeth Barcena, Columbia Southern University
Kendra Bowen, Texas Christian University
Cindy Boyles, University of Tennessee Martin
Joseph Carlson, University of Nebraska at Kearney
Wendelin Hume, University of North Dakota
Coy Johnston, Arizona State University
Iryna Malendevych, University of Central Florida
Norman Rose, Kent State University
Walter Smith, Hazard Community & Tech College

I would also like to thank Dr. Rachel Rock, Dr. Alex Burton, and Dr. John Adams for their assistance and expertise with this textbook. Finally, I would like to extend a special thank you to Steve Helba from Oxford University Press and Patricia Berube from SPi Global for making this project possible.

Douglas Klutz, *University of Alabama*

1

Clearing Up the Many Misconceptions Regarding Criminal Justice Careers

INTRODUCTION

The field of criminal justice provides applicants with many exciting and rewarding career options. These jobs tend to come with good benefit packages and job stability as well. For example, under the Federal Employees Retirement System (FERS), law enforcement officers and firefighters can retire at age 50 with 20 years of service in a qualified position or at any age with 25 years of covered service. Those remaining in covered positions are subject to mandatory retirement when they hit 57 years of age.[1] Lack of jobs and a tight labor market get a lot of press these days, but this does not apply to many areas in the field of criminal justice. In early 2017, U.S. Customs and Border Protection (CBP) announced plans to hire 15,000 more agents.[2] Another recent job headline is that police departments across the country are tremendously short on police officers, and are eagerly looking to hire many more applicants. As of mid-December 2016, the Los Angeles Police Department was short nearly 100 officers.[3] Philadelphia had close to 400 vacancies unfilled for police officers.[4] The Baltimore Police Department even went to Puerto Rico to recruit police officers because it had such a massive shortage of officers.[5]

The cybersecurity world also has numerous employment opportunities. Showing just how intense the hiring demand is in this specific field, the Global Information Security Workforce study found that the field of cybersecurity is going to be 1.8 million workers short by 2022 based on its current hiring pace.[6] Here are a couple of other important findings from this study citing the immense demand for cybersecurity professionals in the workplace today[7]:

From the Real World
I talk with many employers in the cybersecurity space in the public and private sectors, and they consistently state there are many job openings in their field, but it is difficult to find qualified applicants with the specific computer skill sets they are looking for.

- 66% of survey respondents reported not having enough employees to address current cybersecurity threats.
- 70% of companies around the world are looking to increase their hiring of cybersecurity professionals.

With recent security breaches in companies like Equifax, Uber, Alteryx, CashCrate, Disqus, Target, Sony, Staples, P.F. Chang's, J.P. Morgan, Ebay, and Home Depot, the field of cybersecurity is still in its infancy and will be a hot hiring realm in criminal justice careers for years to come. To examine additional misconceptions about criminal justice careers refer to www.oup.com/us/klutz.

---

[1] Tammy Flanagan, "Officers' Options," *Government Executive*. www.govexec.com/pay-benefits/retirement-planning/2011/07/officers-options/34278/.
[2] "White House Orders the Hiring of 15,000 New Immigration Agents," NPR, February 22, 2017.
[3] "Police Departments Struggle to Recruit Enough Officers." *The Economist*, January 5, 2017.
[4] David Gambacorta, "The Philly Police Force Is Short About 400 Officers. What Does That Mean?" *Philadelphia*, April 18, 2016. http://www.phillymag.com/news/2016/04/18/philly-police-force-400-officers/#gbb4gxek4xOodIWm.99.
[5] Kevin Rector, "Baltimore Police to Spend $20K on Recruiting Trip to Puerto Rico," *Baltimore Sun*, June 1, 2016. http://www.baltimoresun.com/news/maryland/baltimore-city/bs-md-ci-police-recruit-puerto-rico-20160601-story.html.
[6] "Global Cybersecurity Workforce Shortage to Reach 1.8 Million as Threats Loom Larger and Stakes Rise Higher," *(ISC)²*, June 7, 2017.
[7] Ibid.

While the work is challenging and tough, there is an abundance of entry-level jobs available for those interested in careers in criminal justice. The criminal justice system also affords you the flexibility to even be your own boss through unique entrepreneurial opportunities. For example, with enough experience one day you might open your own bonds business, private investigation firm, or private practice as an attorney or forensic psychologist. This text will discuss the vast majority of criminal justice career options and how to get there, but first we need to address some "primer" topics as you begin to prepare to work in the criminal justice arena. Media depictions tend to dominate our perceived reality of institutions across society, and this is especially true pertaining to the field of criminal justice. A good example of media distortion and the criminal justice system is illustrated in the wedding cake model theory, where the small piece comprising the top of the wedding cake is glamorous and receives the most attention, but tends to cloud the view of the entire cake. In this case, the top piece of the wedding cake is analogous to famous trial-by-media cases like those of Casey Anthony and O.J. Simpson. Even though these types of cases make up a minute fraction of our overall criminal justice system, these same cases tend to garner the majority of our media's attention and therefore distort the public's perception of our justice system. [8] The large base of the wedding cake is often forgotten because it is not as attention-grabbing, but in reality this is where the majority of action in our criminal justice system takes place, with offenses like misdemeanors usually resulting in plea deals. Most everyone is distracted by looking at the top of the wedding cake when the bottom of the cake is actually where the primary substance is located.

If you want to be successful in your preparation to work in the criminal justice system, you must be able to separate the abundant myths from reality. We live in a world with a lot of hidden agendas, misinformation, and duplicitous intentions. You will need to be able to illuminate reality in order to plan and have a successful career, and to cut out all of the misinformation and distortions that are lurking out there. Chapter 1 will significantly contribute to accomplishing this goal of discarding misinformation in order for you to successfully pursue a career within the criminal justice system.

UNDERSTANDING MYTHS VERSUS REALITIES

Applying to work in the criminal justice system today is a highly competitive venture due in large part to popular television series and films portraying varying components of our criminal justice system viewed by large audiences. However, many of these fictional depictions are factually inaccurate and perpetuate certain myths that viewers mistake for reality. Even more troubling is the fact that younger audiences will often believe these myths when preparing for their future careers working in the criminal justice system, only to be greatly disappointed when the false narratives of these fictional depictions they mistook for fact lead them down the wrong path in planning their careers.

[8]Walker, S. (1985). *Sense and Nonsense about Crime: A Policy Guide* (pp. 24–43). Monterey, CA: Brooks/Cole.

From the Real World
I always ask my Introduction to Criminal Justice courses at the very beginning of the semester if they have heard about famous media trials like those of O.J. Simpson and Casey Anthony. Almost all have; however, very few students can give a basic definition of a plea bargain. Again, the media's influence shapes perceived realities about our criminal justice system.

From the Real World
To illustrate the point that public opinion often conflicts with actual crime data, I always ask students on the first lecture day of the semester whether they think the overall crime rate has increased or decreased based on what they have heard over the years. Almost unanimously, students think it has increased and are shocked to hear it has decreased by almost 50% since the early 1990s. Again, the media and sensationalism are at play here ratcheting up the fear index of unsuspecting viewers.

If you are seriously thinking about working in the criminal justice field, you must be able to separate these common myths from real life. Otherwise, you will waste a large amount of time and money, and ultimately be very frustrated with a likely fruitless outcome with your search for employment. This section of the chapter will focus on dispelling the popular myths lingering out there, and will help illuminate the facts you need to know in order to be successful as you prepare to work in the criminal justice system. Research shows that public opinion often conflicts with factual crime data[9]. This can largely be explained by audiences taking the high amount of sensationalism present in these fictional criminal justice television series and films as reality. Watching many of these fictional depictions of our criminal justice system leaves viewers thinking there are violent crimes occurring everywhere around them at all times. Just count how many times your favorite crime series uses the terms "unsub" (unknown subject)

and "perp" (perpetrator) these days. In fact, television viewership has actually been shown to make people more fearful of crime.[10] But actual crime statistics show that the violent crime rate dropped by 50% between 1993 and 2015.[11] These fictional depictions on television and in film do little to address the reality behind this longitudinal statistical trend of a falling crime rate. After reading Chapter 1, you will not be one of the aforementioned misinformed statistics duped by faulty fictional depictions of our criminal justice system.

Myth #1: The "Criminal Profiler"

In 1991, the film *The Silence of the Lambs* was released to widespread critical acclaim. Due to the popularity of the movie, the Federal Bureau of Investigation (FBI) experienced a surge in the number of applicants wanting to be FBI agents, just like rookie agent Clarice Starling (played by Jodie Foster) in the film. Agent Starling was tasked with tracking the illusive serial killer Buffalo Bill, with the help of the infamous antihero, Dr. Hannibal Lecter. The story behind the creation of this film is an interesting one. In the original novel *The Silence of the Lambs*, author Thomas Harris actually went to the

▲ Jodie Foster plays rookie FBI special agent Clarice Starling in the film *The Silence of the Lambs*.

[9]Julian V. Roberts, "Public Opinion, Crime, and Criminal Justice," *Crime and Justice* 16 (1992): 99–180.
[10]S. Eschholz, T. Chiricos, and M. Gertz, "Television and Fear of Crime: Program Types, Audience Traits, and the Mediating Effect of Perceived Neighborhood Racial Composition," *Social Problems* 50, no. 3 (2003): 395–415. doi:10.1525/sp.2003.50.3.395.
[11]John Gramlich, "5 Facts About Crime In the U.S. Pew Research Center. January 30, 2018. http://www.pewresearch.org/fact-tank/2017/02/21/5-facts-about-crime-in-the-u-s/

FBI and their newly formed Behavioral Science Unit (now called the Behavioral Analysis Unit). Harris wanted to create fictional serial killers for his novel based on real-life serial killers from the Behavioral Science Unit's actual case files. He was intrigued by real-life serial killers like Ted Bundy and Ed Gein and modeled certain aspects of Hannibal Lecter and Buffalo Bill after these real-life serial killers.

In the late 1990s, the fictional television series *Profiler* followed Dr. Samantha Waters, a forensic psychologist working with the FBI's Violent Crimes Task Force. In the show, Dr. Waters has a unique ability to experience visions into the inner workings of the criminal mind. Similarly, *Criminal Minds* has been around since 2005 and has been following fictionalized FBI special agents working in the FBI's Behavioral Analysis Unit. Many people are drawn to the field of criminal justice because they regularly watch these fictional depictions of our criminal justice system. Many viewers have been so intrigued watching the likes of *Criminal Minds* that they would like to become "criminal profilers" themselves. However, this is the first major myth concerning our discussion of careers in our criminal justice system. The reality is that the FBI does not even have a position called a "criminal profiler." Even the FBI's own website specifically says

From the Real World
Many high school students and students beginning their higher education I meet with say they want to be a "criminal profiler" with the FBI. When I ask them why, these students almost always cite popular shows like *Criminal Minds*. These fictional shows greatly influence their perceived realities about criminal justice careers.

▲ Cast of the popular hit show *Criminal Minds*.

their agency does not have a position referred to as a "profiler."[12] Yet many prospective applicants and students planning their careers have no idea about this fact because they base their perceptions on fictional depictions shrouded in myth rather than reality.

Myth #2: CSI Fictional Depictions Are Realistic

Another common myth surrounding our criminal justice system involves the *CSI* effect. CSI stands for crime scene investigations, and the term *CSI* effect was first reported in 2004 in a *USA Today* article with the growing popularity of the television series *CSI*.[13] The *CSI* effect refers to jurors tending to overestimate the importance of forensic testing techniques inside the courtroom due to myths perpetuated by television series like *CSI*. This is largely a product of people believing what they see on television even if it is purely fiction. The *CSI* effect also perpetuates the myth that a case can only be won with advanced forensic testing employed, and if these techniques are not used, the case automatically holds less weight in court. Recent research concerning the *CSI* effect shows that viewership of shows like *CSI* even predicted verdict preferences of prospective jurors. More specifically, viewers that watched primarily fictional depictions of these types of shows rendered more acquittals compared to viewers who did not watch as many fictional depictions of these *CSI*-type shows.[14] Attorneys struggle with correcting these misconceptions of jurors regarding the *CSI* effect. For example, a case might involve simple larceny-theft, yet the *CSI* effect compels some jurors to think there should still be expensive forensic tests conducted that would prove to be exponentially more expensive than the initial monetary value taken in the crime to begin with. The reality is that cases can be won with limited forensic evidence, or no forensic evidence at all. Not every case needs expensive and innovative forensic testing completed in order to be a win, contrary to popular myths involving the *CSI* effect.

Myth #3: Detectives Solve the Majority of Crimes

The next commonly believed myth in the field of criminal justice deals with detective and investigatory work. There are so many compelling films, books, and television series focusing on the detective who always solves and closes the case. Agatha Christie's famed detective Hercule Poirot comes to mind as one of the best examples. Nothing gets by Poirot, not even on the Orient Express.[15] But research tells us something different about detective work entirely. Research findings indicate that detectives actually

---

[12]https://www.fbijobs.gov/career-paths/special-agents, FAQs no. 19: "I want to be an FBI 'Profiler.' Where do I begin the application process?"
[13]Richard Willing, "'CSI Effect' Has Juries Wanting More Evidence," *USA Today*, August 5, 2004.
[14]D. E. Mancini, "The 'CSI effect' in an Actual Juror Sample: Why Crime Show Genre May Matter. *North American Journal of Psychology 15, no.* 3(2013): 543.
[15]One of Agatha Christie's most famed works is *Murder on the Orient Express*. A film adaptation of her famous book was released in November 2017.

solve a very small percentage of crimes.[16] In fact, research also shows that detectives spend the majority of their time chasing cold leads and cases that will likely never be solved. "Expertise" of the detective is not a real factor in whether or not cases are solved either.[17] Yet there are many myths surrounding detective work taken as reality due to the popularity of these fictional depictions of detectives, and many students want to enter detective work simply because they believe these false narratives seen on television and in films. These research findings involving detective work should not come as a complete shock though, considering that much of a detective's time is spent investigating cases that have gone cold. Leads dry up, witnesses move out of the area, and evidence deteriorates over time.

Myth #4: You Can Become a Detective without Relevant Field Experience

While we are on the subject of myths surrounding detective work, it is important to note it is nearly impossible to become a detective/investigator at the local law enforcement level without first putting in significant time as a police officer or deputy sheriff. The reasoning behind this is that your real learning curve in law enforcement occurs on the street with actual hands-on experience in the line of duty. While you obviously learn in the classroom, this is more "book" learning than applied learning. The classroom is not going to teach you how it feels to respond to a domestic violence situation that might have escalated even more seriously after the initial call for help, or the feeling of walking up to a car that you pulled over at 2:00 a.m. as the driver is fidgeting around and reaching under the seat. That type of applied learning occurs with experience in the field and is called experiential learning. This brings up the question, "Do better educated law enforcement officers actually make better overall police officers?" Research studies show that better educated officers do have fewer citizen complaints and are better report writers, but in terms of the overall function of being a highly proficient police officer, expertise is learned through putting in time working the streets.[18] In smaller local law enforcement departments, it can take around 3 to 5 years of experience as a patrol officer in order to be considered qualified to apply to detective/investigator positions. Larger local law enforcement departments have more competition, so it can take up to 4 to 7 years of experience as a patrol officer to be considered competitive for the detective ranks. The notion that you are going to be able to go straight from the classroom with no work experience to becoming an investigator in local law enforcement is a faulty one.

---

[16]Peter W. Greenwood, *The RAND Criminal Investigation Study: Its Findings and Impacts to Date* (Santa Monica, CA: RAND Corporation, 1979). https://www.rand.org/pubs/papers/P6352.html. Also available in print form.

[17]P. Greenwood, J. M. Chaiken, and J. Petersilia, *Criminal Investigation Process* (Lexington, MA: Lexington Books); John S. Dempsey and Linda S. Forst, *An Introduction to Policing* (Clifton Park, NY: Delmar Cengage), 303.

[18]John T. Krimmel, "The Performance of College-Educated Police: A Study of Self-Rated Police Performance Measures," *American Journal of Police* 15, no. 1 (1996): 85–96. https://doi.org/10.1108/07358549610116572.

Myth #5: Police Officers Are Always Immersed in Action Just Like in *Cops*

Yet another commonly believed myth needing to be dispelled comes from the television shows that actually do follow real-life law enforcement personnel, such as *Cops* and *The First 48*. These shows tend to garner more credibility than the purely fictional crime television shows because viewers see real police officers and detectives in their actual jobs. However, the problem with shows like *Cops* and *The First 48* is they only show a small snippet of the total job function in these criminal justice career paths. Usually this involves playing up the more action-oriented elements of the job. Many viewers see this on television, and think all police work involves constant foot-chases, arrests, high-speed car pursuits, and intense interrogation room showdowns. These same shows fail to properly portray the majority of police work involving the less action-oriented elements of policing like writing citations, submitting reports, and testifying in court. These aspects of the job are not exciting enough for television ratings, but are the reality behind the bulk of police work.

Myth #6: *Orange Is the New Black* Is a Realistic Portrayal of Prison

A fictional television series that has been met with great popularity in recent years is *Orange Is the New Black*. This Netflix series focuses on life inside a women's prison;

▲ Netflix's *Orange Is the New Black*.

however, it has been heavily criticized by former inmates about its unrealistic portrayal of prison life, and even how the show falsely glamorizes prison to some extent.[19,20] The show has also received flack about how it portrays correctional officers. *Orange Is the New Black* frequently shows inmates going without any supervision with correctional officers nowhere to be found. This is far from reality, as guards supervise inmates at all times to ensure safety for inmates and correctional staff.[21] *Orange Is the New Black* has also been heavily criticized with how it falsely portrays veterans as villainous correctional officers.[22] This is yet another example of a fictional portrayal of our criminal justice system failing to mesh with reality.

Myth #7: Courtroom Fictional Dramas Are Realistic

The final commonly believed myth pertaining to the field of criminal justice that needs to be clarified involves the *Law and Order* effect. This term refers to the popularity of fictional courtroom dramas like *Law and Order* that make it seem like life inside the courtroom is consistently rife with intense, lengthy, and drawn-out legal battles. In these fictional depictions, the prosecution and defense often have an epic duel worthy of a "You can't handle the truth!" moment during the trial phase of a case.[23] But when examining the realities behind the court system in the United States, we find that reality is far different from these fictional courtroom portrayals. The truth is that approximately 95% of criminal cases end with a plea bargain.[24] This means that a criminal defendant enters a plea of guilty in exchange for a more lenient sentence from the prosecution. There is a catch with this, though, as there is no dramatic courtroom battle once a plea bargain is entered. The case is closed once the plea deal is voluntarily accepted by the defendant. This means that only about 5% of all criminal cases actually find their way to the trial phase, and it represents a much different picture than the intense courtroom battles in fictional television shows and films would lead you to believe. The reality is that the courtroom is much more about quick "assembly-line justice" than it is about having epically long, drawn-out legal showdowns.

It is crucial for individuals thinking about working in the criminal justice system to be able to separate all of these commonly believed myths from the reality of working in real careers in criminal justice. In order to properly structure your career path, you

---

[19]How Real Is "'Orange Is the New Black'? Former Tutwiler Inmates Compare Experiences to TV, Movies," *AL.com*, June 15, 2016. http://www.al.com/entertainment/index.ssf/2014/08/do_tv_and_movies_reflect_reali.html.

[20]Keri Blakinger, "Don't Believe the 'Orange Is the New Black' Hype: How the Netflix Series Misrepresents Life behind Bars," *Salon*, July 11, 2015. https://www.salon.com/2015/07/11/dont_believe_the_orange_is_the_new_black_hype_how_the_netflix_series_misrepresents_life_behind_bars/.

[21]"A Guard's Life: The Reality of 'Orange Is the New Black,'" University of Cincinnati. https://cjonline.uc.edu/resources/news/a-guards-life-the-reality-of-orange-is-the-new-black/.

[22]Bradford Richardson, "Veterans Outraged over Anti-Troop Portrayal in 'Orange Is the New Black.'" *Washington Times*, July 14, 2016. https://www.washingtontimes.com/news/2016/jul/14/veterans-irked-troop-portrayal-orange-new-black/.

[23]If you are unfamiliar with this reference, you need to watch *A Few Good Men*!

[24]Lindsey Devers, *Plea and Charge Bargaining* (Washington, DC: Bureau of Justice Assistance, U.S. Department of Justice, January 24, 2011).

must understand the real-world application of these criminal justice careers, and not base it on what you see in the media, on television, or on the big screen. Turn off the television, finish reading this text, and you are already taking an important step in the correct direction to properly planning your career in the criminal justice system based on facts and reality.

WORK REALITIES IN THE FIELD OF CRIMINAL JUSTICE

The main takeaway from Chapter 1 should be to not base your decision to pursue a career in the field of criminal justice on any fictional depiction pertaining to our criminal justice system. There are certain work realities associated with many career paths in criminal justice which are seldom covered in popular television series and movies. Discussing this topic is not meant to be a "downer," so to speak, but to prevent you from having false expectations about these career fields and what you will encounter on the job. The following three points are work realities in many criminal justice–related jobs that are seldom covered accurately in fictional depictions of our criminal justice system.

1. Stress

In the field of criminal justice you will seldom encounter people at their best. Very rarely does someone call law enforcement when they are having a great day. You will often encounter people in dangerous and stressful situations, and this will also cause potentially stressful situations for you too. How you handle these frequent stressors is critical. Can you tolerate people yelling at you, giving you a hard time, and potentially lying to you? Will you be able to calmly diffuse tense situations as peacefully as possible, and not let anger and frustration get the best of you? How you successfully cope with these stressful situations will be paramount to how you perform your job. You will need to be able to always keep your cool and remain calm under intense pressures. Research shows that stress commonly causes health-related issues in law enforcement officers. Some of the most stressful duties as a law enforcement officer include seeing traumatic events and being involved in physical altercations with suspects.[25] Additionally, due to stress, research shows that law enforcement officers are at an increased risk for obesity, sleeplessness, and even cancer compared to the general population.[26]

Working in the field of criminal justice is often a seemingly thankless job. People might see negative media portrayals of various criminal justice personnel and automatically

---

[25]Maria Korre et al., "A Survey of Stress Levels and Time Spent Across Law Enforcement Duties: Police Chief and Officer Agreement," *Policing: A Journal of Policy and Practice* 8, no. 2 (June 1, 2014): 109–122. https://doi.org/10.1093/police/pau001.
[26]Ellen Goldbaum, "Police Officer Stress Creates Significant Health Risks Compared to General Population, Study Finds," University at Buffalo, July 9, 2012. http://www.buffalo.edu/news/releases/2012/07/13532.html.

think that *all* of these personnel members must perform the same way. You will not be popular with some people and the media will not have your back on many occasions. This brings up the question, "Can you handle a lot of these negative stereotypes concerning your profession and how people might perceive you?" It is pretty common in many criminal justice jobs to also see things that you will want to quickly forget. Will you be able to handle seeing graphic images on a regular basis? For some, this might prove to be too stressful because they cannot shake the stress these images cause to their psyche, but seeing these images is a reality of many criminal justice professions.

You will face many stressors working in the criminal justice arena. These stressors can include poor work-life balance, poor relationships with your supervisors, becoming frustrated with how the legal system really operates, and working long hours.[27] Coping with stressful situations and being able to properly diffuse these situations is a very important part of your job function. Failure to mitigate these stressors can cause premature burnout and negatively affect the overall quality of your life. Just know that by entering this field of work, you will be required to effectively manage highly stressful situations.

2. Work-Life Balance

Working in many criminal justice professions involves working long and irregular hours. Crime does not sleep, considering the peak hour for violent crimes committed by offenders 18 years and older is 10:00 p.m.[28] You might be stuck on a less desirable night-shift schedule for a prolonged period of time in your first job. Or you might be called out to a crime scene in the middle of your night's sleep on a moment's notice. This can prove difficult when it comes to maintaining a proper work-life balance. There is a high amount of burnout in many criminal justice professions largely due to a failure to maintain a proper work-life balance. Research has shown that burnout in policing is largely caused by emotional exhaustion and being over-extended at work.[29] It is important to put a healthy balance between your work and personal lives into perspective as best as possible from the start of your career, so you do not fall victim to early burnout, or even more detrimental consequences. Burnout can also lead to marital problems, issues with substance abuse, and even increased risk of suicide.[30] There will likely be opportunities for voluntary overtime, but tread with caution because taking on too many hours can also lead to premature burnout.

[27]M. H. Anshel, "Coping with Stress in Law Enforcement," in Ronald J. Burke (ed.), *Stress in Policing: Sources, Consequences and Interventions* (New York: Routledge, 2016).

[28]*OJJDP Statistical Briefing Book*. Online. http://www.ojjdp.gov/ojstatbb/offenders/qa03401.asp?qaDate=2010 (released on May 22, 2014).

[29]A. Malach-Pines and G. Keinan, "Stress and Burnout in Israeli Border Police," *International Journal of Stress Management* 13 (2006): 519–540.

[30]P. M. Hart, A. J. Wearing, and B. Headley, "Police Stress and Well-Being: Integrating Personality, Coping and Daily Work Experiences," *Journal of Occupational and Organizational Psychology* 68 (1995): 133–156.

From the Real World
When talking to former students working in the field of law enforcement they almost always cite working on the night shift as one of the most difficult adjustments to make concerning their job. The reality is in many criminal justice careers just starting out in your entry-level job you will be stuck working undesirable shifts and hours. Only through experience and gaining seniority will you be able to get the more desirable shifts.

The reality is that starting off in an entry-level position will likely get you the most undesirable shifts and work hours, but with experience and seniority you will be able to progress into a more desirable schedule. Just know that everyone has to start somewhere, and working the most desirable shift might not be possible in many criminal justice careers when you are just starting out in the field. Work-life balance will be very challenging your first couple of years on the job, but it will become easier as you get more seniority within your organization. It is also important to note that maintaining a quality sleep schedule is critically important. Even if you are working the night shift, you will need to maintain a consistent sleeping schedule during the day. Failure to maintain proper sleeping habits will adversely impact your health and your job performance. Research shows that not sleeping for 17 hours impairs a person's motor skills the same way as having an alcohol level of 0.05% in the bloodstream.[31] Sleep research has also shown that about half of the work-related accidents involving police officers were caused by overall fatigue.[32]

In order to maintain a healthy work-life balance working in this field, you will want to not only get good quality sleep, but also have positive outlets away from your job. Set aside this personal time in advance and do not let work consume you to the point of burnout. This will be very important to remember throughout your career and life as a whole. It will also make you a happier and healthier person if you consistently maintain this healthy work-life balance throughout your entire career. You want to put maximum effort into the quality of your work and job performance, but when it begins to encroach on the overall quality of your personal life, it is time to reassess how you are managing your work-life balance. Research shows that organizations not supporting a proper work-life balance have approximately 27% of their employees ready to leave within two years, while organizations fostering a health balance only have about 17% willing to leave during this same period of time.[33]

3. Danger

There are many inherent dangers you could potentially encounter working in the field of criminal justice. Traffic stops, undercover operations, domestic violence calls, serving warrants, conducting investigations with potential suspects, pursuing speeding motorists, and interacting with people in stressful situations can all come with inherent dangers. You might be confronted with a split-second decision which also proves to be a life-saving situation. There might not be a do-over, so making the correct initial decision is imperative. This is not a video game where you get extra lives or the ability to restart. The wrong decision could cost you your career, or even your life. The dangers in this field are often romanticized in fictional depictions, but in real life the stakes are always high and the margin for error is razor-thin. Scholarly research actually shows that law enforcement officers' life expectancy is lower than the life expectancy of the

---

[31]D. Dawson and K. Reid, "Fatigue, Alcohol and Performance Impairment," Nature 388 (1997): 235.
[32]B. J. Vila. Tired Cops: The Importance of Managing Police Fatigue (Washington, DC: Police Executive Research Forum, 2000).
[33]"Everybody Wins with a Healthy Work-Life Balance," Mark Royal, Hay Group Research Study, CNBC. https://www.cnbc.com/id/100720414.

general population.[34] On October 16, 2017, the FBI released their statistics on law enforcement officers killed and assaulted in the line of duty in 2016. Officers dying as the result of felonious acts increased by almost 60% compared to 2015, and 57,180 officers were victims of on-duty assaults in 2016 as well.[35]

Working in the field of criminal justice means you must always be alert and diligent in your actions. There are no days off, and letting your guard down for even a few seconds could end with tragic results. You must always be thinking one step ahead and be able to anticipate certain scenarios before they potentially occur. Oftentimes tragic consequences can be the result of rushing into a dangerous situation hastily without taking appropriate precautions. Danger in this field can never be completely avoided, but you can take steps to mitigate your risks. For example, instead of responding to a call alone that you do not feel comfortable with, you decide to call for backup and wait for your support to arrive if possible. Just know that in the field of criminal justice encountering danger is part of the job description. Know the potential costs and always be vigilant with your actions. If your job has you complete a training academy, training videos are shown to new recruits where a simple mistake or breach of protocol is met with deadly results. Showing these types of real-life situations to recruits conveys just how high the stakes are in the field of criminal justice.

SUMMARY

Chapter 1 seeks to dispel some of the most prominent myths surrounding our criminal justice system. The intent is to rectify these popular misconceptions before you start seriously preparing for your career in the field of criminal justice, and especially before you start applying to actual jobs with these potential misconceptions in tow. Reality needs to be understood before successful career planning can begin. The point of this chapter is not to discourage the reader about the field of criminal justice, but to clarify the numerous misconceptions and amount of misinformation out there about our field so you can plan your future career correctly. This will give you a huge head start against your competition because unfortunately many people interested in working in criminal justice professions will see these common false portrayals of the criminal justice system, and run with them in planning their future careers. Individuals unable to separate the myths discussed in Chapter 1 with reality will have very frustrating outcomes in their career planning. Television shows and films about our criminal justice system are very entertaining and enticing to watch, but they must be taken with a grain of salt and never used to seriously strategize career planning. You must always focus on reality and facts when it comes to successful strategizing for your future career plans.

---

[34]J. M. Violanti et al., "Life Expectancy in Police Officers: A Comparison with the U.S. General Population," *International Journal of Emergency Mental Health* 15, no. 4 (2013): 217–228.

[35]"FBI Releases 2016 Statistics for Law Enforcement Officers Killed and Assaulted in the Line of Duty." https://www.fbi.gov/news/pressrel/press-releases/fbi-releases-2016-statistics-for-law-enforcement-officers-killed-and-assaulted-in-the-line-of-duty.

Three Key Takeaway Points

1. Do not base your decision to enter the field of criminal justice solely on fictional depictions in television and film. There are too many false depictions out there to glean accurate information for your future career path in the criminal justice system.

2. Talk to real-world practitioners who work in the field, and seek to obtain real-world experiences in the form of internships, to see if you truly like the actual career field and what a specific criminal justice job entails.

3. Understand realities of working in the field of criminal justice. There are real inherent dangers, potential stressors, and difficulty juggling a healthy work-life balance to think about before beginning a career in this line of work.

ASSESSMENT QUESTIONS

1. How well do television shows and movies depict the reality of the criminal justice system?
2. What kind of work experience is needed to become a detective?
3. What is the faulty narrative surrounding "criminal profiler" careers?
4. What is the *CSI* effect?
5. If you are planning to enter the field of forensics, which major area of study will be the most beneficial to you based on the information found in Chapter 1? (Hint: Read the From the Real World sections in this chapter.)

CRITICAL THINKING EXERCISE

Why do you think fictional depictions of criminal justice careers in television shows and movies portray these careers inaccurately?

ACTIVE LEARNING ACTIVITY

Watch an episode of *Criminal Minds*, *CSI*, *NCIS*, or another popular fictional television show or movie pertaining to the criminal justice system. As you watch this fictional depiction, write down three elements that seem sensational or unrealistic. Be prepared to discuss these fictional elements in a class discussion.

KEY TERMS

Sensationalism – Tendency to present information in a manner to gain viewership and attention, but generally at the expense of complete accuracy.

CSI effect – Prospective jurors overstating the importance and amount of forensic evidence needed for a conviction.

Law and Order effect – Overemphasizing the actual criminal trial aspect of the courtroom, and under-emphasizing the amount of criminal cases ending with a plea bargain.

2

Planning Your Next Step in Higher Education

INTRODUCTION

Mapping out a successful higher education plan is vital to obtaining your desired career in the criminal justice system. There will be some variation in terms of who is reading this textbook, and where each reader is in their pursuit of a higher education program. Some readers will be reading this text who are already enrolled in a 4-year bachelor degree–granting college or university, while some other readers will be looking to enter the job market after earning an associate's degree from a 2-year academic institution, and other readers may be looking to enroll in a 4-year institution after completing their associate's degree at a 2-year institution. There may even be a few early college students still in high school reading this material as well, or individuals who have their high school diploma but are still weighing their options for higher education plans. So, to cover all of this potential variation, Chapter 2 will address information concerning 2-year and 4-year academic institutions in higher education. Criminal justice careers vary greatly in terms of the educational requirements needed to secure employment opportunities. Some career paths in the criminal justice system will even require an advanced degree beyond a traditional associate's or bachelor's degree. To make matters more complicated, some minimum education requirements found in job descriptions will technically qualify you for the position, but the applicants actually getting hired far exceed the minimum education requirements advertised. There is no one-size-fits-all approach when it comes to higher education, but the takeaway here is that careers in the criminal justice system require careful higher education planning in order to put yourself at the top of the stack of prospective applicants applying for any given positions.

The pay discrepancy between college graduates and everyone else is at record highs today. In fact, college graduates averaged 56% more in earnings than high school graduates did in 2015.[1] Furthermore, college graduates in the age cohort of 25- to 32-year-olds who are working full-time positions earned approximately $17,500 more per year than this same age cohort only possessing a high school degree.[2] But just simply jumping into a higher education program is by no means a guarantee of a job these days. Whether you are enrolled in a 2-year or 4-year academic institution, you must plot your way methodically through these higher education programs in order to best optimize your chances of securing an entry-level job in the criminal justice system. It is no secret that higher education is not only a big monetary investment, but also a large time investment as well. Recent research shows that almost

---

[1]Christopher S. Rugaber, "Pay Gap between College Grads and Everyone Else at a Record." *USA Today*, January 12, 2017.
[2]"Is College Worth It?" *The Economist*, April 5, 2014. https://www.economist.com/news/united-states/21600131-too-many-degrees-are-waste-money-return-higher-education-would-be-much-better.

70% of students graduating with a bachelor's degree graduated with student loan debt averaging $30,100 per borrower.[3] Thorough planning throughout your degree track will enable you to minimize costs and maximize overall preparedness to be a competitive applicant upon graduation.

Each year you are in a higher education program you are incurring costs and losing out on potential earned income. You want to be certain you are completing your academic career in an efficient manner, and are pursuing a course of study that will actually enable you to attain the career you desire in the field of criminal justice. There are many potential pitfalls out there to be cognizant of when it comes to higher education today. Failing to avoid these pitfalls can result in many years of frustration over things such as failing to qualify for a top job choice, and lost money spent on a poor choice of an academic course of study. Chapter 2 focuses on how to avoid these pitfalls, what steps to take to maximize chances of success in your academic program, and some desirable fields of study for criminal justice careers. For additional information on planning for your career in higher education visit www.oup.com/us/klutz.

WHAT TO DO WHILE WORKING ON YOUR ACADEMIC DEGREE

Enrolling in a higher education program requires a great deal of proactive planning. Make sure to diligently research the degree(s) you are considering attaining, and be sure these degrees meet the qualifications for the jobs you are interested in applying to post-graduation. One of the best ways to accomplish this from an early point in your academic career is to simply look at potential jobs you are interested in applying to in the future by examining actual job postings. See which specific degrees, skills, and abilities these employers are looking for in their job descriptions. Look specifically in the required qualifications section of the vacancy announcement. Use this as a barometer to plan your course of study. If the job vacancy announcement says that an applicant needs to be conversational in the Spanish language and possess computer programming skills, then you know by looking at this job posting that you need to allocate time to attain these skills *before* you start applying to these types of jobs. This underscores the importance of planning ahead to acquire specific job-related skill sets. It is important to note that your competition will be highly educated and skilled, so you need to find out degree paths and skills that are in demand in your

---

[3] "The Average Student Loan Debt in Every State," *USA Today*, April 4, 2017. https://www.usatoday.com/story/money/personal finance/2017/04/28/average-student-loan-debt-every-state/100893668/.

prospective job field, and that will help you stand out from the proverbial crowd of other applicants.

Keep in mind that simply possessing minimum qualifications for a job does not mean that your competition will not significantly exceed these minimum qualifications. More and more applicants are obtaining advanced degrees, certifications, and specific skill sets in areas coveted by employers. Do not make the common mistake of thinking you can take the path of least resistance and still come out on top in the job market. Obtaining desirable jobs in the field of criminal justice these days takes dedication, hard work, and quality career planning. Highly sought-after jobs in the criminal justice system are not easy to attain. There is always a lot of competition, and as a prospective applicant, you must think about how you are going to make your application stand out from the proverbial crowd of other highly qualified applicants. Maximizing your time in a higher education program will help enable you to accomplish this goal and stand out to employers.

TWO-YEAR ACADEMIC INSTITUTIONS VERSUS 4-YEAR ACADEMIC INSTITUTIONS

Two-Year Academic Institutions

Two-year academic institutions at community colleges and vocational colleges typically grant associate's degrees. Often these degrees are called an Associate of Art or an Associate of Science. Many students earning degrees at these 2-year institutions will look to transfer to a 4-year institution upon earning their associate's degree. One primary benefit of this strategy of earning an associate's degree first at a 2-year institution is that it will satisfy most of the basic studies or general education requirements at a 4-year institution for a fraction of the cost. These basic studies or general education requirements generally include courses in English, literature, history, natural sciences, math, and humanities. To illustrate the cost savings of completing these basic studies requirements at a 2-year institution, the average published tuition and fees at a 2-year institution is $3,440 per year for in-district students, as opposed to $9,410 at 4-year public colleges (for in-state students).[4] These annual costs skyrocket even more for out-of-state students, with public 4-year colleges averaging $23,890 per year in tuition and fees and private 4-year colleges costing $32,410 per year. Since two years is the average time frame it takes to complete basic studies and general education requirements at most academic institutions, a breakdown of costs over a 2-year time period at these various institutions is provided in Table 2.1.

---

[4]"College Costs: FAQs," Big Future. https://bigfuture.collegeboard.org/pay-for-college/college-costs/college-costs-faqs.

Table 2.1 Average Published Tuition and Fees for 2 Years[5]
Public 2-year institutions = $6,880
Public 4-year institutions (in-state) = $18,820 ($11,940 more expensive on average when compared to average 2-year institution)
Public 4-year institutions (out-of-state) = $47,780 ($40,900 more expensive on average when compared to average 2-year institution)
Private 4-year institutions = $64,820 ($57,940 more expensive on average when compared to average 2-year institution)

[5]Based on tuition information provided by CollegeBoard.org.

As evidenced by the data in Table 2.1, earning an associate's degree first and therefore completing the majority of your general education requirements at a 2-year institution can come at a tremendous cost savings compared to the average 2-year costs at a 4-year institution. Two-year institutions are sometimes looked down upon in terms of status and overall quality, however recent studies have shown that community colleges are often much underappreciated when it comes to measurements such as graduation rates.[6]

At the end of the day, you cannot worry about what others think of you but what best benefits your personal financial situation. However, if you are planning to earn a degree from a 2-year institution and then transfer to a 4-year institution, you must be sure to check with the 4-year institution prior to enrolling to *make sure* your credits will transfer. If the majority of your credits do not transfer to the 4-year institution from the 2-year institution, this negates the cost-saving aspect of starting at the 2-year institution in the first place. Contact the Registrar's Office at the 4-year institution you plan to enroll in order to get this specific transfer credit information. Getting confirmation in writing or through email is generally preferred so you have it as a matter of public record if any discrepancies arise down the road.

Some states have programs in place now where 2-year institutions and 4-year institutions align requirements so the transfer of credit hours between the two types of institutions is guaranteed. For example, Tennessee has the Tennessee Transfer Pathways program established to guarantee that all 2-year institution courses taken will be accepted at the 4-year institution and counted toward the completion of a specific degree program.[7]

Cost savings are not the only benefit of 2-year institutions compared to 4-year institutions. Two-year institutions generally have much smaller class sizes, and more individualized attention from faculty members because of the smaller student-to-faculty

[6]Kevin Carey, "Revised Data Shows Community Colleges Have Been Underappreciated," *New York Times*, October 31, 2017; Paul Fain, "Graduate, Transfer, Graduate," *Inside Higher Ed*, November 8, 2012. https://www.insidehighered.com/news/2012/11/08/high-graduation-rates-community-college-transfers.
[7]*Tennessee Transfer Pathway*. http://www.tntransferpathway.org.

ratio. At larger 4-year institutions, introductory-level general education courses are regularly taught by graduate students serving as Teaching Assistants (TAs) for faculty members. It is not uncommon at these large 4-year institutions to have your first year of study taught primarily by graduate students. This is not the case at 2-year institutions, where you will have an experienced faculty member teaching you throughout your two years of study. One final benefit of 2-year academic institutions over 4-year institutions is that you will have an associate's degree in hand after only two years of study should you decide to not go on through to a 4-year institution upon earning your associate's degree. If you decide to quit after two years of attending a 4-year institution, you have no degree in hand. There are many jobs available in the criminal justice field with just an associate's degree. These jobs are discussed in much more detail in Chapters 9 through 12. Starting at a 4-year institution will mean you *must* see 4 years' worth of study through in order to obtain a bachelor's degree, while beginning at a 2-year institution gives you the flexibility to stop after 2 years of study and still have an associate's degree in hand, or to continue on to get a bachelor's degree at a 4-year institution if desired.

▲ Earning any degree requires careful planning in order to save as much money as possible in tuition, fees, and expenses.

Four-Year Academic Institutions

Four-year colleges and universities grant bachelor's degrees at the undergraduate level. While a bachelor's degree is designed traditionally to be completed over the course of four years, this time frame can be expedited if a student takes advantage of summer courses, if the student took early college courses while in high school, if the student took advantage of Advanced Placement (AP) courses while in high school, and/or if the student takes advantage of the College-Level Exam Program (CLEP). CLEP offers a student the ability to take a standardized test administered by the College Board and earn course credit hours in lieu of actually taking the class.[8] While 4-year academic institutions cost much more on average annually than 2-year academic institutions, significant cost savings can be had if a student takes advantage of some of these aforementioned mechanisms. Four-year institutions also offer many scholarship opportunities for students. As a prospective or current student at a 4-year institution, one of the things you should do on a regular basis is contact the academic institution's scholarship office, and your major course of study's departmental office to inquire about any available scholarship opportunities. Scholarships can dramatically cut down on your costs at a 4-year academic institution.

Four-year institutions have some distinct advantages over 2-year institutions. The biggest advantage is earning a bachelor's degree instead of an associate's degree. Today's job market is extremely competitive and the reality is that many jobs in the criminal justice system are requiring a minimum of a bachelor's degree to be considered a competitive applicant. An associate's degree alone is not going to open nearly as many employment doors in the field as a bachelor's degree will. The best way to see this for yourself is to look at actual job announcements which will include minimum education requirements. Chapters 9 through 12 in this textbook also provide sample job announcements and their minimum qualifications. And even if a job announcement does not explicitly state that a bachelor's degree is required, you can bet that a lot of your competition will be applying with bachelor's degrees on their résumés.

Another distinct advantage of a bachelor's degree is the fact these degrees are one of the prerequisites to enter advanced degree programs. Without a bachelor's degree you will not be able to enter a law school program, master's degree program, or a PhD program. Many criminal justice careers in today's job market require advanced degrees in order to be a competitive applicant, and to be considered for advancement opportunities within a given organization. An associate's degree alone is not going to gain you entry into an advanced degree program.

Four-year institutions also have an abundance of academic and career resources. While these resources do come at a higher price, 4-year institutions offer extensive resources that can include individualized academic advising, writing centers for students, career fairs, career centers, alumni networks, and internship and research programs through your undergraduate major department. Taking advantage of these resources

---

[8]More information on CLEP tests can be found at clep.collegeboard.org.

provides excellent networking and career-building opportunities that many 2-year institutions do not have available in the same capacity.

One advantage initially attending a 4-year institution has over attending a 2-year institution and then transferring to a 4-year institution involves getting established in research labs early on in your freshman and sophomore years at the 4-year academic institution. Some really competitive graduate programs require a large amount of undergraduate research experience, and in order to obtain this experience you must join an undergraduate research lab. A good example of this is with clinical psychology graduate programs. A student interested in becoming a forensic psychologist would pursue this course of advanced study, and ideally you would join these research labs in your freshman or sophomore year of your undergraduate education at a 4-year academic institution. The goal is to have as much undergraduate research experience as possible over a 4-year degree program. Starting at the 4-year institution enables you to gain more research experience, and to get to know your faculty base in your major area of study better over the course of a 4-year program as opposed to a 2-year program. Two-year academic institutions are not likely to offer these types of research labs and experiences either. If you were to wait to join one of these research labs your junior or senior year when pursuing a bachelor's degree, you would be missing out on prime research time needed to gain admission into very competitive graduate programs.

A final advantage of starting out in a 4-year institution over a 2-year institution involves undergraduate internship opportunities. Many degree programs and major departments at 4-year institutions have internship programs established to enable students to acquire real-world work experience while pursuing a bachelor's degree. Ideally, you would look to start completing internships and building field experience as soon as possible during your bachelor's degree. If you started completing internships as a freshman, you could potentially graduate from a 4-year degree program with three to four internship experiences. Many internships in the field of criminal justice these days require you to be enrolled in an undergraduate institution in a specific major course of study, and some internships even require students to receive credit hours for completing the experience as part of the initial internship agreement between the academic institution and the internship agency. Two-year institutions do not typically offer the same structured internship programs because much of your time is spent completing basic studies requirements in the classroom.

As you can see, both 2-year and 4-year academic institutions have their advantages and disadvantages. There is not one definite correct path to pursue in higher education because there is so much variation in the field of criminal justice in terms of minimum education requirements across different job titles. The main takeaway though is that you need to conduct careful research pertaining to what your desired career path entails when it comes to higher education degrees. Examine actual job postings that interest you and see what is needed in terms of education requirements, and be as precise as possible in planning your higher education degree path.

THE IMPORTANCE OF SEEKING INTERNSHIPS THROUGHOUT YOUR ACADEMIC CAREER

One of your primary focuses while completing a higher education degree should be to complete internships. Internships help you build real-world work experience while you are in school, and they also provide excellent networking opportunities. Recent research shows that approximately 60% of the time a paid internship will turn into a job offer, while about 37% of unpaid internships turn into job offers.[9] Additional research shows that 80% of employers want graduates who have completed a formal internship.[10] You will find that many opportunities come your way in life because of who you know, and completing internships gives you the opportunity to get to know insiders within an organization. The old saying goes, "Who you know is more important than what you know." This will hold true for many opportunities in your future. In fact, a new research survey shows that almost 85% of jobs are filled through networking these days.[11] The need for networking in building your professional career cannot be underscored enough.

Internships also hold the benefit of enabling you to see if you actually like the details of a job before committing to work there full-time. Therefore internships are a great initial screening mechanism. Just think if you went through your degree program without an internship, then started your "dream job," only to find out you did not like the nature of the job once you started full-time work there. Completing internships along the way in your educational degree program will help prevent this type of nightmare scenario from occurring.

You should think about starting to look for internship opportunities as early as possible in your academic career in higher education. See if your academic program offers internships in your field for course credit hours. Many internships in the field of criminal justice require you to be actively enrolled at a college or university, and to also be enrolled in an internship-type course that grants academic credit hours for completing the actual internship. If you are at a 4-year institution, find out if your major or minor department has an internship director, and schedule a meeting with that individual to discuss the specifics about the internship process. If the academic department does not have a specific internship director, schedule a meeting with the undergraduate director of the program to see if they are aware of specific internship opportunities. If you still come up empty, plan to go to the career center at your school to meet with one of their representatives about internship opportunities. You can even contact agencies directly and look to secure your own internships if your educational institution has limited opportunities.

From the Real World
I have had numerous students over the years complete an internship with an agency "just because" to later find out that the student loved the internship and wanted to make a full-time job out of their internship experience one day. I have also had students seem dead-set on a specific future job, but then complete an internship with that agency and immediately have a change of heart about wanting that same job in the future. Think of internships as an excellent screening mechanism to see what you like and do not like in the field.

[9]Susan Adams, "Odds Are Your Internship Will Get You a Job," *Forbes*, July 15, 2012.
[10]Martha C. White, "The Real Reason New College Grads Can't Get Hired," *Time*, November 10, 2013. http://business.time.com/2013/11/10/the-real-reason-new-college-grads-cant-get-hired/.
[11]Lou Adler, "New Survey Reveals 85% of All Jobs Are Filled via Networking," LinkedIn, February 29, 2016.

The more internships you complete throughout your academic career, the better qualified you will be. Many graduates these days are frustrated to find out many jobs require 1–2 years of relevant real-world work experience in order to be fully qualified to apply for the position. The common questions comes up, "How do I get real-world work experience if I have been in school the whole time?" The answer largely has to do with completing internships. Ideally, you will complete your higher education degree with at least two internship experiences at a minimum. But the more internship experiences you have, the better. Completing one internship per year is an excellent strategy to maximize the benefit of internships by gaining directly relevant work experience while pursuing your education. This would likely leave you with three to four internships before you graduate depending on how quickly you complete your degree requirements. Remember to use the summer months wisely as well when it comes to acquiring work experience. Some internship opportunities are only offered over the summer months, and if you are not taking traditional classroom courses in the summer, look to utilize this time productively in a summer internship. For example, the FBI Honors Internship is a very competitive and coveted 10-week internship program offered over the summer months.[12] Applications for the FBI Honors Internship program generally start in August of the previous year for the following summer. Applicants interested in the internship for the summer of 2020 would apply in August of 2019.

Completing multiple internships during your academic career will fill your résumé with quality work experiences. It will also greatly expand your personal contacts and networking base. Should you choose to enter the work world directly after your higher education degree, an ideal situation would be to complete an internship during your last semester of study and then upon graduation, transition directly over to working full-time with that same agency you completed your internship with, or in a similar position with another agency. Internships are an extremely vital component of your academic career in higher education, and they are a necessity in today's extremely competitive job market.

THINKING ABOUT ADVANCED TEST PREPARATION

It is normal for your future career plans to change while pursuing a higher education degree. You might take a class that really intrigues you about a specific niche area, or you might complete an internship that piques your interest in a specific job title. If you are enrolled in a 4-year institution, you also might decide you would like to keep your options of going to graduate or law school on the table after you complete a bachelor's degree. Maybe you hit the job market after earning your degree at a bad time, and there are not a lot of hiring opportunities. Or you discover the career path you really want to pursue requires obtaining a specific advanced degree. These are all very common situations and you should

From the Real World

One of the great misunderstandings I see with students' perceptions about the job market today has to do with classroom experience versus real-world experience. Many students think their degrees alone will immediately secure them a desired job in their field. But most employers today want work experience in addition to the degree. You have to acquire work experience while in school to really be competitive in the job market. The degree alone with no experience will significantly hinder your chances of desired employment in your field.

---

[12]"Beginning a Career with the FBI: Honors Internship Program," *FBI Jobs*. https://www.fbijobs.gov/students/undergrad.

include pursuing an advanced degree program as one of your options for the future. A good strategy is to start preparing for the standardized tests required for entry into these advanced degree programs as early in your higher education career as possible. Entry into advanced degree programs like law school and graduate school programs is largely determined by standardized test scores. Grade point average (GPA) and work experience are also important factors, but scoring well on standardized admissions tests is crucial.

Many students are apprehensive when it comes to preparing for standardized tests. But if you start preparing early, and are diligent with your commitment to prepare, taking the actual standardized test will come as much less of a burden. Think of it in terms of preparing for running a marathon. If you tried to run a marathon with absolutely no training whatsoever until just a few weeks before the actual event, your results in the marathon would most likely not be stellar. But if you prepared consistently for months, or even years in advance for the marathon, you would likely have very positive results. You will find that advanced preparation is a great habit for a successful future, and preparing early for standardized tests is no different.

Identifying which standardized exam you will be taking is extremely important. The two tests you will most likely encounter when applying to advanced degree programs related to the field of criminal justice are the Law School Admission Test (LSAT) and the Graduate Record Examination (GRE). If you want to pursue law school you will need to take the LSAT. For most social science advanced degree programs you will be required to take the GRE. Some graduate programs actually require a subject-specific GRE test as well. The sooner you identify which specific advanced degree program you want to pursue the better. Just remember to start preparing as early as possible in your higher education career for these standardized tests if you think an advanced degree is a future possibility. Advanced degree programs and test preparation strategies are discussed in detail in Chapter 7.

LEARNING A MARKETABLE SKILL WHILE YOU PURSUE A DEGREE

In today's very competitive job market it is critically important to have specific skills that are in demand. Just think how frustrating it would be to find out your higher education degree had no market demand. This is why careful research must be conducted beforehand in order to find the skills and the degree concentration the employment market is demanding at that time. Two of the most marketable skills that have widespread application in the criminal justice career field are in foreign languages and advanced computer skills. These are two skill sets where you can really make yourself stand out from the competition. You should strive to become proficient in a marketable foreign language like Spanish, Mandarin Chinese, or Arabic when thinking about different career options in the criminal justice system. Not only will these languages open up job opportunities for you, but it could also mean more earnings over the course of your career. For example, research suggests that learning Spanish could translate into roughly $51,000 extra in your bank account throughout your professional career.[13]

Becoming proficient in specific advanced computer skills such as cloud and distributed computing, statistical analysis and data mining, and network information security will also help you get hired in today's job market.[14] There are numerous cybersecurity threats as data breaches and hacking incidents continue to increase in scope and sophistication. The key is to look at cybersecurity job postings and see the specific skill sets they are looking for, and then align your educational training accordingly.

An excellent strategy throughout your pursuit of a higher education degree is to work on mastering *at least* one of these in-demand skill sets like a foreign language or specific computer skill. Dedicate time each day to this endeavor. Stay committed and before long you will see impressive results.

Many of these skills can be learned on your own time schedule through language learning software and online tutorials. You can gain access to language learning software through a public library, so be sure to check with your college or university library first. Much like with foreign languages, you do not necessarily have to major or minor in something computer-related to still have marketable computer skills on your résumé. You can self-teach and acquire these basic skills on your own learning time. For example, coding is a marketable computer skill to have on your résumé in today's job market. There are free coding websites online like Code Academy where you can teach yourself how to code without any prior experience in the field.[15] Dedicate at least 30-minutes per day to these personal learning endeavors, and before long you will see impressive results and significantly bolster your résumé at the same time with in-demand criminal justice job skills.

From the Real World
I have personally known individuals who had very little experience with computers use free coding resources like Code Academy to become proficient in coding, and as a result these individuals secured very good-paying job as coders in the broader arena of cyber-security careers. Self-teaching can go a long way if the individual remains diligent with their course of study.

SCHOLARLY RESEARCH EXPERIENCE

While you are pursuing your degree in higher education, one often neglected area through which to gain experience and build your résumé is conducting scholarly research. This could be gained from working with a faculty member directly, or through joining a faculty member's research lab. Your goal here is to work on conducting scholarly research, and to potentially be listed as an author on a research paper and/or present a poster presentation at a research conference. Approach faculty members about working on research with them individually from an early stage in your academic career. Often their research specialties are published on the departmental website, or you can schedule a meeting with them to discuss their research interests directly. If you are a

---

[13]Albert Saiz and Elena Zoido, "The Returns to Speaking a Second Language," Working Paper 02-16, Federal Reserve Bank of Philadelphia, October 2002; "Johnson: What Is a Foreign Language Worth?" *The Economist*, March 11, 2014. https://www.economist.com/blogs/prospero/2014/03/language-study.
[14]Marguerite Ward, "The Top 10 Skills that Will Get You Hired," CNBC, October 20, 2016.
[15]https://www.codecademy.com.

hard-working student showing interest and initiative in the field, often faculty members will be open to you helping out with their active research. This is a great opportunity for you to network with faculty and build research experience on your résumé.

Gaining publications (even if you are listed as second or third author) is a great résumé builder while completing your academic degree. Scholarly research experience is also something graduate school programs really focus on in terms of your qualifications should you choose to apply to an advanced degree program in the future. Attending a research conference to complete a poster presentation is an excellent networking opportunity where you will meet people in your field of study, and it also looks great on your résumé. Scholarly research opportunities serve as a great way to build quality relationships with faculty members, and you will most likely list these individuals for professional references with your future job search. Oftentimes students will ask a faculty member for a letter of recommendation with minimal professional interactions with that same faculty member outside of the classroom. It is difficult for faculty members to write a quality recommendation letter without additional professional interactions with a student in this scenario. Conducting research with faculty members is an excellent means to add additional professional experience and interactions with faculty members outside of the classroom, and therefore strengthen the content of a faculty recommendation letter. Gaining research experience and getting to know your faculty members better is a win-win situation you should maximize while you are pursuing a degree in higher education.

BUILDING POSITIVE RELATIONSHIPS WITH FACULTY MEMBERS

Fostering and maintaining quality professional relationships with faculty members is something you should seek to accomplish throughout any degree program. Your former teachers could be some of the first people contacted by background investigators when you start applying for jobs. These background investigators will talk to former teachers about your personal character, and how you conducted yourself in your professional interactions with that faculty member. This really underscores the need to make a good impression from day one with your teachers. Always treat your interactions as professional business relationships with faculty members. Your reputation will precede you, and a bad report from a faculty member to a background investigator could cost you the job. The reality is that in just finishing your degree, you are likely to list at least two of your former faculty members as professional references on your résumé. But it does not just stop there, because background investigators will often show up in person (or call) other faculty members in your academic department to see what these other individuals have to say about your character and integrity. Next I present a "top-ten" list in order to help you achieve success in your relationships with your faculty members and in your academic career as a whole.

Ten-Step Academic Success Plan

1. Thoroughly read the course syllabus and write down important due dates for assignments and test dates at the very beginning of the semester. It is a bad look on your part to email a faculty member with something trivial that is clearly covered in the course syllabus. Professors take time to put their syllabi together, and you should take the time to review it thoroughly at the beginning of the semester.

2. Always arrive to class and submit assignments on time. Straggling in late to class all the time is not professional, and your faculty members will take mental notes on these kinds of things. Also, always having the excuse "the dog ate my homework" is not professional or responsible. Unforeseen problems do occur, but that is why you should always plan ahead to have your work and assignments completed early. Do not procrastinate and do not always have an excuse.

3. Put full effort into the course (this means preparing ahead of time!). Remember your academic work is laying the foundation for your entry-level career. A lot of success in life simply involves putting in more effort than the next person.

▲ Attending class lectures and remaining actively engaged in the classroom are musts for academic success.

4. Use proper email etiquette when emailing your professors. Faculty members get tons of emails. We live in an "instantaneous" world now with technology, and it might come as a surprise, but professors do not check their emails 24/7. Do not spam a professor with the same email repeatedly in a short period of time. If the professor is not answering your email, there is probably a good reason. Also, always address your faculty member by their proper title (Examples: "Professor, Dr., Mr., Ms., Mrs.). Never start out an email by not putting any proper address in there at all. All emails with faculty members should be treated as official and professional correspondence. Also, get into the habit of checking your email at least once per day. You never know when an important class-related email, or research or internship-type opportunity could come your way, and you want to respond in an expedited manner.

5. Do not make excuses and always take personal accountability. Way too many people have excuses these days (there is a famous saying about that). Taking accountability and responsibility is a great step in building a successful career and making a positive impression on your professors.

6. Never lie, fabricate, plagiarize, or embellish when dealing with faculty members. Word gets around if a student engages in these behaviors; always remember that your reputation precedes you. Engaging in these types of behaviors could also get you in big trouble with a judicial student misconduct board at your college or university. If you are on the fence whether or not something could be considered plagiarism, always check with your professor and the writing center at your academic institution.

7. Do not wait until the end of the semester to start caring about your grade. Care from the first day of class and this means *you* putting in maximum effort to get a top grade. One of the major "pet-peeves" of faculty members is a student who suddenly starts complaining and trying to negotiate their grade at the end of the semester. Grades are earned, not bartered or negotiated.

8. Have positive body language and demeanor while in the classroom and interacting with your faculty members. The last thing a professor wants to see is you slouched over your desk on your phone, sighing audibly in the classroom, or having earbuds in and telling the professor to repeat something. Remember to always convey professionalism, as this will help you stand out from the crowd.

9. Do not engage with other students regarding gossip or negative talk about your professors. Often word spreads about negative talk, and if it spreads to the wrong people, it is a bad look on you. Remember you are trying to avoid burning any bridges, so to speak, and are always engaging in positive impression-management with your future potential references. Avoiding "workplace gossip" is a good strategy to develop at any early point in your career, because it should be avoided as you enter the professional job world as well.

10. Meet with the faculty members in your academic discipline during their office hours (or another meeting time at their convenience) to introduce yourself, explain your career ambitions, and ask for their personal advice about your career plans. When

meeting with a faculty member for the first time, offer a firm handshake and maintain eye contact throughout your conversation. Do not interrupt the faculty member while they are speaking. Meeting with your faculty members is a great early step in your professional networking, and can provide you with valuable insight, giving you an advantage over your competition. One good piece of advice could save you thousands of dollars and years of time.

Maintaining a high GPA throughout your academic career is also very important. This is an easy barometer for employers to look at that shows dedication (or lack thereof) to your quality of work. Research shows that a higher GPA means higher income immediately following graduation.[16] A high GPA can also benefit in giving you certain pre-hire advantages when applying for jobs. For example, over the years the federal government has used the Outstanding Scholar Program as a special hiring authority to place applicants in entry-level positions. In order to qualify for this special hiring authority, applicants need to have a 3.5 GPA or higher on a 4.0 GPA scale for all undergraduate coursework.[17] Following the **10-Step Academic Success Plan** just discussed will go a long way toward ensuring your GPA remains high. You should strive to maintain a high GPA from the first day of your first year of higher education, until the last day of your final semester. Having a low GPA is something that is likely to hurt you professionally when attempting to gain access to competitive internships and employment opportunities. Be proactive and diligent in maintaining your studies, and attaining that high GPA will be well within your reach.

GETTING INVOLVED ON CAMPUS

One strategy to employ during your academic career is to get involved and join student organizations related to your field of study. This is an excellent networking and résumé-building opportunity. Research has shown that students who get involved on campus benefit through a positive impact on their GPA and overall perception of personal academic success while in school.[18] Look to assume leadership roles within these student organizations in order to bolster the leadership experience on your résumé. These kinds of leadership experiences will be a great discussion point to highlight in a future internship or job interview. Employers like to see applicants looking to assume leadership roles from an early stage in their career because it demonstrates drive and initiative. Many student organizations will have guest speakers who work in the field and offer a great networking opportunity. Student organizations also sometimes sponsor

From the Real World

From my experience, students who wish their GPA was higher tend to cite their first semester in college as the semester that had the most negative impact on their overall GPA. This is largely due to having misguided expectations of college work and getting behind in your studies because of improper time management. This underscores the need to take your academic work seriously from the very first day of your degree plan.

[16]Paul Oehrlein, "Determining Future Success of College Students," *The Park Place Economist* XVII: 59–67.
[17]"Outstanding Scholar Program," U.S. Centers for Medicare & Medicaid Services. https://www.cms.gov/About-CMS/Career-Information/CareersatCMS/downloads/osp.pdf.
[18]"Survey Instrument," *National Survey of Student Engagement*, Indiana University Center for Postsecondary Research, 2008. Retrieved from http://nsse.iub.edu/html/survey_instruments.cfm.

career fairs which employers in your field will attend to discuss potential internship and job opportunities. Student organizations present lots of great networking opportunities for your professional development. Take full advantage of career fairs through your academic institution because this offers an excellent networking opportunity for future jobs and potential internships. When attending a career fair, be sure to bring multiple copies of your résumé and do the following:

- Offer a firm handshake and introduce yourself to prospective employers and internship opportunities attending the career fair.
- Be able to articulate what you are studying, and what types of internship or career opportunities you are looking for.
- Ask agency representatives for specific tips related to attaining employment and internships at their agencies.
- Ask agency representatives for their business card, offer them a copy of your résumé, and thank them for their time.

▲ Get to know your fellow students. Doing so can lead to long-lasting friendships and networking opportunities down the road.

BUILDING QUALITY WRITING SKILLS

Take advantage of writing courses, seminars, and workshops offered through your academic institution. Visit your educational institution's writing center on a regular basis. Quality writing skills are extremely important to possess throughout your academic and professional career. Employers are finding writing skills to be in decline among graduates, so demonstrating sound writing skills will help you stand out from your competition.[19] Here are some basic tips to think about when looking to improve your writing skills:

- Practice makes perfect. The more you practice, the more comfortable and confident you will be with your writing skills.
- Be clear and concise. Get to the point without using a bunch of superfluous wording. Incorporate clearly defined, structured, and labeled headings and subheadings to organize your thoughts.
- Always proofread your work. Have a friend or your school's writing center look over your writing after you have proofread it.
- Be able to take constructive feedback. Do not take it personally if someone is offering you advice and suggestions on making changes to your writing. Listen to what they are saying, and look to incorporate their constructive criticism toward making yourself a better writer.

LOOKING TOWARD ADVANCED DEGREE PROGRAMS

It is important to note that many careers in the field of criminal justice do require advanced degrees, and there are really no shortcuts around this time commitment. There are many jobs in the criminal justice field where you must go well beyond an associate's or bachelor's degree to be found qualified and highly competitive for the position. For example, if you are interested in becoming a forensic psychologist and working with criminals sounds interesting to you, there is a lot of advanced academic work to be completed in order to attain a career in this space. On top of a bachelor's degree in psychology, you will need to complete a PhD or PsyD (Doctor of Psychology) degree in a clinical psychology graduate program. These advanced degree programs typically take 5 to 6 years to fully complete. In fields like forensic psychology, there are no real shortcuts to attaining an advanced degree. These degrees require a tremendous time commitment; unfortunately, students often look for the path of "least resistance," leading to frustrating results down the road because they failed to get the necessary advanced degree required for the

---

[19]Joyce E. A. Russell, "Career Coach: Are Writing Skills Necessary Anymore?," *The Washington Post*, May 22, 2011. https://www.washingtonpost.com/business/capitalbusiness/career-coach-are-writing-skills-necessary-anymore/2011/05/18/AFJLUF9G_story.html?utm_term=.af56f284571e.

job. Before you begin any degree path, look at actual job advertisements on career sites like *Indeed* and *Monster*, and examine qualifications required for the job.[20] If you see the job requires a PhD in clinical psychology, stopping after a bachelor's degree and thinking you are going to be the one exception to the rule in getting that job is not going to work.

Final Thoughts on Higher Education Today

There are over 5,000 colleges and universities in the United States today.[21] Often the choice of a higher education institution can leave an applicant feeling overwhelmed. The cost of college has skyrocketed in excess of 500% over the past 30 years.[22] You should do everything in your power to avoid accruing a large debt load throughout your academic career. Keep in mind that student loan debt will have to be paid back in your future *with* interest. A large debt total can hinder your ability to purchase big-ticket items like mortgages and automobile loans in the future as you look to start your professional life. There are numerous headlines published each month about the impending student loan debt crisis that is now surpassing $1.5 *trillion* dollars.[23] But there are many ways to keep your loan debt totals down throughout your academic career in higher education. Some of the best examples are to always search for scholarship opportunities through online resources like *scholarships.com* and your academic institution's scholarship office, look to take general education requirements at a community college after making sure the credit hours will transfer to a 4-year institution if you are pursuing a bachelor's degree, and if you are using financial aid to fund your education, taking out only the loan amounts you actually need for school and living expenses. Living large on student loans is never a good idea. Remember you will have to pay your loans back *plus* interest in the future. Keeping the costs down for your degree will pay significant dividends for your future.

REQUESTING REFERENCES AND LETTERS OF RECOMMENDATION

As you begin to apply to internships, advanced degree programs, and future jobs you will need at least three professional references. References are generally former work supervisors and faculty members who can best attest to your ability as a prospective applicant. Often your references will also need to submit letters of recommendation on your behalf. You need to know the proper etiquette and details when it comes to

---

[20]https://www.indeed.com and https://www.monster.com.
[21]Jeffrey Selingo, "How Many Colleges and Universities Do We Really Need?" *Washington Post*, July 20, 2015.
[22]Carolyn O'Hara, "Is College Worth the Skyrocketing Costs?" *Forbes*, July 10, 2014.
[23]Rick Rieder, "These 3 Charts Explain the Economic Side Effects of the Student Loan Crisis," June 28, 2017; Jeffrey Dorfman, "The Student Loan Default Crisis Is Being Caused by Promises of Debt Forgiveness," *Forbes*, July 7, 2017; Mark Kantrowitz, "Why the Student Loan Crisis Is Even Worse Than People Think," *Time*, January 11, 2016.

asking someone to be a professional reference for you. Here is a list of tips to keep in mind when it comes to requesting references and letters of recommendation:

- Create a list of potential references from former work supervisors and professors who know your work ability best, and that you believe will give you a positive reference. Make sure to select references who have had a lot of interaction with you so they can attest to your skills and the quality of work. A good reference can help you get a position, while a neutral or bad reference can cost you the position.
- Send a professional-sounding email to these potential references with your full name and "reference request" in the subject of the email. Always ask for permission before using someone as a reference. Ask these individuals if they feel comfortable in being a reference or writing a letter of recommendation for you. You do not want to make someone feel cornered and forced to submit a recommendation letter or to provide a reference. Asking someone if they feel comfortable providing a recommendation over email gives them an easier out should they say no than asking them in person. Emails are less personal, but rejection through email is less awkward for both of you.
- Give plenty of advanced notice for a letter of recommendation. A minimum of three weeks should be given to anyone who you are asking for a letter of recommendation. If the letter needs to be mailed, you need to provide the postage, envelope, mailing address, and any additional instructions your letter of recommendation writer needs.
- Provide the writer of your reference and/or letter of recommendation with specific details about what kind of work you have done with them. You should also include your résumé and what specific position you are applying for. Make sure to keep your references updated on what you are doing professionally if you plan on using them in the future. Sending someone an email requesting a reference when you have not corresponded with that person in years is not best practice.
- Send the writer of your reference and/or letter of recommendation a handwritten thank you note for their time and assistance during the application process.

Common Mistakes to Avoid With References and Letters of Recommendation

You just read best practices when it comes to requesting references and letters of recommendation; here are some common mistakes on this same topic that you should avoid at all costs:

- Not asking for permission to use someone as a reference, and that same individual receiving a random email or call telling them to provide a reference for you.
- Not giving a letter of recommendation writer enough time and notice to complete the letter. Three weeks should be given at a minimum.

- Sounding desperate. Telling a potential reference or letter of recommendation writer that they are your last hope. Desperation does not convey professionalism, and acting desperate also makes it seem like you have not properly planned ahead.
- Not providing adequate instructions and information for your reference or letter of recommendation writer with key details like where you are applying, what specifically you need from them, and how they need to submit their reference for you.
- Asking someone to be a reference who you have not had enough professional interactions with in the past. References will be asked for specifics on how they know you and about your work, and the less they know you the less information they will be able to provide. This makes for a weaker overall reference or letter of recommendation.
- Not thanking your references and letter of recommendation writers, and continually spamming them with more reference requests with no new information or updates. Always provide these individuals with updates about where you are applying and thank them for their time.

SUMMARY

Properly planning your academic career in higher education is of critical importance so that you can successfully transition to the next stage of your professional work career. After reading Chapter 2, you should know the specific focal points to pursue while obtaining your degree. These include acquiring field experience in the form of internships, looking to gain scholarly research experience, and joining student organizations where you look to assume leadership positions. You should also be familiar with certain situations to avoid, like not thoroughly researching what types of jobs you can get with your actual degree, not caring about maintaining a high GPA, and not fostering positive relationships with faculty members. Quality planning throughout your academic career will help maximize the opportunity for the start of a successful career. Proactive planning is key here. Always be thinking at least one step ahead.

Three Key Takeaway Points

1. Gain as much real-world experience in the form of internships as possible throughout your academic career. This allows you to network with real-world professionals, build relevant work experience on your résumé, and see if you really like that specific line of work.

2. Get to know your professors on a professional basis, and utilize them as a resource in planning your future career in the field of criminal justice.

3. Be proactive in maintaining a high GPA. It is much easier to lower a GPA than it is to bring one up. The 10-step academic success plan provided in Chapter 2 will help you maintain a high GPA.

ASSESSMENT QUESTIONS

1. Why are internships important to complete during your academic career?
2. What are the main reasons you should look to build positive relationships with your professors while pursuing your academic degree?
3. What are the two marketable skill sets in today's job market that you can teach yourself on your own time discussed in Chapter 2?
4. When should you start preparing for standardized tests required to gain entry into advanced degree programs?
5. What are two "pitfalls" discussed in this chapter that you should avoid while completing your academic degree?

CRITICAL THINKING EXERCISE

What are some specific drawbacks you can think of with an individual choosing not to complete internships during their academic career? And what about the drawbacks of not maintaining positive relationships with your professors?

ACTIVE LEARNING ACTIVITY

Schedule a meeting with your departmental faculty members in your major area of study. Use this as a professional networking opportunity, and as a chance to properly introduce yourself. Be able to articulate your projected career path, and ask these faculty members what suggestions they have for your career progression. Use this as an opportunity to inquire about research and internship opportunities as well. You might find this active learning activity to be a little nerve-racking, but it is good preparation for a future interview.

KEY TERMS

Graduate Record Examination (GRE) – Most widely accepted graduate admissions test worldwide.

Law School Admission Test (LSAT) – Standardized test created to measure skills that are needed to excel in law school.

Internship – A set period of time structured for an individual to gain real-world work experience from an organization.

3

Intense Competition You Will Face

INTRODUCTION

Competition is fierce in the field of criminal justice. One job vacancy can have hundreds, or even thousands, of prospective applicants. The Federal Bureau of Investigation (FBI) alone, on average, receives approximately 70,000 applications per year. But some years are even more competitive than others. A few years ago the FBI announced a mass hiring of approximately 3,000 new jobs and received 270,000 applications for those new positions![1] And the intense competition does not just center on jobs at the FBI. Thinking about applying to law school? About 350,000 people applied to law school in 2015.[2] Many career paths in the criminal justice system are extremely competitive, so you really need to think about how you are going to stand out in the sea of other applicants. This underscores the importance of conducting quality career planning. One very beneficial habit to get into early in your academic career is to begin looking at job announcements and the qualifications these jobs require. If your dream job requires a specific skill set, you should do everything in your power to attain that skill set before you officially apply for the job. This is where the proactive career planning comes into play. Chapter 3 will cover additional strategies and tips to help succeed against the intense competition you will face when applying to criminal justice careers.

It is also important to note that you should have contingency plans in place in case your first career option does not work out. There is little you can do if there is a hiring freeze, or an agency is simply not hiring at the time you are getting ready to apply for jobs. The old saying "Never put all of your eggs into one basket" applies to your job search. Having contingency plans should your first job choice not come to fruition will help limit disappointment and frustration because you will have backup plans to apply to many different jobs. Always have as many options at your disposal as possible. The more job options you are open to applying to, the greater the chance you will get hired and be off the ground running with the start of your career. Unfortunately, many students make the mistake of limiting their job options so much that it turns into being too restrictive and limiting when they apply to the job market. Chapter 3 will cover some other potential "roadblocks" to avoid when applying to the job market, and strategies to employ to help separate yourself from the bevy of other applicants in the search for criminal justice jobs. For additional strategies on separating yourself from the competition go to www.oup.com/us/klutz.

---

[1] "FBI Gets 270,000 Applications for 3,000 Jobs," *CNN.com*. http://edition.cnn.com/2009/US/03/17/fbi.hiring/.
[2] Christopher P. Banks, *The American Legal Profession: The Myths and Realities of Practicing Law* Washington,DC. (SAGE Publications, 2017).

TALKING TO "INSIDERS"

One of the first steps you should take to start separating yourself from the competition is to consult with individuals possessing work experience in the same field in which you are seeking employment. Discuss with them how they got to their specific positions, and ask for recommendations they might have for you to reach a similar position. These tips and strategies from insiders can prove to be very beneficial in planning your career entry point. Two of the most beneficial questions to ask any insider are:

1. What are some of the best pieces of advice you have concerning career preparation and how to be a competitive applicant entering this line of work?
2. What are specific pitfalls to avoid when formulating career planning to enter this line of work?

Another great mechanism to glean insight from insiders is to utilize online career forums. Sites like *FederalSoup.com* and *Officer.com* enable you to correspond with current and former real-world practitioners in the field of criminal justice.[3] Sites like *Glass-Door.com* and *Indeed.com* also have valuable hiring information and feedback from current and former employees working in similar positions to the ones to which you will be applying.[4]

LinkedIn is a professional networking site that offers a good medium to connect with real-world professionals in the field. Look up professionals on LinkedIn in the criminal justice jobs you are interested in applying to, and send them a personal message asking if they have any specific tips for you to be a competitive applicant. The worst they can say is no, or they may simply not respond. Taking the time to talk to real-world practitioners possessing work experience in the field you would like to enter can prove to be a huge advantage over your competition. Not only for the "insider" tips and tricks you will glean, but also for the networking opportunities as well.

When it comes to talking to insiders, contacting employers and seeking job-shadowing opportunities can provide excellent networking experience. Job-shadowing does not have to be a formal internship program, but just some time throughout the week where you follow a criminal justice practitioner in their line of work. This will enable you to meet people in the field and build your contact base. Volunteering is also a great mechanism for networking and meeting new contacts. Contact agencies where you would like to work or complete an internship in the future, and inquire about job-shadowing and potential volunteer-type opportunities. This can be the beginning of the foot-in-the-door approach discussed in the next section. Completing

---

[3] https://forum.federalsoup.com and https://forum.officer.com.
[4] https://www.glassdoor.com/index.htm and https://www.indeed.com.

internships throughout your academic career is also an excellent strategy for meeting and working with active criminal justice professionals. Internships provide real-world experience on your résumé and build your networking base.

FOOT-IN-THE-DOOR APPROACH

The foot-in-the-door approach refers to taking an entry-level job in order to start building full-time work experience. The reason this approach is important to discuss is that some of your competition will make the mistake of holding out for their absolute dream job instead of focusing on building entry-level work experience. It is perfectly fine to have top job choices, but when you pass up job opportunities or bypass looking at entry-level jobs because you become too enamored by a handful of dream jobs, that becomes very problematic and limiting with a job search. It is very difficult to land your ultimate dream job right away out of your educational career. The majority of the time you will need to work your way up the corporate ladder, starting with an entry-level position first in order to reach more desirable career opportunities. With this said, sometimes it is best strategy to simply get your foot in the door of the agency where your dream job is located, but again this will generally involve beginning at an entry-level position. The advantage with this strategy is you will be an employee of the institution where your ultimate dream job is located, and this will enable you to apply for future vacancies at your employer as an internal applicant. Applying internally comes with many benefits external applicants do not necessarily have access to. These benefits include already being in the agency system, knowing hiring personnel within the office, and having access to job announcements as soon as they are released.

▲ The foot-in-the-door approach is a very important strategy when it comes to entry-level employment opportunities. You will find it is far easier to work your way up inside an organization than if you were applying as an external applicant.

Another reality of the job market is that you will most likely not be coming out of your degree program making a six-figure salary and working in a coveted position requiring years of real-world experience. Many students tend to have unrealistic expectations when it comes to the prospects of their first "real" job. Overvaluing initial starting salary for an entry-level position is very common. Remember, it is referred to as "entry"-level for a reason. Having the notion that you can circumvent entry-level positions and automatically gain access to the higher-paying supervisory ranks is a common false perception students often have. You need significant work experience to gain access to the better paying jobs. The more professional work experience you have will only add to your value with prospective employers in the job market. Never look down on any job opportunity that builds experience on your résumé in your field when better opportunities are not present. It is better to be gaining valuable work experience in some related field to your career path, than it is to scoff at a job prospect while unemployed or because the job does not pay top dollar. Avoid gaps in employment on your résumé, and do not have the mentality that you are holding out for the perfect job. The perfect job opportunity may never come, or if it does, it is likely to require entry-level work experience.

And finally, be very careful about becoming a perpetual lateral "job-hopper." A lateral job-hopper refers to someone taking similar positions at different agencies because they always think a better job exists at a different agency in almost the exact same job role as their previous agency. An applicant who changes jobs every few months is a big red flag to prospective employers. Employers are looking for work experience, but they are also looking for applicants who will be stable and likely remain in their organization for some quality time. Put greater emphasis on staying in one organization and working your way up the ranks, than simply changing organizations all the time for similar job positions.

KEEPING YOUR RECORD CLEAN—BACKGROUND RECORD/CLEARANCE DISCUSSION

Working in the criminal justice system usually requires a very thorough and extensive applicant background check before an official hiring decision is made. One of the most important aspects of beginning to prepare to work in the competitive field of criminal justice careers is knowing what to expect and planning ahead for your background clearance process. Preparing for a background clearance is something you should strategize about and actively manage for many years in advance, and you should actively maintain a clean background throughout your entire professional career. Think of it as consistently maintaining a professional, clean, and law-abiding image. Many applicants are surprised to find out just how thorough and detailed a background clearance process can be with criminal justice jobs. There is good reason for how thorough clearance checks are, as hiring agencies want to make sure they are getting an applicant with strong integrity and with no major red flags on their record. Employers want to mitigate the chances of employee liability down the road. Background clearances are also expensive and resource-intensive. A Top Secret clearance costs the federal government on average $3,959 per background check.[5] With this cost in mind, employers want to

From the Real World
The reality is you are not going to be making $80K+ as a Special Agent in the FBI, or similar coveted positions, straight out of school without significant work experience. This is not meant to be deflating, but to interject reality into your perceptions of the job market. Your best plan of action coming out of a degree program is to take an entry-level position, gain full-time work experience, and then with more work experience look to advance to more coveted and higher-paying positions.

[5]Brian Fung, "5.1 Million Americans Have Security Clearances. . . ," *Washington Post*, March 24, 2014. https://www.washingtonpost.com/news/the-switch/wp/2014/03/24/5-1-million-americans-have-security-clearances-thats-more-than-the-entire-population-of-norway/?utm_term=.305ff4d55daf.

find the right applicant with a clean background history to avoid having to conduct multiple background checks on different applicants.

Many background checks now go back 7 to 10 years in an applicant's personal history. Background investigators will talk to your friends, former and current roommates, neighbors, present and former bosses and supervisors, former teachers and professors, and even other professors in the same academic department not even listed on your reference list. Investigators will ask these individuals about your personal character and integrity, how they personally know you, and about any potential red flags concerning your personal character. This underscores the need to constantly engage in impression-management, and to build quality relationships, stay out of legal trouble, and convey professionalism at all times. One misstep could potentially cost you a job. Often these missteps occur when hanging out with friends and succumbing to peer pressure, and engaging in questionable behaviors you would not ordinarily partake in on your own. If something seems questionable, risky, or makes you feel uncomfortable from a legal standpoint, simply do not engage in this behavior. Always avoid "burning bridges" in your personal and professional relationships; one severed relationship and bad recommendation could cost you a future job too. Negative perceptions and anecdotes can certainly come back to haunt you during your background clearance process. No one is perfect, but keep the blips on your background radar to a minimum.

During the background investigation phase, investigators frequently inquire about any kind of known drug and illegal substance usage by the applicant. The use of certain illegal substances and drugs can serve as an automatic disqualifier during the application phase. This can include using prescription medication in the absence of having an actual prescription. For example, Adderall is a prescription medication containing a combination of amphetamines and dextroamphetamines, and is frequently used to treat ADHD, and in some cases to treat narcolepsy. It is no secret that Adderall is also a popular "study/cram" aid for college students, and is commonly used by students for these purposes without a prescription. Using Adderall, and other prescription medications, without a prescription is an automatic disqualifier for some criminal justice agencies. Anabolic steroids used without a prescription from a licensed practicing physician are also considered an automatic disqualifier for many criminal justice agencies. Choosing to use prescription drugs in the absence of an actual prescription can come with serious ramifications during the hiring process and catches many prospective applicants off-guard. Think about the potential consequences *before* using these substances without a prescription.

Another popular topic in the vein of drug use pertains to marijuana. Twenty-nine states and the District of Columbia have now legalized marijuana use either medically or recreationally.[6] But even though many states have legalized marijuana use, the federal government has not. Prospective federal applicants need to keep this in mind. When asked during a federal background clearance process about prior marijuana use, and you

---

[6]"State Marijuana Laws in 2017 Map," *Governing*, September 14, 2017.

say, "But it is legal in my home state!" that will not be considered a valid excuse in the eyes of the federal government. Hiring policies regarding marijuana use have become more lax in recent years, but it is still not advisable to have used marijuana within the past three years when applying to most criminal justice agencies. The FBI defines varying forms of marijuana use as "the various forms of marijuana including cannabis, hashish, hash oil, and tetrahydrocannabinol (THC), in both synthetic and natural forms. A candidate's use of marijuana in its various forms for medical reasons, regardless of whether or not it was prescribed by a licensed practicing physician, cannot be used as a mitigating factor."[7] An example of agencies relaxing marijuana use policy actually comes directly from the FBI itself. The FBI used to have a policy where if you had smoked marijuana more than 15 times in your lifetime, that served as an automatic disqualifier for employment with the Bureau. That all changed in 2007 when the FBI loosened their marijuana use policy to allow applicants who had not smoked marijuana within the previous 3 years prior to their application to be qualified for employment.[8] Criminal justice agencies vary widely when it comes to their marijuana use policies, but best practice is just not to partake in any illegal drug use if you are planning on working in the field of criminal justice (or legal marijuana use if your state has legalized it, and you are planning to work in another state or in the federal government). It would be a shame to meet all other qualifications and then be disqualified because you had used an illegal substance.

While you are completing your initial background clearance paperwork it is very important to be honest and engage in full disclosure. Lying or purposefully omitting information regarding your background can actually result in legal action being taken against you. Even if you think a prior mishap on your record has been expunged, you still need to include this information on your background paperwork because some criminal background databases might still show this information to background investigators. Lying or omitting this information is almost always an automatic disqualification for your application, and could potentially result in additional legal consequences if the agency you misinformed decides to take legal action against you. Since the stakes are high when applying to criminal justice careers, always be upfront and honest when it comes to your background investigation, and when discussing personal information with background investigators.

Many agencies in the criminal justice field will use a polygraph examination to screen applicants in greater detail. Facing a polygraph examination is an intimidating experience, but as the old saying goes, if you are telling the truth you do not have much to be worried about. If you are administered a polygraph test, be honest, remain calm, and keep your breathing steady. Rapid changes in your breathing patterns can cause your pulse to elevate and this could send a signal to the polygraph examiner that something could be

---

[7]"Eligibility," FBI jobs, https://www.fbijobs.gov/working-at-FBI/eligibility.
[8]Massimo Calabresi and Zeke J Miller, "Up in Smoke: FBI Won't Change Rules on Pot Smoking Recruits," *Time*, May 21, 2014.

I have had numerous students over the years disqualified from an internship or job because of something they posted on social media. Keep your social media profiles professional and clean. I have also talked with many employers in the criminal justice field who say their first step with a prospective applicant is to conduct an online search to see what the employer can find about the applicant. The first hits in the search will usually be social media accounts because they tend to rank at the top of online search results. My advice is to deactivate all social media accounts when actively applying to jobs with the exception of a LinkedIn account containing information about your education and professional work experience. Especially avoid posting about controversial topics like political and religious debates on social media that a prospective employer could access.

amiss with your responses. Never attempt to beat a polygraph test. Full disclosure and honesty is paramount in the polygraph phase of a background clearance process.

One final area of your background investigation that is receiving a lot of attention in today's job market pertains to your credit history. In order to work in the field of criminal justice you want to maintain a meticulous credit record. A quality credit history tells a background investigator that you are most likely a responsible individual when it comes to your finances. Large amounts of delinquent unpaid debt not only sends the message to your prospective employer that you might lack responsibility, but it also means you could be at a greater risk of being compromised by another party because of your debt liability. In order to ensure your credit file is accurate and in good standing, use *Annualcreditreport.com* to check your credit history, and which credit accounts are currently active and inactive on your credit report.[9] This free resource gives you access to your credit report through the three main credit-reporting bureaus—Equifax, Experian, and TransUnion. You can get one report from each of these three companies every twelve months for free using *Annualcreditreport.com*. Having access to these credit reports will help ensure the information on your credit record is accurate, and you have not been a victim of identity theft where someone has taken out accounts under your name and ruined your credit record. Monitoring credit reports is a means to help thwart potential surprises during a background clearance. Always remember to be responsible with your finances, pay bills on time, and avoid delinquent debt.

A SPECIAL NOTE ON SOCIAL MEDIA

Social media is a very easy mechanism for employers to screen and disqualify prospective applicants based on what they post and what their social media profiles look like. A lot of your competition will be ensnared in making mistakes through their social media accounts, but you need to be cognizant of avoiding these pitfalls because of just how prominent screening social media profiles has become throughout the application process. Anything you post in the realm of social media can and will be used against you during the application and hiring process. In 2017, employer survey results showed that 70% of companies were looking through social media accounts to screen applicants before hiring.[10] It cannot be underscored enough that you need to think multiple times about something before you post it to the world of the internet. So many jobs, internships, and other employment opportunities have been lost due to just one questionable post to social media.[11] Simply think before you post anything to these sites, and how it can and

---

[9]https://www.annualcreditreport.com/index.action is federally authorized and a great credit resource.
[10]Lauren Salm, "70% of Employers Are Snooping Candidates' Social Media Profiles," *CareerBuilder.com*, June 15, 2017.
[11]Stacy Rapacon, "How Using Social Media Can Get You Fired," *CNBC.com*, February 5, 2016. https://www.cnbc.com/2016/02/05/how-using-social-media-can-get-you-fired.html.

will impact your future career. Is losing a potential job or internship really worth a controversial status update?

Many employers will start the screening process by simply using an internet search engine to search for an applicant's name. These employers will look at the social media accounts to see if there are any questionable images or posts they can find related to the applicant. Make sure to always be careful in the social media realm not just during your job application process, but also throughout your entire career. A questionable social media post or photo could cost someone their career even if they have 20 years of experience on the job. Some employers might also ask you to provide them with login credentials, or actually login yourself to your social media accounts during an interview. These employers will then look through your social media profiles in more detail focusing on previous posts, groups liked and followed, and even

▲ Using social media in a positive manner can lead to vital professional networking opportunities. But keep in mind that social media has many potential pitfalls if caution is not exercised.

personal messages. There is no federal law against employers engaging in these practices, but some states have restricted employer access to this information. It is important to keep this information in mind and watch what you post and send through social media accounts, and always remember to have a positive online presence.

One of the best ways to start having a positive online presence is to have a LinkedIn profile publicly available with a professional headshot, and a basic breakdown of your education and work experiences. Your LinkedIn profile will be accessible through an online search of your name and will help convey professionalism. If you have the least amount of doubt whether or not you should post or share something in a social media account, the best advice is to simply not do it. Always err on the side of caution when it comes to managing your online image. Once questionable content appears on the internet it can be very difficult to fully remove.

IN-DEMAND AREAS OF STUDY

There are certain academic disciplines that are really in demand across various criminal justice careers these days, and earning a degree in these disciplines can make your résumé stand out and help separate you from the competition. While there is never a one-size-fits-all approach, specific in-demand areas of study are computer science and cybersecurity, foreign languages, and accounting. Numerous cybersecurity threats have greatly driven up the demand for applicants with advanced computer-related backgrounds. Domestic and international threats have also increased the demand for knowledge about specific foreign languages. For example, the FBI has a critical language list on their website seeking applicants possessing proficiency in the languages listed in Figure 3.1.

FIGURE 3.1

FBI Critical Language List[12]

Arabic

Chinese

Farsi

Korean

Punjabi

Russian

Spanish

Urdu

Vietnamese

---

[12]"More than Talk: All about FBI Linguists," Federal Bureau of Investigation. https://archives.fbi.gov/archives/news/stories/2008/july/linguists_072908.

The Central Intelligence Agency (CIA) also has a mission-critical language list on their website, and they are looking for applicants proficient in the languages listed in Figure 3.2.

FIGURE 3.2

Sample Languages from the CIA's Critical Language List[13]

Arabic

Dari

Chinese

Indonesian

Kurdish

Korean

Pushto (Pashtu)

Persian (Farsi)

Russian

Turkish

Urdu

---

[13]"CIA Values Language Capabilities among Employees," Central Intelligence Agency. https://www.cia.gov/news-information/featured-story-archive/2010-featured-story-archive/cia-values-language-capabilities.html.

The CIA also offers a "Language Hiring Bonus Program" where an applicant can earn up to a one-time $35,000 payment for possessing superior language skills in the various languages listed in Figure 3.2. Many criminal justice agencies offer bonus payments and/or additional monetary compensation for proficiency in foreign languages.

Accounting is another in-demand area of expertise in the field of criminal justice. Choosing to pursue a degree in accounting needs to be combined with becoming a Certified Public Account (CPA). The requirements for sitting for the CPA exam differ between states, but the varying requirements can be found detailed in link provided in the footnote below.[14]

In terms of specific computer skills desired in the field of criminal justice, look to complete training courses offered through your academic institution or complete internships advertising the use of commonly used technologies in the criminal justice field. Having these specific technology skills and experiences on your résumé will make you a more competitive applicant. Here is a list of some technologies frequently used in the criminal justice system today:

Microsoft Excel—This software program, developed by Microsoft, allows users to organize, format, and run calculations on data in a spreadsheet system.[15] Graphs, charts, and histograms are easily created using Microsoft Excel. Many colleges and universities offer courses in Microsoft Excel, and some will even offer a certificate program in the software program.

IBM i2 Analyst Notebook—Provides analysts with multidimensional visual analysis capabilities to uncover connections and patterns in data.[16] According to IBM's website, the i2 Analyst Notebook provides innovative features like connected network visualizations, social network analysis, and geospatial views, giving you the ability to identify and disrupt criminal, cyber, and fraudulent threats.

GIS (Geographic Information System)—Lets users visualize, analyze, and interpret data to better understand patterns, relationships, and trends.[17] When it comes to the criminal justice system, GIS is especially beneficial in mapping crime trends. The National Institute of Justice (NIJ) states that GIS crime mapping enables crime analysts to analyze and investigate the causes of crime and to develop appropriate responses.[18] Many colleges and universities offer courses in GIS, and some even offer GIS certificate programs.

---

[14] "A Career in Accounting," *accountingedu.org.* https://www.accountingedu.org.

[15] https://products.office.com/en-us/excel.

[16] https://www.ibm.com/us-en/marketplace/analysts-notebook.

[17] http://www.esri.com/what-is-gis.

[18] *Mapping and Analysis for Public Safety,* National Institute of Justice, July 31, 2017. https://www.nij.gov/topics/technology/maps/pages/welcome.aspx.

Compstat—This performance management system is used to reduce crime, and emphasizes information-sharing, responsibility, accountability, and improving the efficiency and effectiveness of operations.[19] The following are four core components of Compstat:

- Timely and accurate information or intelligence
- Rapid deployment of resources
- Effective tactics
- Relentless follow-up

Biometrics—This is the technical term for body measurements and calculations, and these calculations can be used to authenticate an individual based on these specific characteristics. In the criminal justice system, one of the most common historical examples of biometrics measured is fingerprints. But this is changing rapidly according to the FBI's Next Generation Identification (NGI) where palm prints, irises, and facial recognition are all different forms of current biometrics.[20] According to the FBI, the NGI provides criminal justice practitioners with the world's largest and most efficient electronic database of biometric and criminal history information.

Computer Programming or "Coding"—Computer programming, also known as "coding," enables programmers to create websites, software programs, and user applications. Cybersecurity is a huge concern for the public and private sectors looking into the future. Hacking events and data thefts are occurring on a regular basis, and the cybersecurity industry anticipates a workforce gap of 1.8 million cybersecurity jobs because this industry cannot find enough qualified applicants.[21] The employment opportunities in the cybersecurity field are plentiful as government agencies and private companies attempt to strengthen the security on their websites, data, and networks before they are the victim of the next cybercrime. Websites like *Code Academy* will teach you the basics of coding, and you can also look to supplement computer programming skills by majoring in computer programming or computer science.[22]

A NOTE ON VETERANS' PREFERENCE

Many companies and agencies give preference to military veterans who meet specific criteria based on their service in the military. Veterans need to be familiar with these hiring preference initiatives because they have earned these hiring preferences through

---

[19] *COMPSTATE: Its Origins, Evolution, and Future in Law Enforcement Agencies.* Bureau of Justice Assistance. Police Executive Research Forum. https://www.bja.gov/Publications/PERF-Compstat.pdf.

[20] *Next Generation Identification (NGI)*, Federal Bureau of Investigation. https://www.fbi.gov/services/cjis/fingerprints-and-other-biometrics/ngi.

[21] "Global Cybersecurity Workforce Shortage to Reach 1.8 Million as Threats Loom Larger and Stakes Rise Higher," *(ISC)*2, June 7, 2017.

[22] https://www.codecademy.com.

▲ Many employers give preference to military veterans. If you are a veteran, contact potential employers or examine employer websites to see whether they offer preferential hiring for veterans.

their service to our country. Military veterans should consult company websites in the private sector for the specifics on their veteran hiring initiatives; these benefits will differ between various private companies. For federal jobs, the federal government has outlined specific criteria needed for veterans to quality for certain preference considerations. The following information on Veterans' Preference comes directly from FedsHireVets.gov/[23]:

> "Only veterans discharged or released from active duty in the armed forces under honorable conditions are eligible for veterans' preference. This means you must have been discharged under an honorable or general discharge.
>
> If you are a "retired member of the armed forces" you are not included in the definition of preference eligible unless you are a disabled veteran OR you retired below the rank of major or its equivalent."

---

[23] "Veterans: Veterans' Preference," *fedshirevets.gov*. https://www.fedshirevets.gov/job/vetpref/.

There are basically three types of preference eligibles, disabled (10 point preference eligible), non-disabled (5 point preference eligible) and sole survivorship preference (0 point preference eligible).

You are a **0-point Preference eligible** - no points are added to the **passing** score or rating of a veteran who is the only surviving child in a family in which the father or mother or one or more siblings:

1. Served in the armed forces, **and**

2. Was killed, died as a result of wounds, accident, or disease, is in a captured or missing in action status, or is permanently 100 percent disabled or hospitalized on a continuing basis (and is not employed gainfully because of the disability or hospitalization), **where**

3. The death, status, or disability did not result from the intentional misconduct or willful neglect of the parent or sibling and was not incurred during a period of unauthorized absence.

You are a **5 point preference eligible** if your active duty service meets any of the following:

1. For more than 180 consecutive days, other than for training, any part of which occurred during the period beginning September 11, 2001, and ending on August 31, 2010, the last day of Operation Iraqi Freedom, **OR**

2. Between August 2, 1990 and January 2, 1992, **OR**

3. For more than 180 consecutive days, other than for training, any part of which occurred after January 31, 1955 and before October 15, 1976.

4. In a war, campaign or expedition for which a campaign badge has been authorized or between April 28, 1952 and July 1, 1955.

You are a **10 point preference eligible** if you served at any time, and you:

1. have a service connected disability, **OR**

2. received a Purple Heart."[24]

If you are not sure of your preference eligibility, visit the Department of Labor's Veterans' Preference Advisor.

Now that we have discussed your preference eligibility and the associated points, let's discuss preference groups. Preference eligibles are divided into five basic groups as follows:

- CPS - Disability rating of 30% or more (10 points)
- CP - Disability rating of at least 10% but less than 30% (10 points)
- XP - Disability rating less than 10% (10 points)

---

[24]Ibid.

- TP - Preference eligibles with no disability rating (5 points)
- SSP - Sole Survivorship Preference (0 points)

NOTE: Disabled veterans receive 10 points regardless of their disability rating.

When agencies use a numerical rating and ranking system to determine the best qualified applicants for a position, an additional 5 or 10 points are added to the numerical score of qualified preference eligible veterans.

When an agency does not use a numerical rating system, preference eligibles who have a compensable service-connected disability of 10 percent or more (CPS, CP) are placed at the top of the highest category on the referral list (except for scientific or professional positions at the GS-9 level or higher). XP and TP preference eligibles are placed above non-preference eligibles within their assigned category.

You must provide acceptable documentation of your preference or appointment eligibility. Acceptable documentation may be:

A copy of your DD-214, "Certificate of Release or Discharge from Active Duty," which shows dates of service and discharge under honorable conditions

A "certification" that is a written document from the armed forces that certifies the service member is expected to be discharged or released from active duty service in the armed forces under honorable conditions not later than 120 days after the date the certification is signed.

You may obtain a letter from the Department of Veterans Affairs reflecting your level of disability for preference eligibility by visiting a VA Regional Office, contacting a VA call center or online.

NOTE: Prior to appointment, an agency will require the service member to provide a copy of the DD-214.

If claiming 10 point preference, you will need to submit a Standard Form (SF-15) "Application for 10-point Veterans' Preference."

From the Real World
I meet with many military veterans who are unaware of many forms of Veterans' Preference. If you are a veteran, you have earned this preference by serving our country, so be sure to know how to specifically use and apply these hiring benefits.

GEOGRAPHICAL FLEXIBILITY

One final way to help better manage all of the competition you will face when applying to careers in criminal justice is to have geographical flexibility when applying to jobs. This means being open to job opportunities all over the country, and not restricting yourself to a specific geographical area. The more places you are open to possibly moving to, the more opportunities you will have to find job openings. Being geographically flexible does not mean you must live for years in a locale you do not desire, but remember it is important to get a foot in the door and to start building that full-time work experience. This might mean living for a few years in a geographical location that would

From the Real World
As a whole, I find that students are way too geographically restrictive when beginning their job searches. Often, students will come to me and say they want a job with a specific agency in a specific city. If that agency is extremely competitive, I will tell the student they are better off purchasing a lottery ticket because they have about the same odds of winning the lotto as they do of getting that specific of a job. One of the best pieces of advice I can give students coming out of a degree program and looking for employment opportunities is to have a lot of geographical flexibility.

ordinarily not be at the top of your living location list. After working for a few years, though, you will have built up a nice level of work experience, and can start looking at applying to other, more desirable living locations. Just remember that really popular living locations will have more applicants and job competition. Sometimes applying to a sparsely populated or less desirable living location is a good plan to circumvent a lot of your competition because there will be fewer applicants in these locations. Be geographically flexible in your job search, and you will find that more potential employment opportunities come your way.

NOT GETTING THE JOB

Since the field of criminal justice is so competitive, the unfortunate reality is that you will apply to jobs where you either get rejected or receive no response at all. This can be disheartening for applicants just beginning their job search, but you cannot let a rejection or lack of a response bring you down. Do not get too attached to one job application. Simply apply, and move on to the next desirable position you find. It can take many weeks or even months to hear back from some job announcements. The internet and online job postings have made it much easier for numerous applicants to apply to job openings. Approximately 98% of applicants are eliminated after the initial résumé screening process, meaning that only about 2% of applicants make it to the interview phase.[25] So do not take a rejection personally because it is a game of numbers. When applying for jobs, keep spending time looking for more job opportunities and continue to submit more applications. You can start applying for jobs a few months before your actual graduation date since research shows the job search process can take over 30 weeks in today's job market.[26] If you are applying to jobs before your date of graduation, make sure to put your anticipated graduation date on your résumé so employers know you have not officially completed your degree at the time of your application.

SUMMARY

The field of criminal justice is so competitive that you need to always be asking yourself, "How am I going to stand out from the numerous other applicants out there applying to the same jobs as me?" In order to stand out, you need to possess desired skills and qualifications the criminal justice job market demands. Talk with

[25] "Why Only 2% of Applicants Actually Get Interviews," *Workopolis*, November 10, 2016. https://careers.workopolis.com/advice/only-2-of-applicants-actually-get-interviews-heres-how-to-be-one-of-them/

[26] "Job Market Expert Explains Why Only 2% of Job Seekers Get Interviewed," Webwire, January 7, 2014. https://www.webwire.com/ViewPressRel.asp?aId=184277#.Usw5G7GEit9.

insiders to get inside tips and strategies on how to secure employment in their given field of work. Look to keep your personal record clean as well. There is not much room for error either. One mistake in your personal background could cost you the job, and basically all future jobs in the field if the mistake is serious enough. Criminal justice is a high-stakes career field that takes dedication, diligence, and personal integrity. Always carry yourself professionally regardless of whether you think someone is watching you or not. You want to always maintain a positive and professional image everywhere you go, including your time spent online and on social media. Your reputation precedes you in all of life's endeavors, and especially when it comes to rising above your competition in criminal justice careers.

Three Key Takeaway Points

1. Talk with insiders who work in the types of jobs you would like to obtain in the future. Gain as much insight as you can from them in terms of what specific qualifications you should be looking to gain, and knowledge about inside hiring tips and advice.
2. Keep your background clean. Always have this in mind, and carefully think about questionable situations before you enter them. One mistake could cost you access to the career of your dreams.
3. Be careful with your online presence on social media. Know that employers go here first when they are reviewing your application. Anything questionable should not be posted or shared.

ASSESSMENT QUESTIONS

1. Why is it important to talk with insiders in the types of jobs you would like to have in the future?
2. What are two potential pitfalls to look out for in managing your personal background?
3. What are some benefits of using LinkedIn as a professional networking site?
4. Why should you be extremely careful with your social media accounts?
5. What is the significance of having good credit during your background clearance process?

CRITICAL THINKING EXERCISE

Compile a list of three specific strategies you can start employing today to help stand out from your future competition in a job search.

ACTIVE LEARNING ACTIVITY

Create a LinkedIn profile that includes your basic education, professional work experience, and internship experience. Look for real-world practitioners on LinkedIn working at employers where you would like to work in the future. Send them a message through LinkedIn, and ask these insiders for specific tips and advice they have for you to increase your chances of working for that agency in the future. For this activity, send at least three practitioners a professional-sounding message soliciting feedback on your career planning.

KEY TERMS

Foot-in-the-Door Approach – Getting an entry-level position in an organization with the goal of gaining work experience above all else.

Geographical flexibility – Openness to move to many different geographical areas for employment opportunities.

Veterans' Preference – Preference given in hiring to military veterans for their service in the military.

Coding – Computer programming, also known as "coding," enables programmers to create websites, software programs, and user applications.

4

Cover Letters and Résumés

INTRODUCTION

When it comes to marketing yourself in the professional world, having a well-crafted cover letter and résumé are vital components in your professional portfolio. Everyone should have an active résumé on file because you never know when opportunity will knock on your door. If someone asks to see your résumé, you should be able to provide them with one in a timely manner. It is far easier to update an existing résumé with new work experiences and qualifications than it is to rush to create one from scratch.[1] A cover letter and résumé represent your marketability in answering the proverbial question "Why should we hire you?" These documents are also important because they display your writing ability and written communication skills to a prospective employer.[2]

Special attention to detail and general formatting guidelines need to be followed when crafting your cover letters and résumé. One grammatical mistake or misspelled word could potentially cost you an employment opportunity. You also want to avoid using the same wording in cover letters sent out for multiple jobs. An ideal cover letter should be individually tailored to the job you are applying for. Recruiters spend an average of 6.25 seconds looking at your résumé, and 80% of those seconds are spent looking at your name, current job title and company (if applicable), previous job title and company, previous position start and end dates, current position start and end dates, and education.[3] Seconds are of the essence here, and this underscores the need for a well-formatted cover letter and résumé. Following the formatting advice found in Chapter 4 will put you on the correct track to creating great cover letters and résumés. To review more tips on cover letters and résumés visit www.oup.com/us/klutz.

THE ART OF THE COVER LETTER

A cover letter represents the opportunity to detail specific selling points about you, the applicant, to the prospective employer. With a cover letter, you are tasked with identifying what you specifically bring to the table that differentiates you from other applicants. You should also discuss why the employer should in fact hire *you* for the job. Be specific! Typically, cover letters are approximately two to three paragraphs in length. The cover letter should focus on the most relevant experiences and qualifications in your résumé related to the job you are applying to. You should not simply copy-and-paste material from your résumé, but use the cover letter as your "elevator pitch" that is personal and to the point about why *you* are in fact the best applicant for the job. Think of the cover letter as your "elevator pitch." If a prospective employer were to ask you to sell them on why

---

[1] Erin Greenawald, "6 Good Reasons to (Always!) Keep Your Resume Updated," *The Muse.* https://www.themuse.com/advice/6-good-reasons-to-always-keep-your-resume-updated.
[2] Brittany Helms, "Importance of Writing Skills for Business Communication," *Tech Guru Daily*, November 21, 2017. http://www.tgdaily.com/enterprise/biz/importance-of-writing-skills-for-business-communication.
[3] Susan Adams, "What Your Résumé Is Up Against," *Forbes*, March 26, 2012. https://www.forbes.com/sites/susanadams/2012/03/26/what-your-resume-is-up-against/#e65e6893f9ca.

you are the best applicant out there for the job, you should be able to tell them in 30 to 60 seconds.[4] A good elevator pitch should be brief, clear, concise, and extend an invitation to continue the conversation.[5] In this case the extended conversation is an interview.

When composing a cover letter you should address it to the specific person/people in charge of hiring if you know their name(s). Often these details are listed in the actual job advertisement, or can be discovered by directly contacting the hiring agency. If you are unable to find a specific name, a generic "To Whom It May Concern" is appropriate in this situation. In the text of the cover letter be specific, citing what you will bring to that agency in terms of skills and abilities based on your work and educational experiences. A cover letter's main purpose is to literally cover the résumé, and highlight the most marketable aspects of you, the applicant.

A good cover letter lets the reader know why you are the best applicant for the position and what specific skill set makes you a desirable candidate. A well-crafted cover letter is not simply a copy-and-paste from your résumé, but should be individually tailored to the specific job vacancy announcement. Figure 4.1 provides a cover letter with good formatting and structure. This specific cover letter builds on the information provided in the sample résumé in Figure 4.3.

FIGURE 4.1

Sample Cover Letter—Good Formatting and Structure
(including notes in *italic*)

Angelica Smith (*Start with your basic contact information*)

555 Lakeview Drive

Tuscaloosa, AL 35487

555-555-5555

angelica.smith@email.com (*Make sure your email address sounds professional*)

May 5, 2019 (*Date application is submitted*)

Special Agent Green (*Employer contact information. If no name is known for the selecting official, leave this space blank. The more personally specific the address in a cover letter the better, though.*)

Hiring Official (*Job title*)

Internal Revenue Service (*Name of employer*)

1111 Constitution Ave NW (*Address of employer where the job announcement is located*)

continues

---

[4]Tom Deierlein, "Why Everyone Needs a Good 60-Second Elevator Pitch," LinkedIn, September 13, 2014.
[5]Jacqueline Whitmore, "7 Essentials for an Elevator Pitch That Gets People to Listen," *Entrepreneur*, August 21, 2015. https://www.entrepreneur.com/article/249750.

continued

Washington, DC 20224

Dear Special Agent Green: (*A specific contact is preferred for an address in a cover letter. If no specific contact is known, "To Whom It May Concern" is sufficient.*)

I am interested in applying for the Customer Support Specialist position with the Internal Revenue Service in Washington, DC. I recently attended a career fair at the University of Florida where I will be earning a Bachelor's of Arts degree in criminal justice on May 8, 2019. At the career fair, I met Special Agent Moore with the IRS who informed me about this job opening. Based on the educational career, professional work experience, and internship and volunteer work I have completed, I strongly believe I am a prime candidate for the Customer Support Specialist position with the Internal Revenue Service.

The first paragraph provides information on why you are submitting your application, the position you are applying for, and a basic introduction of yourself.

In terms of what makes me qualified for this specific position, I have almost two years of professional work experience in the legal field. I have served as a Law Clerk for Jones and Jones Law Firm in Gainesville, Florida. Through this position I have gained experience working directly with clients, and preparing reports for attorneys to present at trial. Through my hard work and dedication to my job, I was awarded "Employee of the Year" in 2018 at the law firm. I will have earned a bachelor's degree in criminal justice in a few days and also currently hold an associate's degree. Throughout my education, I have worked extremely hard, and was awarded the Smith Scholarship, which goes to the student in the criminal justice department with the highest GPA.

The second paragraph provides information on why you are an ideal fit for the position. Be sure to cite specific examples, and do not just copy-and-paste from your résumé.

I thank you for taking the time to review my application package. I feel my professional educational and work experiences make me an ideal fit for the Customer Support Specialist, and I will be an asset to your team at the IRS. Thank you for your time and for reviewing my additional qualifications and experiences found in the résumé attached with this application package.

The third paragraph concludes the cover letter, references more information to be found in your résumé, and thanks the selecting official for their time.

Sincerely,

(*Place handwritten signature here for a personal touch.*)

Angelica Smith

FIGURE 4.2

Sample Cover Letter—With Common Cover Letter Mistakes
(comments in *italic*)

*No personal contact information or employer contact information provided

May 5, 2019

To Whom It May Concern: (**A generic introduction is not necessarily a mistake, but remember to include the name of the agency contact/hiring official when able. The more specific, the better.*)

   I am interested in this position because I am a hard-worker and strongly believe I will be a good fit for your agency. I am a college graduate with many work experiences that make me qualified for this job. I have included a copy of my résumé for your review. Thank you for your time and consideration, and I look forward to your response.

Sincerely,

Angelica Smith

* This cover letter includes many common mistakes. The biggest mistake is that it is non-specific, and reads like it has been spammed out to numerous different job openings. There is no mention of the specific position the applicant is applying to, and no individual tailoring to the actual position being advertised. There is also no specific information included about the applicant's qualifications and skills, and why this applicant in particular is a great fit for this job and the agency as a whole. The reader takes very little information away from this cover letter, aside from the fact that it is generic and vague. Cover letters are your chance to shine and highlight specific details regarding your qualifications that expand on points listed in your résumé.

THE ART OF THE PROFESSIONAL RÉSUMÉ

The purpose of a résumé is to highlight your entire body of work throughout your educational and professional careers. Special attention should be given to having separate sections in your résumé including education, professional work experience, internship and volunteer experiences, specific skill sets, and honors and awards received. A résumé should typically be around one-page in length for entry-level positions. Mid-career professionals will have longer résumés based on more professional work experience. Research and academic-focused jobs will require a longer résumé as well (usually referred to as a CV, or curriculum vitae, for academic jobs) in order to detail publication and research history and experience. Here is the basic structure of how a professional résumé should read:

1. Full name and professional-sounding contact information centered at the top
2. Education
3. Professional work experience
4. Internship and volunteer experiences
5. Honors and awards received

From the Real World
Most students I meet with concerning career preparation have never constructed a cover letter before. Hiring officials only spend a handful of seconds initially screening your application package. Your cover letter needs to grab their attention right away so they continue with your application package.

▲ A well-designed and properly formatted cover letter and résumé are essential when applying to internships and jobs.

6. Specific skills, including computer skills and proficiency in foreign languages
7. Professional references

For any professional work experience or internship/volunteer experience, you should include bulleted points describing some specifics of what you did in that role. A maximum of two or three bulleted points per experience. Bullets help to consolidate major points you are trying to highlight in your résumé, and help avoid lengthy text for the reader. Figure 4.3 offers some additional tips for your résumé.

FIGURE 4.3

Sample Résumé—With Good Formatting and Structure
(including notes in *italic*)

Use a traditional format and font when creating a résumé. Using really obscure or non-traditional résumé formatting can work against you with some hiring managers. Cambria and Times New Roman are good traditional choices. Avoid having too much white space in your résumé. Save résumés as a PDF file in order to avoid distortions of text and formatting in different versions of other software programs. Many agencies use résumé and keyword scanners, and you do not want your résumé text distorted or unreadable during this screening process since having proper formatting is critical to having your application package properly reviewed.

Angelica Smith *(name in bold and centered 16-point font)*

555-555-5555   *(personal phone number)*

angelica.smith@email.com *(professional-sounding email address)*

Education *(section headings left-justified and in bold)*

University of Florida – Gainesville, FL

- Bachelor of Arts in Criminal Justice – May 2019 – GPA 3.8 *(Include date earned. If not earned yet, put "anticipated in" then list month and year for anticipated graduation date. Include minors and Latin honors if applicable.)*

Cape Fear Community College - Wilmington, NC

- Associate's degree - May 2017 – GPA 3.8

Professional Work Experience

Jones and Jones Law Firm—Law Clerk – July 2017–present *(Include name of employer, position title, and dates employed. If still employed write, "present" for the end date.)*

- Assist attorneys with administrative assignments around the office such as typing and reviewing reports, managing a filing system, and preparing paperwork for the courtroom.

- Prepare court presentations, and provide initial screening with prospective clients. *(Provide a minimum of one bullet point per experience, and then list specific duties performed at your employer. Two or three bullet points maximum per experience. If currently employed, put duty descriptions in present tense.)*

Internship and Volunteer Experience *(List internship and volunteer experience separately from professional work experience.)*

New York City Police Department – Intern – May 2018–August 2018

- Completed police ride-along program with sworn police officers. Rotated between 5 departments within the NYPD including homicide, narcotics, patrol, mounted-patrol, and criminal investigations divisions. *(Provide at least one bullet point with duties performed in the internship.)*

Helping Friends Afterschool Program – Volunteer – January 2016–May 2017

- Helped 4th and 5th grade students with their homework. Read books with students to encourage interest in student-centered learning.

continues

continued

Student Clubs and Organizations

Criminal Justice Student Association (CJSA) – President – August 2018–May 2019

- Served as the head official for the Criminal Justice Student Organization, and was in charge of organizing 15 meetings for a total of 100 student members. Coordinated a spring career fair for students where 10 employers from the field of criminal justice came to discuss internship and career opportunities with students. *(Including numbers and specific data points in a résumé is recommended because this stands out to the reader and is easy to quantify.)*

Awards and Honors *(Be specific, describe brief details of each award/honor, and include the dates you received them.)*

- Dean's List – 2017–2019; Given to students who maintain over a 3.6 GPA each semester
- 2018 Employee of the year at Jones and Jones law firm – Received December 2018
- Smith Scholarship – Received August 2018 – Given to student with highest GPA in the criminal justice department each year

Relevant Skills *(Be as specific as possible; avoid saying vague blanket statements like "proficient in Microsoft Office," "team player," and "hard worker.")*

- Conversational in Spanish – Three 100–200 level Spanish courses taken during bachelor's degree
- Proficient in Microsoft Excel and Microsoft Access
- 2-years of experience using the statistical software program SPSS

References *(Include at least three references from your educational career, professional work experience, or internship and volunteer experiences. Include their full name, institution where the reference is employed, position title of reference, and email/phone contact information for your reference. Providing this information in your résumé saves a step for interested employers from having to ask you for it later).*

Dr. Jane Smith – Success College – Chair – Jane.Smith@successcollege.com – 555-555-5555

Ms. Quinn Walters – New York Police Department – Internship Supervisor – quinnwalters@nypd.com – 555-5555

Mr. Lindsey Jones – Jones and Jones law firm – Attorney and Owner – Lindsey.jones@joneslaw.com – 555-555-5555

Additional General Résumé Success Tips

1. Be specific! Avoid using vague, non-descriptive terminology. Quantify completed assignments when applicable (e.g., successfully completed 20 reports with a 5-star rating on each report).

2. Avoid using obscure fonts.

3. Do not include a headshot of yourself. It comes across as conceited. If anything, include a link to your LinkedIn profile, and have your LinkedIn profile feature a professional headshot.

4. Avoid droning on in your résumé about superfluous information. Being wordy and having a lot of filler content is not advisable. A résumé needs to be informative, but should not read like *War and Peace*. Typically, résumés for entry-level jobs should be approximately one page in length. A mid-career professional will have a longer résumé because of more work experience, and research and academic jobs require a much longer résumé or CV because of more details about research and publication experience.

5. Avoid spelling and grammatical mistakes. One mistake could potentially cost you a job. Have at least two different people look over your résumé before you start sending out job applications.

6. Do not spam or "shotgun" your résumé for prospective jobs. Hitting "submit" on 100 job applications at the same time, with the exact same cover letter and résumé, is most likely going to end in a lot of frustration. Take some time to individually craft and tailor a cover letter and résumé for each individual job based on the duties and qualifications stated in the specific job description.

7. Including key words and phrases from the job vacancy announcement is extremely important for your résumé. If you possess the qualifications listed in a job announcement, you need to include this in your résumé based on the wording in the job description (usually found in the duties-and-qualifications section of a job posting). For example, if a job advertisement states that an employer is looking for an applicant who has "worked with SPSS to conduct statistical analyses," and you have this specific experience in your work history, your résumé should include a line that says, "Worked with SPSS to conduct statistical analyses" and then describe what you specifically did with this work in slightly more detail. Many résumés are now put through electronic keyword scanners, and failing to include precise language found in a job announcement could cost you the chance of your résumé being forwarded to the second round of the selection process.

Figure 4.4 contains common résumé mistakes. Making mistakes on your résumé can cost you the chance of having it forwarded to the next round of the hiring process. This sample résumé also covers how to avoid making these common mistakes. This sample is for the same applicant, possessing the same qualifications and work history as Figure 4.3, but this sample résumé is filled with common résumé errors.

FIGURE 4.4

Sample Résumé—With Common Résumé Mistakes
(including notes in italic)

Angelica Smith *(name same size of rest of text and not in bold. Does not stand out to the reader.)*

*No contact phone number

partygirl@email.com *(unprofessional-sounding email address)*

Education
University of Florida and Cape Fear Community College

* Sub-headings not in bold. Poor spacing not fully highlighting educational institutions or specific degrees earned at these institutions. The résumé reader has no idea about subject areas studied, dates attended, or if the degrees have actually been completed.

Professional Work Experience
Jones and Jones Law Firm – July 2017–present
Complete general office administrative work on a daily basis while helping attorneys.

* Does not include title of your employment position. Does not include bullet points for the description of work duties, and also is a very vague and non-descriptive attempt of explaining work completed at this position.

Intern – May 2018–August 2018

- Completed an internship with a police department. *(Fails to include name of internship site. A vague attempt at describing actually duties performed through the internship. Also, internship experience should be categorized under its own heading of "Internship and Volunteer Experience" separate from professional work experience.)*

Afterschool Program – Volunteer

* No name of actual afterschool program, and no dates of volunteer experience included. No description of actual volunteer work performed through a bulleted formatting. Leaves the reader with almost no information. Also, volunteer work should be categorized under its own separate title of "Internship and Volunteer Experience" separate from professional work experience.

Student Clubs and Organizations
CJSA President – August 2018–May 2019

*Reader has no idea what CJSA stands for. Need to write out, "Criminal Justice Student Association" for the reader. No description of duties and accomplishments of the given position in a bulleted formatting.

Awards and Honors
Dean's List
2018 Employee of the year
Smith Scholarship

Very vague and non-descriptive. No specific dates provided on any of the awards or honors. Reader is left wondering what each accomplishment actually means. Need at least one descriptive sentence explaining what each award or honor actually entails.

Relevant Skills

Spanish

Microsoft Office

Good with computers

Not descriptive at all. With any foreign language listed, you should include what skill level you have attained in speaking that language. Never simply list "Microsoft Office." Which programs do you specifically have experience working with? And do not include an extremely vague statement such as "good with computers." Instead, include specific work experience you have with a certain software program like, "2-years of experience using SPSS." The more specific you can be for the résumé reader, the better.

References

Provided upon request

Many applicants put this line in their résumés, but if an employer is interested in your application, providing the actual references beforehand saves them a step and time instead of having to contact you to actually provide your references "upon request."

The Importance of Using Key Words and Phrases in Résumés

One final note about résumés involves using key words and phrases found in a job description in the text of your actual résumé. The reason this is suggested is that many employers are inundated with applications these days. Because of the large number of applications, numerous employers are utilizing résumé-screening software that looks for key words and phrases in your résumé. This screening software basically screens the quality match between your résumé and the actual wording in the job description. The better the match, the better chance you have of being referred to the selecting official, and then having your résumé meet a set of human eyes. Even if you are a great fit for an open job, failing to use these key words and phrases can result in having your résumé fail to make it out of the keyword software-screening portion of the application process.

From the Real World
You might find this surprising, but many students I meet with are not familiar with the contents of their own résumés! Know all aspects of your résumé. If an employer asks you about a specific experience, be fully prepared to discuss the details of that experience.

GENERAL APPLICATION TIPS

Applying to jobs can be a stressful process with many unknowns; however, if you keep the following application tips in mind, it will make your application process less stressful and burdensome:

- * Be geographically flexible when applying to jobs. The wider you cast your net in terms of geographical areas, the more opportunities you will have for desired employment. Limiting yourself to a small geographical area substantially limits your chances of finding a job. Keep in mind that applying to large cities and popular living areas will also garner more competition for you to compete against. Smaller cities and less popular living areas will have less competition overall.

From the Real World
I find one the biggest limiting factors for students and recent graduates in terms of finding employment involves limiting themselves to a very small geographical area when applying. Often a student will say, "I want to work for X company in X city." Your chances of that happening are pretty small, so make sure to widen your application range as wide as possible to increase your employment chances.

- * Do not become fixated on one specific job when applying. While it is perfectly fine to have a "dream job" in mind, do not put all of your eggs into one basket when you start applying for jobs. Apply to similar types of positions at many different agencies and companies. The more you confine yourself to one specific job, the less likely you are to get hired.

- * Do not adopt the "shotgun" or "spam" approach when applying for jobs. While you do not want to limit yourself applying to just a select few jobs, you also do not want to submit your application en masse to a bunch of different jobs without tailoring your cover letter and résumé accordingly. You do not need to spend a tremendous amount of time on each individual application, but you do want to personalize your application to some extent and at least include agency-specific information in your cover letter. Spamming or shotgunning the same cover letter and résumé to many different jobs at one time is likely to produce less-than-favorable results. Spend some time on each individual application, and customize your applications to some extent.

- * Make sure to use key words and phrases from the actual job announcement in your cover letter and résumé. These key words are generally found in the duties-and-qualifications sections in a job advertisement.

- * Utilize job sites like *Indeed, Monster, Simply Hired, Glassdoor*, and *USAjobs.gov* on a regular basis to look for open job opportunities. There are thousands of new jobs posted on these sites each day, so actively search these sites for new job announcements on a daily basis.[6] If you are applying to federal jobs, you will need to create a free account on USAjobs.gov.

- * Make sure to follow directions on a job application. For example, if the application states to upload all documents in PDF format, make sure all of your documents are uploaded correctly in the proper format requested by the employer. Not following directions carefully will likely exclude you from being considered for the job.

- * Before you actively begin applying for jobs, have a professional voicemail set up clearly stating your name and cell phone number. Do not sound unprofessional or have music playing during any part of your voicemail. Remember that first impressions are lasting impressions, and everything about your application package needs to convey professionalism.

---

[6]https://www.indeed.com; https://www.monster.com; https://www.simplyhired.com; https://www.glassdoor.com/index .htm; https://www.usajobs.gov.

FINDING JOB OPENINGS

Finding job openings to apply to can be an intimidating process. Knowing the right resources to find and apply to job openings will make your application process easier and more efficient. The following five steps will help you maximize finding job vacancies:

1. Decide on the types and titles of jobs you are looking for. For example, job titles such as *police officer, forensic scientist, cyber security analyst, probation officer,* and *law clerk* will be simple to find in search results on job websites.

2. Utilize job websites like *Indeed.com, SimplyHired.com,* and *Monster.com.* Each one of these online job sites has a search engine where you can input the types of jobs and job titles you are searching for.

3. In order to find federal jobs you will need to utilize *USAjobs.gov.* Pay special attention to the federal government's new hiring program for current students and recent graduates called the Pathways Program.[7] This program offers internships, part-time and full-time jobs, and the Presidential Management Fellows (PMF) Program. Pathways positions are for current college students or recent college graduates who have graduated from their qualifying educational institution within the past two years (marked by their graduation date). Veterans have up to 6 years to apply to these Pathways positions given their military service obligation. The PMF program is for recent graduates with an advanced degree such as a master's, PhD, or JD (law) degree. In order to find Pathways vacancy announcements on *USAjobs.gov,* you can simply input the term "Pathways" into the search function on the website.

4. Use the website *Glassdoor.com* to find job opportunities, interview questions from specific employers, feedback from current employees on working conditions within a given organization, and salary and benefit information. Create a LinkedIn account to access job opportunities as well. LinkedIn is an excellent professional networking site.

5. Visit your college or university career center to find additional job opportunities. Many colleges and universities now have online portals with job postings. Take advantage of alumni networking opportunities as well. Connecting with alumni organizations can lead to additional job leads.

INTERVIEW PREPARATION AND TIPS

It is not enough to simply have a great cover letter and résumé. You must also be skilled in the art of interviewing in order to maximize your chances of employment. In an interview setting, utilizing and conveying quality interpersonal skills is of critical

---

[7]Specific information on the Pathways Program is found here: https://www.usajobs.gov/Help/working-in-government/unique-hiring-paths/students/.

importance. This is where you will employ the "soft skills" you have developed. Soft skills are discussed in more detail in Chapter 5, but they are essentially your interpersonal communication skills. Someone who lacks proper interpersonal skills will raise a red flag to most employers because employers want someone who can effectively communicate in their job role. These days employers are finding soft skills in short supply with applicants.[8] Having good interpersonal skills will go a long way in an interview setting and will help you stand out from your competition.

Nervousness is common in an interview setting, but you want to have as much confidence as possible. In the field of criminal justice you will often encounter panel interviews where you might be interviewed by several agency personnel at one time. These panel interviews can be even more nerve-racking for applicants. Here are some basic interview tips for in-person interviews to help ease the process.

In-Person Interviews

1. Thoroughly research the agency you are applying to and the actual job description days before the in-person interview.
2. Print off at least five copies of your cover letter and résumé, and put them in a professional binder or brief case to take with you on your interview day.
3. Plan your professional business attire the night before. Have your clothes neatly pressed and on hangers so they do not become wrinkled overnight.
4. Get a good night's sleep so you feel well rested before the interview.
5. Eat a good quality meal before your interview so you feel energized and ready to go.
6. Plan to arrive at least 15 minutes early to your interview site to account for traffic delays.
7. Make sure your cell phone is turned off once you enter the building. Never check your cell phone during any interview.
8. Once you enter the facility make sure to smile, have a friendly demeanor, treat everyone you meet with respect, and offer a firm handshake (not too hard or soft) to everyone you directly meet. Again, this is displaying your soft skills.
9. Once you sit down for the interview, offer the individual(s) conducting the interview a copy of your cover letter and résumé.
10. Keep a friendly and positive demeanor during your interview. Maintain eye contact with your interviewer. If it is a panel interview, be sure to make eye contact with the different panel members throughout the interview process and conversation. Do not interrupt the person speaking. Be confident in your answers.

From the Real World
One of my personal suggestions on how to build interview skills and other soft skills is to practice your employment pitches with friends and family. Practice makes perfect, and the more comfortable you are with marketing your major selling points the better. Also, visit your college or university's career center and see if they offer mock interview preparation. If your educational institution does not offer mock interviews, sit down with friends and family and conduct one. Complete a couple of mock interviews before you face an official interview process.

---

[8]Kate Davidson, "Employers Find 'Soft Skills' Like Critical Thinking in Short Supply," *Wall Street Journal*, August 30, 2016. https://www.wsj.com/articles/employers-find-soft-skills-like-critical-thinking-in-short-supply-1472549400.

11. At the end of the interview be sure you have a couple of questions for the interviewer(s). Make sure to think of a couple of insightful questions a couple of days before your actual interview. Not asking any questions at the end of your interview is viewed negatively. Here are a few sample questions you could ask:
    o   What soft skills would best serve this position I am applying to?
    o   What do you (the interviewer) like best about working for this company?
    o   What are the major challenges for this specific position I am interviewing for?
    You can provide follow-up statements to the interviewer's answers to your questions. This is a great way to demonstrate your soft skills in action, and discuss further why you feel you are the best fit for the position.[9]
12. Ask for the interviewers' email addresses so you can send them a follow-up thank you email for taking the time to interview you, and reiterate your interest in the position and what you will bring to the agency should they hire you.

A Note on Phone Interviews

Phone interviews are a little different from traditional in-person interviews. Some specific factors should be taken into consideration:

1.   Make sure you have scheduled the interview time correctly if the employer is located in a different time zone. Have your phone by your side and ready to go at least 15 minutes before your scheduled interview time.
2.   Ensure you have quality phone reception.
3.   Be sure your phone interview area is quiet and free of distractions.
4.   Wear professional dress clothes even during a phone interview so it feels "real."
5.   Print out a copy of the job announcement and your résumé to have in front of you throughout the interview in case you have to refer to these documents.
6.   Try not to interrupt or talk over the interviewer(s).
7.   Cover the same basic advice for in-person interviews mentioned previously.
8.   Ask for the interviewers' email addresses so you can send them a follow-up thank you email for taking the time to interview you, and reiterate your interest in the position and what you will bring to the agency should they hire you.

Be prepared for common interview questions. You do not want to sound too rehearsed, but you do want to be well prepared so you do not stumble on your answers. Prepare in advance for these types of questions and you will feel confident when interview day comes. The following list includes some common interview questions you should be familiar with.

---

[9]Jacquelyn Smith, "28 brilliant questions to ask at the end of every job interview," *Business Insider*, May 2, 2016. http://www.businessinsider.com/questions-to-ask-at-end-of-job-interview-2016-4/#-1.

Common Interview Questions

1. **"Tell me about yourself"** – By stating this, employers want to see what relevant experiences you bring to the table and why you are a good fit for the position.
2. **"Why should we hire you?"** – Employers want to hear about your specific skills related to the job. What sets you apart from other applicants?
3. **"Tell us what you know about our agency"** – This statement serves to see if you have done your own homework and how familiar you are with the agency/job.
4. **"What is your greatest strength/weakness?"** – Do not be overly arrogant with your answer to your greatest strength, but cite something where you can give a specific example of your strength in action. For the weakness part of the question, be somewhat humble and cite a real weakness, but also talk about how you are working on turning that weakness into a stronger point in your life.
5. **"Why do you want this job?"** – Again, be specific! What skills do you possess that will enable you to be successful in this specific position?

You should also be familiar with some common interview mistakes that should definitely be avoided if you want your interview to go smoothly and if you want to have a chance at landing the job. The following list includes some of the worst interview mistakes you can possibly make.

Top Five Interview Mistakes to Avoid

1. Arriving late to your interview.
2. Not bringing enough copies of your cover letter and résumé to an interview.
3. Not doing your homework before the interview and lacking knowledge about the company and the specific position being advertised.
4. Lacking proper soft skills like not maintaining eye contact, speaking over and interrupting the interviewer(s).
5. Not having follow-up questions at the end of the job interview for the interviewer(s).

SUMMARY

You must have a properly formatted cover letter and résumé that read well in order to have a complete application package and to be competitive in the hiring process in today's job market. These documents enable you to show off all of the hard work you have completed over the years. This is your opportunity to effectively market yourself. You must also be skilled in the art of interviewing to maximize your employment chances. Just looking great on paper is not enough. Employers want to see that you can effectively communicate interpersonally, and you know what you are talking about before they hire you. Chapter 4 provides the basic foundation to excel in these areas and increase your chances of attaining desired employment options in the future.

Three Key Takeaway Points

1. Cover letters are basically your "elevator pitch" on paper. The cover letter should be concise and market specifically why you are a great fit for the position you are applying to.
2. Résumés are your chance to summarize all of your relevant career experiences. Make sure you expand on your experiences enough so that the reader will be familiar with what you have actually accomplished and completed in your career.
3. Interviews require you to be able to bring your experiences on paper into discussion points with your prospective employer. Know your experiences and what you will specifically bring to that organization well.

ASSESSMENT QUESTIONS

1. What is the importance of a cover letter?
2. Why should you elaborate on your professional experiences in your résumé?
3. Why should you include key words and phrases from a job description into your résumé?
4. What is a panel interview?
5. What type of answer is an employer looking for when they say, "Tell me about yourself"?

CRITICAL THINKING EXERCISE

Formulate a good introduction line or "hook" for your cover letter to get the reader interested and intrigued with reading the rest of your application package.

ACTIVE LEARNING ACTIVITY

Select a job advertisement that interests you on a job website like *Indeed.com* or *USAjobs.gov*. Create a cover letter formatted to specifically apply for this job, and a résumé specifically tailored for this job as well. Treat it like a real job application. Meet with your professor or your academic institution's career center to solicit feedback on this exercise.

KEY TERMS

Cover letter – Used to highlight specific skills and accomplishments from your résumé in a narrative format.

Résumé – Document designed to highlight your professional accomplishments in areas including professional work experience, education, professional skill sets, and honors and awards received.

Professional references – Individuals who can attest to your work ability and professional character.

Résumé-screening software – Software used by employers that looks for specific key words and phrases in an applicant's résumé.

5

Chapter Outline

The Importance of Networking

INTRODUCTION

We live in a "who you know" world. Often, who you know becomes even more important than what you know! Networking refers to building connections and professional relationships in the professional work world. Since the field of criminal justice is highly competitive, networking is one of the most important aspects in your professional development. You should always be thinking about networking. You never know when a personal contact, or someone you have just met, might have a great opportunity waiting for you. Look to create an extensive network of contacts and quality professional relationships in order to maximize your chances of benefiting from the "who you know" aspects of life. Effective interpersonal and communication skills are needed in order to successfully build your networking base. These communication skills are referred to as "soft-skills," and are vitally important to have throughout your entire professional career. Chapter 5 will cover basic networking strategies, and how to utilize soft skills to bolster your networking abilities to a greater extent. For more networking strategies refer to the companion website at www.oup.com/us/klutz.

THE SIGNIFICANCE OF NETWORKING

Many jobs are attained through referrals. A recent study from Jobvite showed that an incredible 78% of recruiters find their best quality candidates through referrals.[1] Another recent study showed that a staggering 85% of all jobs are filled

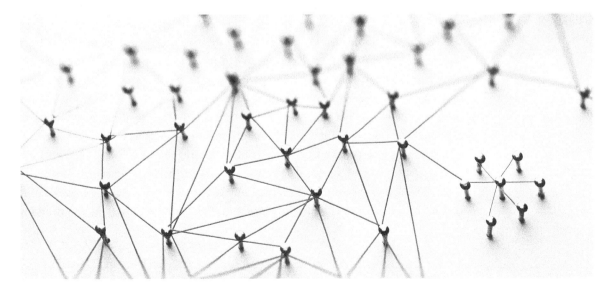

▲ In our interconnected world, networking is vital to professional development and attaining desired employment opportunities.

---

[1]"In a Competitive and Complex Job Market, Relationships Reign Supreme," *2015 Recruiter Nation* Survey. https://www.jobvite.com/wp-content/uploads/2015/09/jobvite_recruiter_nation_2015.pdf.

via networking.[2] Now do you think networking is important in your professional development? But all too often the art of networking is glossed over, and the application process quickly leads to frustration for applicants when no desired outcomes are attained largely due to a lack of proper networking. It is important to note that networking is something you need to begin engaging in today, and not something you put off until you actually need a job and desperation starts to creep into the equation.[3] In today's job market you must engage in networking to really bolster your chances of obtaining desired employment opportunities.

HOW TO EFFECTIVELY NETWORK

Networking comes in many different forms. For starters, taking advantage of building a network with your professors and internship supervisors is a great starting resource for building a base of professional contacts. Make sure to impress these individuals with your hard work and responsibility. Being responsible and dedicated to your work will help you stand out from the crowd. Your professors and internship supervisors will remember your positive traits, and if you impress them enough and an opportunity becomes available, you might just be the first person they contact about that new opportunity. While you are pursuing your degree in higher education, try to obtain as many internship opportunities as possible throughout your academic career. Internships are some of the best networking channels you have at your disposal as a student. In fact, statistics show that up to 60% of college graduates who completed a paid internship had a least one job offer upon graduation.[4] Additional research concerning the importance of internships shows that 80% of employers want recent graduates to have completed a formal internship.[5]

Networking should also be engaged in with personal acquaintances, alumni from your academic institutions, and even people from your personal hobbies and interests. The point is to keep a conversation going with these individuals, and to keep these people up-to-date on your career path. But these relationships should also be a two-way street, meaning that you do not simply call in favors from others all the time, but you look to help out others as well. This could be forwarding your contacts an interesting career article, job postings, or simply staying in touch on a regular basis.[6] Creating a business card to distribute to your growing contact base while networking is a good strategy to employ. Your business card should include your name, basic professional-sounding contact information, and a link to your LinkedIn profile. Another basic networking

From the Real World
I have had numerous students gain employment opportunities simply because they completed an internship while in school. The importance of networking through internships cannot be underscored enough. Treat everyone you meet as a networking opportunity. Always remember to make positive impressions throughout your entire career.

---

[2]Lou Adler, "New Survey Reveals 85% of All Jobs are Filled Via Networking," *LinkedIn*, February 29, 2016. https://www.linkedin.com/pulse/new-survey-reveals-85-all-jobs-filled-via-networking-lou-adler.
[3]Andrew Vest, "How to Network the Right Way: Eight Tips," *Forbes*, July 28, 2014. https://www.forbes.com/sites/theyec/2014/07/28/how-to-network-the-right-way-eight-tips/#42d5716f6d47.
[4]Penny Loretto, "Survey Says Paid Internships Lead to Full-Time Job Offers," *The Balance*. June 26, 2017. https://www.thebalance.com/paid-internship-full-time-1987131.
[5]Martha C. White, "The Real Reason New College Grads Can't Get Hired," *Time*, November 10, 2013. http://business.time.com/2013/11/10/the-real-reason-new-college-grads-cant-get-hired/.
[6]Allison Doyle, "The Importance of Career Networking," *thebalance.com*, June 22, 2017. https://www.thebalance.com/top-career-networking-tips-2062604.

▲ LinkedIn is an excellent professional networking site. Create a LinkedIn account today and start your online professional networking.

tip is to remember names of people you meet. This demonstrates a personal touch on your part, and calling someone by his or her name actually causes unique activation functioning in that person's brain.[7] Maybe it is even enough lasting brain activation to land you a future job when the light goes on in their head thinking about a personable prospective job applicant they met in the past!

You should look to create a LinkedIn profile as part of your networking strategy. You will find many professionals in your desired career field on LinkedIn. Connect with these individuals, and send them a message articulating your specific career plans. Research shows 35% of LinkedIn members have found a new career opportunity because of a conversation they had on LinkedIn.[8] Ask for any specific advice these working professionals on LinkedIn have for you concerning what you should be doing in building your qualifications. This demonstrates initiative and also serves as a professional networking opportunity.

---

[7]D. P. Carmody and M. Lewis, "Brain Activation When Hearing One's Own and Others' Names," *Brain Research* 1116, no. 1 (2006): 153–158. http://doi.org/10.1016/j.brainres.2006.07.121.
[8]"Eighty-Percent of Professionals Consider Networking Important to Career Success," *LinkedIn*, June 22, 2017. LinkedIn Corporate Communications Team. https://news.linkedin.com/2017/6/eighty-percent-of-professionals-consider-networking-important-to-career-success.

BEST NETWORKING METHODS

- **Join a professional organization**—Professional organizations enable you to meet practitioners working in your field of interest. Be active in the organization, and look to attend organizational conferences and meetings to effectively network. Here is a list of some professional organizations related to the criminal justice system:
  - Academy of Criminal Justice Sciences (ACJS)
  - American Society of Criminology (ASC)
  - American Academy of Forensic Science (AAFS)
  - National Criminal Justice Association (NCJA)
  - Alpha Phi Sigma: The National Criminal Justice Honor Society
- **Internships**—Not only do internships allow you to build relevant work experience in school, but they also enable you to network with working professionals in the field. When completing an internship, always ask for business cards or contact information from people you meet. Internships also afford you the opportunity to see if you really like what the job requires before you "sign on the dotted line" as a full-time employee. Contact agencies and employers directly about internship opportunities. Jobs websites like *Indeed.com* and *Monster.com* always have internships posted. Just simply search for "internships" in the search menu.
- **Volunteering**—Even if an employer you are interested in working for in the future does not have a formal internship available, contact the employer to see if they would be willing to have you volunteer at their organization. This shows initiative and will still give you excellent networking opportunities. Treat the volunteer experience seriously, and make sure supervisors know you ultimately desire a full-time position within the company.

BUILDING "SOFT SKILLS"

Employers are finding soft skills to be in short supply with today's job applicants.[9] Soft skills are essentially interpersonal skills, and soft skills encompass how well you work and interact with other people. Skills like proper communication and leadership abilities are becoming a lost art in today's ever-increasing digital age. Research shows that up to 60% of employers believe applicants lack basic communication and interpersonal skills—an increase of 10% in only two years.[10] Having strong soft skills is a necessary ingredient for success in the professional work world. Acquiring these skills will take

---

[9]Kate Davidson, "Employers Find 'Soft Skills' Like Critical Thinking in Short Supply," *Wall Street Journal*, August 30, 2016. https://www.wsj.com/articles/employers-find-soft-skills-like-critical-thinking-in-short-supply-1472549400.
[10]Martha C. White, "The Real Reason New College Grads Can't Get Hired," *Time*, November 10, 2013. http://business.time.com/2013/11/10/the-real-reason-new-college-grads-cant-get-hired/

practice, but once you have them they will prove easy to maintain. Here is a list of desirable soft skills employers currently seek.

Communication—When it comes to having successful interactions with people, communication is key. Communication can take many forms, but it essentially means how well you can correspond and engage with people. Employer survey results are showing that employers are frequently complaining about candidates' inability to speak and write clearly.[11] It is important to be articulate in your verbal communication skills in the professional world as well. You need to be able to engage in a meaningful conversation with colleagues, supervisors, and prospective employers. Effective communication skills also include writing skills. Seventy-three percent of employers want an applicant with strong writing skills.[12] Professional communication skills are also needed on the phone and over email. When leaving a voice message for someone, make sure you clearly state your name and number in a quiet environment. If you are talking to someone over the phone, make sure to also be somewhere quiet and have a notepad handy to write down important information. Have a professional-sounding voicemail clearly stating your name and telephone number without any noise or music in the background. Emails should always be treated as professional correspondence. In any email, properly address someone by their title and do not use shorthand or slang words. Make sure the tone of your email is polite and friendly. Always thank people for their time when communicating with them.

Listening—Can you listen to people without interrupting them? Are you able to listen to instructions about how to complete a task, and then go out and complete this task successfully? Listening skills are in great demand these days because many people are self-proclaimed experts who rarely listen to anything outside of their own mind. Research shows that most people only listen with approximately 25% efficiency.[13] If someone has a ton of experience in the field, you might want to at least listen to the advice that person is giving. According to research on good listening skills, asking insightful questions and engaging in a two-way dialogue are also important.[14] The point is to glean as much knowledge as possible through a conversation, and not just simply sit and nod your head while retaining nothing. When you have meetings with people, take materials to write down notes so you

---

[11]Kelley Holland, "Why Johnny Can't Write, and Why Employers Are Mad," NBC News, November 11, 2013. https://www.nbcnews.com/business/why-johnny-cant-write-why-employers-are-mad-2d11577444.

[12]Kaleigh Moore, "Study: 73% of Employers Want Candidates with This Skill," *Inc.com*, April 7, 2016. https://www.inc.com/kaleigh-moore/study-73-of-employers-want-candidates-with-this-skill.html.

[13]R. C. Husman, J. M. Lahiff, and J. M. Penrose, *Business Communication: Strategies and Skills* (Chicago: Dryden Press, 1988).

[14]Jack Zenger and Joseph Folkman, "What Great Listeners Actually Do," *Harvard Business Review*, July 14, 2016. https://hbr.org/2016/07/what-great-listeners-actually-do.

get specific instructions right the first time, and show active listening skills by asking insightful questions.

Responsibility—You should always be responsible in your actions. Show up to work when expected, put in maximum effort where expected, and earn the trust of your supervisors to demonstrate that you are a responsible person. Can your supervisor count on you to put in full effort to complete a quality work product? If so, you are likely to benefit from desirable work assignments and opportunities because your supervisor knows you will meet your end of the bargain. Opportunities will come your way if you convey you are a responsible worker. Be sure to always keep your word if you give it to someone in a professional setting. Empty promises are not a sign of a responsible person.

Accountability—Take ownership if you make a mistake or need improvement in a specific area. Too many people these days try to defer blame and always claim it is someone else's fault. Own up to shortcomings and employers will appreciate your accountability. In fact, accountability can even lead to improved workplace performance.[15] Be able to accept constructive criticism as well, and use this criticism as a learning and personal building experience. Some individuals fall to pieces with any amount of criticism directed their way, and employers will not find this to be a desirable trait.

Appearance—Ever heard the saying "People judge a book by its cover?" Workplace appearance is very important, and research actually shows that those who dress more nicely actually achieve more success.[16] This same research also showed that people who dress down were less sure of their delivery and were less respected by peers. Appearance also includes consistently maintaining proper hygiene and grooming standards. Make sure you clothes are neatly pressed, and when in doubt you should over-dress versus under-dress. Dress professionally and this will help you in terms of how people perceive you throughout your professional career. Like it or not, most corporate cultures are into appearance. Be mindful of visible tattoos and body piercings; a potential employer could view these negatively. Some agencies actually prohibit visible tattoos. For example, the U.S. Secret Service prohibits tattoos on the head, face, neck, hand, and fingers.[17]

---

[15]"Performance Management: Reference Materials," Office of Personnel Management. https://www.opm.gov/policy-data-oversight/performance-management/reference-materials/more-topics/accountability-can-have-positive-results/.
[16]Ray A. Smith, "Why Dressing for Success Leads to Success," *Wall Street Journal*, February 21, 2016. https://www.wsj.com/articles/why-dressing-for-success-leads-to-success-1456110340.
[17]https://www.secretservice.gov/join/careers/agents.

Positivity—Having a positive mindset and outlook will go a long way in conveying positivity in the workplace. Practice a "can-do" attitude at work, and actively employ mind over matter. Research shows that workers with a positive outlook are more productive than workers possessing a negative outlook.[18]

"HARD FAULTS" TO AVOID

Engaging in certain behaviors in professional settings is a good way to get canned from a job or interview. These same behaviors will also impede efforts to successfully network. We will refer to these undesirable behaviors as "hard faults." Avoid committing them at all costs because sometimes you only get one chance to impress, and committing a hard fault will simply not impress in the professional world. The following list contains common hard faults you should completely avoid.

Interrupting People When They Are Speaking—Someone who interrupts another person speaking is not only irritating but it is also highly disrespectful. Show the speaker respect and afford them the opportunity to finish their thoughts without interruption. If both parties start speaking at the same time, make sure to apologize and tell them they can go ahead with their thoughts. Be patient; your time to talk will come.

Negativity/Complaining—Very few people desire to be around someone who is always negative. Constant complaining and being a "downer" is not good for your professional appearance, and it will not get you far with networking. Persistent negativity suppresses your immune system, leads to an increased chance of heart attacks and strokes, and can actually kill you![19] So cease the negative thoughts and actions before they kill your career too.

Gossiping—Talking about others behind their backs is a recipe for disaster in the workplace. Yes, it is very common, but no, you should never engage in gossip. Leave it to others and distance yourself from the drama. There are few faster bridge-burners than talking negatively about people and that same negative rhetoric getting back to them. A recent psychological research study showed gossipers are disliked by colleagues and perceived as being weak.[20]

From the Real World
From my personal experience and working with students over the years, I can tell you that a lot of your professional career development involves showing up, putting in effort, and conveying an overall positive image. If you can accomplish these three simple things, you are way ahead of a lot of your competition these days.

---

[18]Emma Seppala, "Positive Teams Are More Productive," *Harvard Business Review*, March 18, 2015. https://hbr.org/2015/03/positive-teams-are-more-productive.

[19]Jessica Stillman, "Chronic Negativity Can Literally Kill You, Science Shows," *Inc.com*, October 13, 2015. https://www.inc.com/jessica-stillman/science-the-negative-people-in-your-life-are-literally-killing-you.html.

[20]S. Farley, "Is Gossip Power? The Inverse Relationships between Gossip, Power, and Likability. *European Journal of Social Psychology* 41, no. 5 (2011): 574–579, doi:10.1002/ejsp.821.

Profanity/Swearing—Do you swear like a salty pirate? If so, leave it at home and out of the workplace. After all, your work probably does not involve acting in a remake of *Pulp Fiction*.[21] Cursing is not good for your professional appearance in the workplace. In fact, a survey by Career Builder showed that 64% of employers view employees who curse negatively, and 57% of employers said they would be less likely to give an employee with a salty mouth a promotion.[22]

SUMMARY

The importance of networking in your professional career cannot be underscored enough. Look to build your list of professional contacts at all times. There are always chance encounters in life that open up doors you never thought possible, but you have to get out into the real world and meet people. The more people you know and have quality relationships with, the better chances you will have of benefiting from these connections. Utilize professors, internship supervisors, and work supervisors to start building your networking base. Reach out to people and tell them about your interests and qualifications. Word of mouth is a very powerful tool in the professional work world. Utilize online professional networking sites like LinkedIn in your networking endeavors. Effective networking is something that should start for you today and continue throughout your entire career. You must also have strong soft skills to successfully engage in quality networking and relationship-building. It only takes one opportunity to change the entire trajectory of your career.

Three Key Takeaway Points

1. Networking is something that never stops during any part of your career. You should treat everyone you meet as a networking opportunity.
2. Effective networking includes completing internships in your field to get to know working professionals, and utilizing social media sites like LinkedIn to connect with people working in the field.
3. Soft skills are in high demand these days because of how technology has taken over our society. Possessing quality people-skills will put you a step ahead of much of your competition.

---

[21]The film *Pulp Fiction* has around 429 curse words in it. http://www.vulture.com/2011/06/pulp_fiction_cursing_supercut.html.

[22]"Swearing at Work Can Harm Your Career Prospects, Finds CareerBuilder Survey," *CareerBuilder.com*, July 25, 2012. https://www.careerbuilder.com/share/aboutus/pressreleasesdetail.aspx?ed=12%2F31%2F2012&id=pr709&sd=7%2F25%2F2012.

ASSESSMENT QUESTIONS

1. What does the word "networking" mean?
2. Why is it so important to effectively network?
3. What are two specific networking strategies?
4. What are "soft skills"?
5. Give two examples of specific soft skills.

CRITICAL THINKING EXERCISE

Think about three specific soft skills you can start building today. What are they? How are you going to start applying and practicing these soft skills? Provide specific details.

ACTIVE LEARNING ACTIVITY

Think about a semester or summer where you will have enough time to complete an internship or volunteer opportunity to start building your work experience and networking base. Develop a list of three potential employers or types of jobs you could see yourself working in the future. If the agencies have a website, go online and see if they have information about their internship or volunteer application process. If not, find the contact information for these agencies. Call the agencies and ask to speak with the individual who handles interns and volunteers. Get the specifics and plan to complete an internship or volunteer experience soon. Often it is best to apply for these positions months in advance to get ahead of your competition, and to have enough time to complete the background clearance process.

KEY TERMS

Networking – Building connections and relationships in the professional work world.

Soft skills – Interpersonal and communication skills needed to be successful in the workplace.

Hard faults – Behaviors and thought patterns to avoid in the workplace.

6

Chapter Outline

Physical Fitness Requirements and the Importance of Overall Health Working in the Field of Criminal Justice

Disclaimer: Before you begin any physical fitness training or dietary program consult with a medical professional. The information in this chapter is not intended or implied to be a substitute for professional medical advice, diagnosis or treatment. Only your doctor can determine what is right for you. Consult with your doctor before starting any physical fitness or dietary program.

INTRODUCTION

The field of criminal justice is often very physically and mentally demanding. In order to maintain proper health and fitness levels, many criminal justice careers demand a consistently high level of physical fitness. Attention to healthy eating habits and quality sleeping schedules is also very important in this line of work. There are many careers in the criminal justice system that require you to be in top physical and mental condition in order to perform the job to the best of your ability. Some of the most sought-after positions in the field of criminal justice require the completion of a rigorous training academy, which can include the mandate to successfully complete stringent physical fitness requirements. You may meet all of the job requirements on the paper part of your application, but if you cannot pass the demanding physical fitness tests you will find yourself out of the running for the job.

Physical fitness level can come with life-or-death outcomes; research by the FBI has shown that physical fitness level is a critical factor in police survival of shooting incidences.[1] A California Peace Officer Standards and Training (POST) study also showed that physical fitness conditioning is a significant factor in reducing police injuries and deaths.[2] Some positions within the criminal justice field will even give additional recognition to those applicants who score the highest marks on the physical fitness tests. For example, at the Federal Law Enforcement Training Centers (FLETC), scoring 90% or higher in all of the fitness and body composition tests will earn you a Certificate of Distinguished Fitness and your name will be added to the fitness honor role.[3] Preparing well ahead of time with a consistent physical fitness routine is vital to ensure succeeding on these physical fitness requirements, both for pre-employment assessment and for maintaining fitness levels throughout your career. Chapter 6 will cover two specific types of physical fitness tests used in the field of criminal justice: The Cooper Institute Standards and the FBI's own physical fitness test.

Many criminal justice careers come with a high level of stress and strain. Maintaining a consistent physical fitness routine will enable you to mitigate some of these

[1] A. J. Pinizzotto, E. F. Davis, and E. C. Miller, *In the Line of Fire* (Washington, D.C: U.S. Department of Justice, Federal Bureau of Investigation, 1997).

[2] *California Law Enforcement Officers Killed and Assaulted in the Line of Duty* (California Commission on Peace Officer Standards and Training, 2001).

[3] *Physical Efficiency Batter (PEB)* (Federal Law Enforcement Training Centers, U.S. Department of Homeland Security). https://www.fletc.gov/physical-efficiency-battery-peb.

stressors, as research has shown cortisol levels decrease with a regular workout schedule.[4] Additionally, research also shows that getting enough sleep decreases cortisol levels.[5] Eating a healthy diet is also linked to decreased stress levels.[6] Eating healthy foods consistently can even boost your productivity at work![7] And this is just the tip of the iceberg in terms of what focusing on these specific areas related to your overall health can do for your future career. Focusing on these areas of physical fitness, healthy eating habits, and maintaining the proper amount of sleep will maximize your chances of landing a job and later excelling in your specific job description. Chapter 6 will concentrate on strategies needed to formulate the proper physical fitness regime, adhere to a healthy diet, and maintain a consistent quality amount of sleep. To learn more about physical fitness requirements and the importance of overall health working in the field of criminal justice go to www.oup.com/us/klutz.

MENTALLY APPROACHING PHYSICAL FITNESS REQUIREMENTS

If the job you are seeking in the future requires certain physical qualification standards, you may need an ample amount of preparation time in order to properly train to pass these requirements, depending on your current fitness abilities. Fitness training should be viewed similarly to preparing for a standardized test. The more preparation time the better, and the more likely you will achieve successful results. Failure to properly prepare for a physical qualification test could literally cost you the job even if you pass every other component of the application process with flying colors.

Physical fitness is not just something you should prepare for once and then forget about. It should be maintained throughout your entire career so you can enjoy the many positive benefits associated with an active lifestyle and exercising on a consistent basis. The benefits from consistent exercise include preventing chronic diseases such as diabetes, cardiovascular diseases, cancer, obesity, hypertension, depression, and osteoporosis.[8] Regular exercise has also been shown to make positive changes in the brain, including better thinking skills and improved memory function.[9] However, most people do not get nearly enough exercise. A research study conducted by the Centers for Disease Control and Prevention (CDC) indicates that 80% of Americans do not get

[4]"Exercising to Relax," *Harvard Men's Health Watch* (Cambridge, MA: Harvard Health Publishing, Harvard Medical School, February 2011).
[5]R. Leproult, G. Copinschi, O. Buxton, and E. Van Cauter, "Sleep Loss Results in an Elevation of Cortisol Levels the Next Evening," *Sleep* 20,no. 10 (1997): 865–870.
[6]Joshua Cook, "Breathe, Eat Well to Reduce Stress," University of Texas at Austin.
[7]Ron Friedman, "What You Eat Affects Your Productivity," *Harvard Business Review*, October 17, 2014.
[8]D. E. R. Warburton, C. W. Nicol, and S. S. D. Bredin, "Health Benefits of Physical Activity: The Evidence," *Canadian Medical Association Journal* 174, no. 6 (2006): 801–809. http://doi.org/10.1503/cmaj.051351.
[9]Heidi Godman, "Regular Exercise Changes the Brain to Improve Memory, Thinking Skills," Harvard Health Blog, April 9, 2014. https://www.health.harvard.edu/blog/regular-exercise-changes-brain-improve-memory-thinking-skills-201404097110.

the recommended amount of exercise each week, and therefore increasing their likelihood of major health issues later on down the road.[10] Physical inactivity has been linked to approximately 5.3 million deaths worldwide annually.[11] Consistent exercise is a key component to living a healthy life and having a long, successful career.

There is a lot of variation within criminal justice careers in terms of physical requirements and how intensive the pre-hire physical fitness tests will be. Some criminal justice careers have stringent standards, while some jobs have no physical standards at all. We will focus on some of the more rigorous physical fitness standards because if you are prepared for these, you will be prepared for almost any physical fitness test in the criminal justice system.

The Federal Bureau of Investigation (FBI) has challenging physical fitness requirements to become a Special Agent. These requirements are publicly posted on the FBI's website, and the site goes into quite a bit of detail in terms of what to expect when it comes to their fitness tests.[12] The information that follows pertaining to physical fitness standards for the FBI will be helpful in training for the majority of physical fitness requirements in criminal justice careers across the board because the FBI requirements are so rigorous.

Physical fitness tests can be intimidating experiences, especially without proper preparation and training. But these fitness tests are certainly doable, and the more confidence you have in yourself the better off you'll be when it comes to successfully completing the fitness requirements needed for employment within the field of criminal justice. A positive, can-do attitude will go a long way. In fact, recent research has shown that having a positive mindset while pursuing fitness training can change your workout results for the better.[13] The last thing you want to do is employ negativity and create a mental barrier in getting the task completed. Mental toughness and perseverance are important when it comes to performance in athletic activities, so convince yourself you will be able to pass these physical fitness requirements because you will have put in the time and effort into adequately preparing for them beforehand. Advanced preparation is key here as with just about anything in life. Prepare early for seemingly daunting tasks and your advanced preparation will help set your mind at ease with increased levels of confidence.

ACTUAL PHYSICAL FITNESS REQUIREMENTS

There is a lot of variation between various criminal justice careers and specific physical fitness requirements. The idea, though, is that if you can pass the requirements for the most stringent of physical fitness tests in the field, you will be prepared for

---

[10]Ryan Jaslow, "CDC: 80 Percent of Americans Don't Get Recommended Amount of Exercise," CBS News, May 3, 2013. https://www.cbsnews.com/news/cdc-80-percent-of-american-adults-dont-get-recommended-exercise/.

[11]Ryan Jaslow, "Inactivity Tied to 5.3 Million Deaths Worldwide, Similar to Smoking," CBS News, July 18, 2012. https://www.cbsnews.com/news/inactivity-tied-to-53-million-deaths-worldwide-similar-to-smoking/.

[12]https://www.fbijobs.gov/sites/default/files/PFT_Guide.pdf.

[13]Octavia H .Zahrt and Alia J. Crum, "Perceived Physical Activity and Mortality: Evidence from Three Nationally Representative U.S. Samples," *Health Psychology* 36, no. 11 (2017): 1017–1025.

▲ Many criminal justice careers require intense physical fitness standards. Simply looking good on paper is not enough to win the race for employment opportunities in this field.

almost anything a criminal justice job might throw your way with regard to physical requirements. The FBI has very stringent standards, and they are publicly posted on their website, FBIjobs.gov.[14] The fitness test components and the scaled scoring ranges for the FBI are listed in Tables 6.1 through 6.5, and they come directly from FBIjobs.gov as well.

To attain a passing scoring on this physical fitness test, the FBI states that you must earn at least 1 point in each one of the physical fitness events listed in the figures, and a minimum cumulative score of 12 in each of the four events.[15] Tactical Recruitment Program applicants must score a minimum of 20 points, and at least 1 point in each of the five events (pull-ups included as the fifth event). According to the FBI, their physical fitness test is designed to measure both muscular strength and endurance with the sit-ups,

---

[14]The information on this page is found on https://www.fbijobs.gov/sites/default/files/PFT_Guide.pdf.
[15]https://www.fbijobs.gov/sites/default/files/PFT_Guide.pdf.

Table 6.1 Maximum Number of Sit-Ups in One Minute (Total Number)

Score	Female Range	Male Range
−2	29 and below	31 and below
0	30–34	32–37
1	35–36	38
2	37–40	39–42
3	41–42	43–44
4	43–46	45–47
5	47–48	48–49
6	49–50	50–51
7	51–52	52–53
8	53–54	54–55
9	55–56	56–57
10	57 and over	58 and over

Source: FBIjobs.gov.

Table 6.2 Timed 300-Meter Sprint (in Seconds)

Score	Female Range	Male Range
−2	67.5 and over	55.1 and over
0	67.4–65.0	55.0–52.5
1	64.9–62.5	52.4–51.1
2	62.4–60.0	51.0–49.5
3	59.9–57.5	49.4–48.0
4	57.4–56.0	47.9–46.1
5	55.9–54.0	46.0–45.0
6	53.9–53.0	44.9–44.0
7	52.9–52.0	43.9–43.0
8	51.9–51.0	42.9–42.0
9	50.9–50.0	41.9–41.0
10	49.9 and below	40.9 and below

Source: FBIjobs.gov.

Table 6.3 Maximum Number of Continuous Push-Ups (Untimed; Total Number)

Score	Female Range	Male Range
−2	4 and below	19 and below
0	5–13	20–29
1	14–18	30–32
2	19–21	33–39
3	22–26	40–43
4	27–29	44–49
5	30–32	50–53
6	33–35	54–56
7	36–38	57–60
8	39–41	61–64
9	42–44	65–70
10	45 and over	71 and over

Source: FBIjobs.gov.

Table 6.4 Timed One and One-Half Mile (1.5 Mile) Run (in Minutes:Seconds)

Score	Female Range	Male Range
−2	15:00 and over	13:30 and over
0	14:59–14:00	13:29–12:25
1	13:59–13:35	12:24–12:15
2	13:34–13:00	12:14–11:35
3	12:59–12:30	11:34–11:10
4	12:29–11:57	11:09–10:35
5	11:56–11:35	10:34–10:15
6	11:34–11:15	10:14–9:55
7	11:14–11:06	9:54–9:35
8	11:05–10:45	9:34–9:20
9	10:44–10:35	9:19–9:00
10	10:34 and below	8:59 and below

Source: FBIjobs.gov.

Table 6.5 Pull-Ups (Tactical Recruitment Program Applicants Only—Untimed; Total Number)*

Score	Female Range	Male Range
0	0	0–1
1	1	2–3
2	2	4–5
3	3	6–7
4	4	8–9
5	5	10–11
6	6	12–13
7	7	14–15
8	8	16–17
9	9	18–19
10	10 and over	20 and over

Source: FBIjobs.gov.

push-ups, and pull-ups. Anaerobic power (higher-intensity exercise) is measured with the 300-meter sprint, and aerobic power (adequate fuel and oxygen) is measured with the 1.5-mile run. There are only 5 minutes of rest between each event.

The FBI also gives specific advice for training for this type of intense physical fitness test. They break their recommendations down into four core training principles:

1. **Overload**–The FBI defines overload as challenging the body beyond its current capacity. Overload can further be broken down into training frequency, intensity of training, and duration of training.
2. **Progression**–The FBI defines progression as gradually increasing overload in order to see positive gains in physical performance.
3. **Specificity**–The FBI defines specificity as focusing physical training to the components of the actual physical test, including the sprint, long distance run, sit-ups, push-ups, and pull-ups if required. Furthermore, according to the FBI, these events should not be performed in isolation but completed in their sum totality, just as will be required on the actual fitness test.
4. **Reversibility**–The FBI defines reversibility as essentially atrophy, or the wasting away of muscles back to their previous state. When physical training stops, physical ability returns to pre-training levels.

Before you begin your physical training exercises, the FBI recommends you warm up your body for 5 to 10 minutes in order to increase your body temperature and get a sweat going. The warm-up period also serves to get your joints and nervous system firing correctly. The FBI suggests incorporating moderate-intensity aerobic activities in the form of light running and biking, and some of the specific movements to be trained that day such as push-ups and sit-ups. After your workout is completed, the FBI recommends finishing with a 5- to 10-minute period of moderate physical activity before transitioning to a resting state.

Warming up and cooling down properly will help you avoid injury. It is important to note that while you are training to pass the physical fitness portion of your application process, you do not want to overdo your training to such a degree that you may injure yourself. An appropriate workout schedule should be formulated in order to maximize gains and minimize the chances of injury.

Formulating a Training Schedule to Pass Physical Fitness Tests

On *FBIjobs.gov,* the FBI provides a physical fitness test sample workout program. They recommend focusing your training on four specific areas:[16]

1. **Muscular Strength and Endurance**–Targeting specific muscle groups by performing push-ups, sit-ups, and pull-ups in order to exert force and resist fatigue.
2. **Aerobic Power**–Increases capacity of cardiovascular, respiratory, and musculoskeletal systems in order to maximize oxygen delivery for increased energy. The FBI specifically recommends sustained running periods for building aerobic power.
3. **Anaerobic Power**–Increases the body's ability to engage in high-intensity workouts. The FBI specifically recommends burst training to increase anaerobic power, and 30 to 90 seconds of sprinting activity.
4. **Circuit Training**–Combines all elements of training including muscular strength and endurance, aerobic power, and anaerobic power with limited rest periods in order to directly simulate what a physical fitness test will actually be like on test day. The FBI recommends a circuit training session consisting of the following activities:
   1. Run for 90 seconds
   2. Maximum sit-ups in 30 seconds
   3. Run for 90 seconds
   4. Maximum continuous push-ups
   5. Run for 90 seconds
   6. Maximum continuous pull-ups
   7. Run for 90 seconds
   8. Maximum body weight squats or lunges in 30 seconds

In terms of an actual training schedule, the FBI recommends to train for muscular strength and endurance 2 to 3 days per week on non-consecutive days. Anaerobic training

---

[16]https://www.fbijobs.gov/sites/default/files/PFT_Guide.pdf.

should occur 1 to 2 days per week, and aerobic power 3 to 5 days per week. Some of these training sessions will overlap on the same day. Special attention should be given to having at least 1 to 2 rest days per week to allow your body to repair and recover from your training schedule. The FBI's physical fitness test is one of the more rigorous to pass. If you feel comfortable with the physical requirements discussed herein, you will be more than ready for the vast majority of physical fitness tests found in the criminal justice career field.

The Cooper Institute Standards

Another common physical fitness test used in the field of criminal justice is known as The Cooper Institute Standards. This fitness test was originally designed by Kenneth H. Cooper in 1968 for military use, and is both gender- and age-specific in terms of its requirements and assessment structure.[17] The scoring and assessment structure of this specific test is shown in Figures 6.1 and 6.2 and linked in note 18.[18] The Cooper Institute Standards are now used as the physical fitness test for numerous local, state, and federal law enforcement agencies. The following list includes the physical exercises required in the Cooper Institute Standards[19]:

- **Vertical jump test**—Measures jumping and explosive power. To train for this test you should do squats with a straight bar or dumbbells. Doing four sets of 10 to 12 repetitions with weight you can manage comfortably is ideal for training purposes. This training exercise should be completed once per week.[20]
- **Maximum sit-ups in 1 minute**—Measures muscular endurance in the abdominal muscles. In order to train for this exercise, set a goal for the total number of sit-ups you would like to complete and break this up into five smaller sets totaling your overall target amount of sit-ups. Initially take a 45-second rest between each of these sets, and over time, gradually cut this rest time down between sets until you are not resting between sets at all. (45 seconds, 30 seconds, 15 seconds, 0 seconds). Each week of training you can cut down the rest period by 15 seconds until you are at no rest period between sets. No rest period between sets will translate into one continuous set where you are trying to complete as many sit-ups as possible in 1 minute. Perform your sit-up training three times per week.
- **300-meter run test**—Measures anaerobic power. In order to train for this exercise, start by completing three sets of 100-meter sprints. Rest for three minutes between sets. After two weeks of training, condense your sprints into two 150-meter sprints with a three-minute rest period between the two sets. After two more weeks of training, run the full 300-meter sprint as part of your weekly training routine. This training exercise should be completed at least twice per week.

[17]Kenneth H. Cooper, Aerobics (New York: Bantam Books, 1969). ISBN 978-0-553-14490-1.
[18]https://www.tucsonaz.gov/files/police/CooperStandards.pdf.
[19]This information was retrieved from http://www.cooperinstitute.org.
[20]Training recommendations given by the Minnesota State Patrol. https://dps.mn.gov/divisions/msp/join-the-state-patrol/trooper-careers/Documents/applicant-fitness-testing-standards.pdf.

- **Maximum push-ups in 1 minute**—Measures muscular endurance and strength in upper-body muscles including chest, shoulders, and triceps. Attaining gains with push-ups should be treated the same way as sit-ups. Set a goal for the total number of push-ups you would like to complete and break this up into five smaller sets totaling your overall target amount of push-ups. Initially take a 45-second rest between each of these sets, and gradually cut this rest time down to no rest between sets (45 seconds, 30 seconds, 15 seconds, 0 seconds). Each week of training you can cut down the rest period by 15 seconds until you are at no rest period between sets. No rest period between sets will translate into one continuous set where you are trying to complete as many push-ups as possible in 1-minute. Perform your push-up training three times per week.
- **1.5-mile run**—Measures and tests aerobic endurance and ability. In order to train for this distance run, you should run 2-mile distances at least two times per week. Training for 2 miles will make a 1.5-mile run seem much more manageable. To start your training, run at a comfortable pace, and look to limit walking as much as possible. After a couple of weeks of training, you should not be walking at all and looking to increase your running speed during your 2-mile training intervals.

▲ Working out consistently not only helps you feel better, but it could also be the necessary link to attain a career in the field of criminal justice.

Point Value	Vertical Jump (Inches)	1-Minute Sit-ups	300 Meter Run (Seconds)	1-Minute Push-ups	1.5 Mile Run
			Figure 6.1 Cooper Institute Standards for Females, Ages 20–29[21]		
20	19.0	>51	54.0	53	9:23
19	18.8	51	54.3	42	10:20
18	18.1	49	56.0	37	10:59
17	18.0	45	58.0	33	11:34
16	17.7	44	58.3	28	11:56
15	17.0	42	59.7	27	12:07
14	16.3	41	60.0	24	12:51
13	16.0	39	61.0	23	13:01
12	15.9	38	61.0	21	13:25
11	15.5	37	62.7	19	13:58
10	15.2	35	64.0	18	14:15
9	14.3	34	68.5	17	14:33
8	14.0	32	71.0	15	15:05
7	13.9	31	74.5	14	15:32
6	13.5	30	75.0	13	15:56
5	13.0	28	76.0	11	16:43
4	12.6	24	78.0	10	17:11
3	12.0	23	88.0	9	17:53
2	12.0	21	97.0	8	18:39
1	11.4	18	106.7	6	21:05

[21]https://dps.mn.gov/divisions/msp/join-the-state-patrol/trooper-careers/Documents/applicant-fitness-testing-standards.pdf.

Practice makes perfect on this training exercise. Make sure you conduct a proper warm-up and cool-down routine before and after running distance runs.

- *Some agencies will require a one-rep max (1RM) bench press. In order to train for a one-rep max bench press, one recommended method by strength coach Bill Starr is the 5×5.[22] Starr's book, *The Strongest Shall Survive: Strength Training for Football*, is an excellent read for strength training. The 5×5 training method means you lift an amount of weight that you can lift doing 5 sets of 5 repetitions on a bench press, with the final repetition of each set causing you fatigue. The final repetition causing fatigue is what will ultimately build strength. Make sure you *always* have a spotter when training on a bench press. This is an absolute must.

[22]Bill Starr, *The Strongest Shall Survive: Strength Training for Football. Fitness Consultatnts and Supply.* (1999).

Figure 6.2 This table shows the Cooper Institute Standards as part of the Minnesota State Patrol applicant testing standards for male applicants 20 to 29 years old[23].

Point Value	Vertical Jump (Inches)	1-Minute Sit-ups	300 Meter Run (Seconds)	1-Minute Push-ups	1.5 Mile Run
20	30.3	>55	42.6	100	8:22
19	26.5	55	46.0	62	9:10
18	25.0	52	48.0	57	9:34
17	25.0	49	49.0	51	9:52
16	24.0	47	50.3	47	10:08
15	23.0	46	51.0	44	10:34
14	22.5	45	52.0	41	10:49
13	22.0	44	53.5	39	11:09
12	21.5	42	54.0	37	11:27
11	21.0	41	55.0	35	11:34
10	20.5	40	56.0	33	11:58
9	20.0	39	57.5	31	12:11
8	20.0	38	59.0	29	12:29
7	19.0	37	60.0	27	12:53
6	18.0	35	62.1	26	13:08
5	18.0	35	64.0	24	13:25
4	17.5	33	66.0	22	13:28
3	17.0	32	69.0	19	14:33
2	16.0	30	73.4	18	15:14
1	13.6	27	81.3	13	16:46

[23]https://dps.mn.gov/divisions/msp/join-the-state-patrol/trooper-careers/Documents/applicant-fitness-testing-standards.pdf.

IMPORTANCE OF DIET

"You are what you eat" is an old saying meaning that in order to perform optimally you need to eat healthy foods. People can physically train all the time, but if they are not putting the right foods in their system they will not maximize potential gains. Food is directly linked to our overall well-being and even to how we perform on the job. Often a healthy diet gets placed on the back burner because we are in a rush and simply grab the quickest thing to eat. Most of the time this is something unhealthy, and does not provide the sustained energy and nutrition our bodies demand. Working in the field of criminal justice places great demands on a person physically and mentally, and it is imperative that you fuel your body correctly in order to stay healthy and fit. It might come as a shock to many, but police officers statistically are 25 times more likely to die from cardiovascular disease (CVD) than from the action of a suspect.[24] According to research, nearly 50% of police officers will die from heart disease within five years of retirement as well.[25] This underscores the need for criminal justice practitioners to take healthy eating habits very seriously from an early stage in their career.

Heart-Healthy Foods

Approximately 610,000 people in the United States die from heart disease every year— that is 1 out of every 4 deaths in the U.S.[26] The Centers for Disease Control and Prevention (CDC) note that heart disease is the leading cause of death for both men and women.[27] Heart disease is an epidemic that does not receive nearly as much coverage as it should with these types of alarming statistics. Heart health is important when it comes to many criminal justice careers. Regular exercise, blood circulation in the body, and proper brain function are impacted by overall heart health. Imagine if all of a sudden you need to chase down a suspect. You are going to want a healthy heart. Regular exercise contributes to heart health, and so does a healthy diet. Here are some heart-healthy foods, according to research, that you should try to incorporate into your diet:[28,29]

1. Salmon
2. Oatmeal
3. Blueberries
4. Citrus fruits (lemons, oranges, limes, kiwis)
5. Nuts (almonds and walnuts)

And here is a list of some foods that are detrimental to your overall heart health, and should be avoided as much as possible[30,31]:

1. Deep-fried foods
2. Candy
3. Soft drinks and diet sodas
4. Cookies and pastries
5. Sugary cereals

---

[24]Tom Tracy, "Fit for Duty: Demand It," *Police* (March 1993): 18.

[25]Ibid.

[26]https://www.cdc.gov/heartdisease/facts.htm, November 28, 2017.

[27]Ibid.

[28]"Study Says Heart-Healthy Diet Isn't Only About Fat," *Health Essentials* (Cleveland Clinic), July 9, 2014. https://health .clevelandclinic.org/2014/07/study-says-heart-healthy-diet-isnt-only-about-the-fat/.

[29]"Heart-Healthy Diet," University of Maryland Medical Center. http://www.umm.edu/health/medical/reports/articles/ hearthealthy-diet.

[30]"Avoid These Foods for a Healthier Heart," *Healthbeat* (Harvard Health Publishing, Harvard Medical School, n.d.). https://www.health.harvard.edu/healthbeat/avoid-these-foods-for-a-healthier-heart.

[31]Amanda MacMillan, "The 10 Worst Foods for Your Heart," *Time*, February 13, 2017. http://time.com/4669635/ worst-foods-for-heart/.

Brain-Healthy Foods

Working in the field of criminal justice requires your brain to be firing on all cylinders at any given time. There will be many occasions mandating a split-second decision, and if your brain is feeling sluggish you might make a very costly mistake. Treat your brain well when it comes to your diet, and focus on foods that bolster overall brain health. The following foods are some good choices to keep your synapses firing[32,33]:

1. Oily fish such as salmon and sardines
2. Blueberries
3. Tomatoes
4. Pumpkin seeds
5. Broccoli

Immune-Boosting Foods

The stress that is inherent in many criminal justice jobs can negatively impact your immune system.[34] You need to be feeling well in order to perform your job optimally and to be functioning at your peak ability at all times. You do not want to get run down and stifled by an illness. Here are some good dietary choices that will give an extra boost to your immune system:[35,36]

1. Chicken soup
2. Yogurt with live and active cultures
3. Foods rich in zinc like eggs and pumpkin seeds
4. Fruits and vegetables high in Vitamin C (citrus fruits, tomatoes and bell peppers)
5. Plenty of water. Staying hydrated is extremely important for your body. Water needs vary, but traditionally the four-to-six cup rule is for healthy individuals.[37]

Eating a healthy diet will produce many positive benefits for you in terms of your overall well-being. You will feel better physically and mentally, and you will also be paving a way toward achieving long-term health. Healthy eating will also cut down on

---

[32]Michael Roizen, "Food for Brain Health," *clevelandclinic.org*, n.d. https://my.clevelandclinic.org/ccf/media/files/Neurological_Institute/Cleveland-Clinic-Food-for-Brain-Health-Michael-Roizen.pdf.

[33]"Boost Your Memory by Eating Right," *Harvard Women's Health Watch* (Harvard Health Publishing, Harvard Medical School, August, 2012). https://www.health.harvard.edu/mind-and-mood/boost-your-memory-by-eating-right.

[34]Michael D. Wirth, Michael E. Andrew, Cecil M. Burchfiel, James B. Burch, Desta Fekedulegn, Tara A. Hartley, Luenda E. Charles & John M. Violanti, "Association of Shiftwork and Immune Cells among Police Officers from the Buffalo Cardio-Metabolic Occupational Police Stress Study," *Chronobiology International* 34, no. 6 (2017).

[35]"Healthy Diet Fights Infection by Boosting Immune System," *Health and Nutrition Letter*, Tufts University, May 2013. https://www.nutritionletter.tufts.edu/issues/9_5/current-articles/Healthy-Diet-Fights-Infection-by-Boosting-Immune-System_981-1.html.

[36]Laura Newcomer, "Eight Foods to Superpower Your Immune System," CNN.com, February 7, 2017. http://www.cnn.com/2017/02/06/health/foods-boost-immune-system-diet-partner/index.html.

[37]Heidi Godman, "How Much Water Should You Drink?" *Harvard Health Letter* (Harvard Health Publishing, Harvard Medical School, September 2016). https://www.health.harvard.edu/staying-healthy/how-much-water-should-you-drink.

the time you feel fatigued due to a poor diet and the chances of getting sick. Practice healthy eating habits now for a healthy future.

IMPORTANCE OF SLEEP

Quality sleep plays an extremely important role toward our overall health. Adequate sleep protects our mental health, physical health, and overall quality of life.[38] Failure to get the proper amount of sleep will negatively affect your immune system, and it will significantly decrease your job performance.[39] Working long hours in the field of criminal justice will challenge your time management abilities, but you will always want to prioritize getting quality sleep.

Sleep deprivation in the field of criminal justice is a serious issue. Often criminal justice personnel are required to work long and irregular hours. A research study on sleep deprivation found that not sleeping for 17 hours impaired an individual's motor skills to the same degree as having an alcohol toxicity of 0.05% would, and not sleeping for 24 hours had the equivalency of 0.10% when it came to alcohol toxicity levels.[40]

Additional research has shown sleep deprivation to contribute to work-related accidents. A research study found that four out of eight officers with on-the-job accidents and injuries were impaired because of sleep deprivation.[41] Another research study showed that sleep-deprived officers used force inappropriately more often, and had more difficulties dealing with community members.[42] All of these research studies underscore the need for quality sleep to perform your job at peak ability and to maintain overall health and well-being.

Individuals vary with regard to how much sleep they need in order to feel refreshed, but a general guideline would be between 7 and 8 hours of sleep per night (same hour amount if you are working night shift and sleep during the day).[43] Here are some tips for better sleep from the National Sleep Foundation:[44]

1. Avoid consuming caffeine before bedtime
2. Avoid electronics and loud noises before bedtime
3. Go to bed at a consistent time each day

---

[38]"Why Is Sleep Important?" National Heart, Lung, and Blood Institute, National Institutes of Health, U.S. Department of Health and Human Services, n.d. https://www.nhlbi.nih.gov/node/4605.

[39]L. Besedovsky, T. Lange, and J. Born, "Sleep and Immune Function," *Pflugers Archiv*, 463, no. 1 (2012): 121–137. http://doi.org/10.1007/s00424-011-1044-0; P. Alhola and P. Polo-Kantola, "Sleep Deprivation: Impact on Cognitive Performance," *Neuropsychiatric Disease and Treatment* 3, no. 5 (2012): 553–567.

[40]D. Dawson and K. Reid, "Fatigue, Alcohol and Performance Impairment," *Nature* 388:235.

[41]B. J. Vila, *Tired Cops: The Importance of Managing Police Fatigue* (Washington DC: Police Executive Research Forum, 2000).

[42]B. J. Vila and D. J. Kenney, Tired Cops: The Prevalence and Potential Consequences of Police Fatigue (pdf, 6 pages). *National Institute of Justice Journal* 248: 16–21.

[43]"How Much Sleep Is Enough?" National Heart, Lung, and Blood Institute, National Institutes of Health, U.S. Department of Health and Human Services, June 7, 2017. https://www.nhlbi.nih.gov/health/health-topics/topics/sdd/howmuch.

[44]"Healthy Sleep Tips," National Sleep Foundation, n.d. https://sleepfoundation.org/sleep-tools-tips/healthy-sleep-tips.

4. Practice a relaxing bedtime ritual
5. Exercise daily for better sleep

IMPORTANCE OF SOCIAL RELATIONSHIPS

Research shows that having quality social relationships has a positive impact on physical and mental health.[45] Strong quality personal relationships with friends have even been shown to reduce heart disease and lead to a longer life![46] It is important to establish and maintain consistent relationships within a network of friends. Working in the criminal justice system can often lead to feelings of isolation and detachment from society. Recent research has shown that a lack of social relationships is as detrimental to your health as smoking up to 15 cigarettes every day.[47] Additionally, some criminal justice practitioners fall into the trap of only maintaining friendships within their own profession. It is important to guard against this temptation and to broaden your circle of social relationships away from the job.[48] Make sure the relationships you seek are healthy in nature, and look to avoid individuals who are negative and will only bring you and everyone around them down. Quality personal relationships have even been shown to impact metabolism, where people with positive relationships burn more calories than individuals consumed with negative relationships.[49] Look to build your social networks with activities that will encourage meeting new people such as joining a recreational sports league or through volunteering for a cause that is personally important to you.

IMPORTANCE OF MENTAL HEALTH

Working in the field of criminal justice can take a great toll on your mental health. Maintaining mental health is often overlooked in this field, but it is a critical component in promoting physical and emotional well-being. Criminal justice practitioners frequently encounter people at their worst, and are exposed to traumatic experiences of others, known as vicarious trauma.[50] Suicides, post-traumatic stress disorder (PTSD),

[45]D. Umberson and J. K. Montez, "Social Relationships and Health: A Flashpoint for Health Policy," *Journal of Health and Social Behavior* 51(2010, Supplement): S54–S66. http://doi.org/10.1177/0022146510383501.

[46]Emily Sohn, "More and More Research Shows Friends Are Good for Your Health," *Washington Post*, May 26, 2016. https://www.washingtonpost.com/national/health-science/more-and-more-research-shows-friends-are-good-for-your-health/2016/05/26/f249e754-204d-11e6-9e7f-57890b612299_story.html?utm_term=.1d152fcb73f0.

[47]Julianne Holt-Lunstad, Timothy B. Smith, Mark Baker, Tyler Harris, and David Stephenson, "Loneliness and Social Isolation as Risk Factors for Mortality: A Meta-Analytic Review," *Perspectives on Psychological Science* 10, no. 2 (2015): 227–237.

[48]Michael Wasilewski and Althea Olson, "The Importance of Friendship," *Officer.com*, July 4, 2015. https://www.officer.com/training-careers/article/12089602/the-importance-of-friendship.

[49]Janice K. Kiecolt-Glaser et al., "Marital Discord, Past Depression, and Metabolic Responses to High-Fat Meals: Interpersonal Pathways to Obesity," *Psychoneuroendocrinology* 52 (2015): 239–250. Published online December 3, 2014. doi:10.1016/j.psyneuen.2014.11.018.

[50]"Mental Wellness," International Association of Chiefs of Police. http://www.theiacp.org/Cosw-Mental-Health.

depression, and other mental health issues are an underreported sector of the criminal justice system.[51] Law enforcement officers are at an increased risk for suicide due to experiencing risk factors such as work-related stressors, exposure to violence, anxiety, and depression.[52] In May 2017, the Senate passed the Law Enforcement Mental Health and Wellness Act. This Act calls for the Department of Justice (DOJ) to report on Department of Defense (DOD) and Department of Veterans Affairs mental health practices and services that can be adopted by law enforcement agencies.[53] Furthermore, the DOJ is tasked with reviewing existing crisis hotlines, providing recommended improvements, and researching the quality of annual mental health checks for law enforcement officials under this same bill.

Each year on average, there are 130 police officer suicides, and for every police suicide, there are at least 1,000 police officers suffering from some symptoms of PTSD.[54] In fact, research shows that more officers die of suicide than from gunfire and traffic accidents combined.[55] From 2008 to 2012, research showed that two times more officers committed suicide than were killed by felons.[56] When there is an officer suicide or attempted suicide, another research study found that coworkers had a higher incidence of mental illness.[57] The Badge of Life (badgeoflife.com) is a nonprofit 501(c)3 organization whose mission is to mitigate the impact of stress and trauma on active and retired law enforcement officials. This nonprofit organization recommends annual mental health checkups to help get ahead of mental health issues in the criminal justice workplace. These checkups would be on a voluntary basis and would have criminal justice practitioners visit a licensed therapist at least once per year.[58]

In September 2015, the FBI addressed the topic of mental health issues and suicide on their law enforcement bulletin publication. In doing this, the FBI discussed a nonprofit organization called *Safe Call Now*, whose mission is to offer 24/7 crisis intervention services for public safety employees experiencing crises. Safe Call Now is a confidential, comprehensive, 24-hour crisis referral service.[59] Communication is the first step to suicide prevention, and in addressing various forms of mental health issues that can impact criminal justice professionals. Keep open channels of communication

---

[51]Simone Weichselbaum, "A New Emphasis on Mental Health for Cops, Other Officers," *USA Today*, June 14, 2017. https://www.usatoday.com/story/news/2017/06/14/new-emphasis-mental-health-cops-other-officers/102677982/.

[52]Dell P. Hackett and John M. Violanti, *Police Suicide: Tactics for Prevention* (Springfield, IL: Charles C Thomas Pub Ltd., 2003).

[53]https://www.congress.gov/bill/115th-congress/senate-bill/867.

[54]"Police Suicides and Mental Health," *The Badge of Life*. http://www.badgeoflife.com.

[55]http://www.badgeoflife.com/#.

[56]"Tracking Police Suicides 2008, 2009, 2012," *The Badge of Life. http://www.badgeoflife.com/suicides.php* (accessed March 11, 2015); "A Study of Police Suicide 2008–2012," *The Badge of Life. www.policesuicidestudy.com* (accessed March 11, 2015; and John M. Violanti, *Police Suicide: Epidemic in Blue*, 2nd ed. (Springfield, IL: Charles C. Thomas, 2007).

[57]. O. Bär, C. Pahlke, P. Dahm, U. Weiss, and G. Z. Heuft, "[Secondary prevention for police officers involved in job-related psychologically stressful or traumatic situations]," *Psychosom Med Psychother* 50, no. 2 (2004): 190–202.

[58]http://www.badgeoflife.com/prescription-police-mental-health/.

[59]https://www.safecallnow.org.

with family, friends, colleagues and supervisors. Do not be ashamed or embarrassed to seek professional help when it comes to mental health. Seeking help with a professional at a minimum of an annual basis is something you should do while working in the criminal justice field. Remain vigilant in maintaining your mental health.

SUMMARY

Taking care of your overall well-being is extremely important when working in the field of criminal justice. This requires special attention to your physical fitness and exercise routine, eating habits and sleeping patterns. These areas in your life require long-term attention, as there are no quick fixes in these departments. Start healthy habits today and maintain consistency. This will enable you to maximize your chances for long-term health and success. Also, remember that mental health and keeping an active social network are very important when working in the criminal justice field. Do not be ashamed to seek professional help when it comes to discussing stressors you encounter on the job and in your personal life.

Three Key Takeaway Points

1. Start training for physical fitness tests months in advance. It takes time to build proper muscles and the endurance needed to pass many of these tests.
2. Practice healthy eating habits now for long-term health in the future. A poor diet will really hinder your overall well-being and job performance.
3. Get 7 to 10 hours of sleep each day. Quality sleep is essential when it comes to maintaining wellness and a healthy lifestyle.

ASSESSMENT QUESTIONS

1. Why is it important to train for physical fitness tests far in advance, as opposed to starting your training close to the academy date?
2. What is the difference between anaerobic and aerobic power?
3. What is "circuit training"?
4. How many people die in the United States from heart disease each year?
5. How many hours of sleep should you ideally get each day?

CRITICAL THINKING EXERCISE

As you begin to think about applying to criminal justice career positions in the future, strategize and develop physical fitness workout and healthy eating programs. Start today with strategizing exercising more and eating better foods. Developing good habits today will prepare you well in advance for the rigorous fitness requirements discussed in Chapter 6. Maybe your future criminal justice job does not require as intense of a physical fitness test as the FBI's requirements, but eating well and exercising will provide long-term health benefits regardless of your career path. How will you start eating better and exercising today?

ACTIVE LEARNING ACTIVITY

Put your designed plan of workout and dietary strategy from the Chapter 6 Critical Thinking Activity to the test. Begin a low-intensity workout regimen and dietary plan in order to start preparing for any physical fitness test thrown your way down the application road. Start small and gradually increase intensity over time in order to see progress. Results will not be immediate, but through consistent training, you will be better prepared for your future fitness test, or simply for overall healthier mental and physical well-being.

Disclaimer: Before you begin any physical fitness training or dietary program consult with a medical professional. The information in this chapter is not intended or implied to be a substitute for professional medical advice, diagnosis or treatment. Only your doctor can determine what is right for you. Consult with your doctor before starting any physical fitness or dietary program.

KEY TERMS

Cooper Institute Standards – Physical fitness requirements used by many law enforcement departments at the local and state levels as part of their pre-hire screening process.

Circuit training – Physical fitness training involving high-intensity workouts designed to build strength and muscular endurance.

Aerobic Power – Increases capacity of cardiovascular, respiratory, and musculoskeletal systems in order to maximize oxygen delivery for increased energy. The FBI specifically recommends sustained running periods for building aerobic power.

Anaerobic Power – Increases the body's ability to engage in high-intensity workouts. The FBI specifically recommends burst training to increase anaerobic power, and 30 to 90 seconds of sprinting activity.

Reversibility – The FBI defines reversibility as essentially atrophy, or the wasting away of muscles back to their previous state. When physical training stops, physical ability returns to pre-training levels.

Preparing and Applying to Advanced Degree Programs

INTRODUCTION

Many criminal justice careers have become so competitive in recent years that earning an advanced degree is often needed in order to really put yourself into the top tier of the applicant pool. Even jobs not explicitly stating they require an advanced degree could have the majority of their competitive applicants applying with an advanced degree in hand. Federal law enforcement agencies are now routinely only posting job vacancies at the GS-9 level or higher, meaning you are qualified to apply as a GS-9 with at least 2 years of work experience that is directly relevant to a GS-7 level in that same job role, or you are qualified to apply based on the fact you have an advanced degree.[1] The need for attaining an advanced degree is often evidenced by employees looking for advancement opportunities within their agency or organization. In order to get into the supervisory and administrative ranks, an advanced degree will likely be required at some point in your future career field. More Americans have college degrees than ever before, so earning an advanced degree might be part of the equation for what you need to distance yourself from the sea of other applicants out there.[2]

Some popular criminal justice career paths do explicitly state that an advanced degree is required to perform the job function, and to even be considered for the position based on minimum qualifications. For example, if you are interested in becoming a forensic psychologist, most of these jobs require a PhD in clinical psychology with hundreds of supervised clinical hours in order to attain the desired jobs in this field. Additionally, if you are interested in practicing law and having a legal career, you will most likely have to earn a law degree (Juris Doctor) in order to sit for the bar exam.[3] It is very important to properly research your desired career field and to see about the hiring requirements, employment trends, and minimum qualifications of job postings to see if an advanced degree is necessary for your career.

Conducting careful research into an advanced degree program and how it will specifically benefit your career objectives is essential before you decide to enroll in any program. Advanced degree programs are not all created equally when it comes to quality, and simply getting an advanced degree is certainly no guarantee of a job in today's employment market. When you really boil it down for some jobs, an advanced degree checks a requirement box, but there are other factors in a hiring decision as well. The advanced degree will open some doors for you in terms of the specific jobs you are qualified to apply for, but employers are still focusing on what you bring to the table with

[1] GS stands for General Schedule in the federal government. Typically with just a bachelor's degree and no relevant work experience you are qualified to apply to GS-5 jobs or lower. There have been some exceptions with GS-7 postings over the years where you can apply with just a bachelor's degree if you have "Superior Academic Achievement."
[2] Reid Wilson, "Census: More Americans Have College Degrees than Ever Before," *The Hill*, April 3, 2017. http://thehill.com/homenews/state-watch/326995-census-more-americans-have-college-degrees-than-ever-before.
[3] There are a few states where you do not have to earn a law degree in order to sit for the bar. In California, Vermont, Virginia, and Washington you can complete an apprenticeship in the legal field for a specific amount of time and then take the bar exam.

prior work experience and marketable skill-sets such as foreign language experience and advanced computer knowledge. You could have multiple advanced degrees, but if you lack real-world experience and basic interpersonal and professional skills, you are still going to have difficulties getting hired for the competitive jobs out there. An advanced degree should be seen as just one component of your overall professional package as an applicant. If you rely strictly on any degree to give yourself a job, your employment search is likely to be filled with frustrating results.

Before you invest a tremendous amount of time and money into any advanced degree program, you must properly vet the program you are intending to pursue. The goal is to try to determine if the advanced degree is going to benefit you enough to justify the cost and the time of earning the advanced degree. One of the worst mistakes you can make is to simply apply to a program without any research, and to expect positive results just because you are earning an advanced degree. Not properly vetting an advanced degree program can lead to a lot of problems, including lost time and money. Chapter 7 will help you to navigate through the process of preparing for and applying to advanced degree programs for the best possible results in your career. For additional preparation tips and advice on applying to advanced degree programs visit www.oup.com/us/klutz.

BIGGEST MISCONCEPTIONS AND PITFALLS ABOUT ADVANCED DEGREE PROGRAMS

Before we discuss how to properly prepare for and apply to advanced degree programs, some pitfalls and popular misconceptions need to be addressed that students tend to have regarding advanced degree programs. The following is a "top" list of common mistakes students make concerning advanced degree programs:

1. **Thinking an advanced degree program will guarantee you a job or will be the automatic solution to your application woes**. While an advanced degree can certainly help your application package, it is in no way a magic bullet for a guaranteed job in today's job market. Employers are still focusing on experience, soft skills, and other specific skill sets including foreign languages and specific computer skills.

2. **Taking on too much debt**. You must carefully consider the cost/benefit analysis of an advanced degree program before entering said program. Crunch the numbers and think about what that debt burden (plus interest) is going to look like for your financial future. If you are going to be $200,000 in debt, and only making $50,000 per year, those numbers do not add up. Think about the prospective debt load *before* you enter an advanced degree program. About 40% of the $1.5-trillion–dollar total outstanding student loan debt was used to finance graduate and professional degrees.[4]

From the Real World

One of the biggest mistakes I see students make is simply not adequately researching prospective advanced degree programs in terms of cost, time, and mental commitment before they apply to and enter the program. Often I see students apply due merely to a lack of other job options, or because their parents want them to enroll in an advanced degree program when in reality the student is on the fence. Simply hoping an advanced degree program is going to produce a job for you is not an adequate solution. Entering an advanced degree program means 100% commitment. You should always find out about where a program is placing their graduates, and talk to current and former students about the quality of the overall program before enrolling in any advanced degree program.

---

[4]"A Look at the Shocking Student Loan Debt Statistics for 2017," *Student Loan Hero*, September 13, 2017. https://studentloanhero.com/student-loan-debt-statistics/.

3. **Entering the wrong advanced degree program for your career path due to inadequate research**. This happens a lot more than one might think because many students will rush into an advanced degree program without conducting the proper amount of research, only to find out later the advanced program does not really help them in pursuing their ultimate career goals. For example, if you are planning to be a forensic psychologist, pursuing a graduate degree in criminal justice is not going to help. Instead you should be pursuing a PhD in clinical psychology where you can obtain supervised forensic experiences and obtain the advanced degree that is actually required for the job. In this same situation, if you cannot get accepted right away into a PhD program in clinical psychology, then you should look for quality clinical/forensic psychology master's programs. Completing a master's degree can be your stepping stone to the PhD program in clinical psychology, but the point is you are still pursuing a master's degree in the correct field of study—in this case, clinical/forensic psychology. Find out specific job and degree requirements while you are pursuing your undergraduate degree and *before* you even think about applying to an advanced degree program. A good way to find out these specific requirements for jobs is to spend some time looking at multiple job vacancies for the types of jobs you will be applying to in the future. What specific requirements (including advanced degrees) are the employers looking for?

4. **Lateral degree-hopping in similarly titled advanced degrees.** This means students who are unsatisfied with the results after one advanced degree program automatically looking for the solution in another advanced degree program at the same lateral level (e.g., obtaining two master's degrees in similar areas of study). Students need to be cautious of simply hopping between lateral degrees, because this will often produce the same frustrating results with lack of employment opportunities. Getting two lateral advanced degrees in almost the same field is probably not going to help you much in the employment search. For example, an applicant obtaining a master's degree in criminal justice fails to have readily available employment opportunities, so that same applicant decides to get a second master's degree in criminology, thinking that will make them more competitive for jobs. These two degrees are so close it is not going to make much difference in their application, and most employers are not going to be wowed that they hold two master's degrees in similarly titled fields.

5. **Entering an advanced degree program due to lack of options.** Many students are being caught in this pitfall today. Due to limited options after their undergraduate degree is earned, students will simply choose an advanced degree program "just because." Often the lack of options for students after their undergraduate career is due to poor strategic planning (not pursuing internships, not earning an in-demand undergraduate degree, not networking, etc.). Simply obtaining an advanced degree by itself is not going to change much unless students change their

overall strategy to become more marketable in terms of networking and gaining real-world experience. If you do not have a specific plan in place for your future, jumping into an advanced degree program can prove to be an expensive mistake. If you are really unsure of your future career plans, and do not have a clear strategy in place, your time would be better served getting an entry-level job in your field, building some real-world work experience, and holding off on those advanced degree plans until you formulate a concrete plan of action as to how a specific advanced degree program is going to benefit your career.

6. **Not adequately preparing for the standardized tests required for entry into advanced degree programs.** This largely has to do with the rush decision-making factor where a student decides to apply to an advanced degree program at the very last minute without proper research and preparation. Failure to properly prepare for the standardized tests can cost you a lot of money when you think about losing out on funding packages many advanced degree programs offer based on test scores. These funding packages can include working as graduate teaching and research assistantships, and there are even scholarships in some cases. But these funding opportunities are largely based on excellent performance on standardized tests like the Graduate Record Examination (GRE) and the Law School Admissions Test (LSAT). Rushing test preparation and getting a low score on a standardized test will often cost you access to various funding opportunities, making an advanced degree program much more expensive.

   Inadequate test preparation can also cost you admission into your desired program due to a low standardized test score. Then it becomes a snowball effect of bad decision-making for many students because they feel compelled to enroll in a program of lesser quality just to "get in" to any advanced degree program. Simply enrolling wherever you get accepted is not a good strategy if you have not properly screened the degree program. You want to make sure the advanced degree program is well regarded and has a quality reputation in order to maximize your future career opportunities. The big takeaway here is that you must begin your test preparation early, and be diligent during the course of your test-preparation time. Failing to properly prepare for a standardized test required for entry into an advanced degree program can come with many consequences and drastically limit your future career options.

7. **Not applying to enough advanced degree programs.** You should plan on applying to at least 5 to 10 programs in order to see what types of financial packages programs are willing to offer you. Yes, application fees can be expensive, but it is much cheaper to pay hundreds of dollars in application fees than it is to only apply to one program, and potentially miss out on thousands of dollars of funding opportunities another competitive program might have offered you. When you are applying to programs, you are the consumer, and you should be looking

for the best deal and fit for your future career plans. Limiting yourself to only applying to one or two degree programs is not likely going to afford you the opportunity to see a good variety of different funding options. View applying to an advanced degree program like shopping for any other big-ticket purchase item. Do a lot of research and take your time making a final decision.

Be very cognizant of these common mistakes and pitfalls students encounter when formulating their advanced degree plans (or lack of a plan). Side-stepping these mistakes can save you a lot of time, stress, and money. Always try to be proactive in your planning and avoid the big pitfalls discussed herein.

THOROUGHLY RESEARCHING ADVANCED DEGREE PROGRAMS

Prospective homebuyers usually want to have a house inspected before purchasing it. The foundation is checked along with the structural integrity and "guts" of the home. Careful research is done beforehand because no one wants to find themselves in a money pit. You should view shopping around for an advanced degree program the same way as investing in a house, and try to check out the specifics of the program as much as you can before officially enrolling in that degree program. Many advanced degree programs these days cost approximately the same as a starter-home. You would probably think twice about buying a house without a home inspection, but unfortunately many students these days are not thinking twice before enrolling in an advanced degree program without thoroughly researching the overall quality of the program beforehand. A poor choice with an advanced degree program can become a "money pit" just like investing in a house that has a poor structural foundation.

So how do you ensure to the best of your ability that the advanced degree program at the top of your list is a good-quality program with a solid foundation? Here are some tips that will help you as the "investor" before you actually make the investment and decide to enroll in the program:

1. If you are applying to a graduate program, email or schedule a meeting with the graduate program director to inquire about where the program is placing their graduates in terms of employment. You should also ask about the structure of the degree program and if it offers internship-type opportunities (sometimes called externships, co-ops, or practicum placements) through the program because of the importance of gaining real-world experience and networking. The importance of acquiring internships and real-world experience holds true for both undergraduate and advanced degree programs. Additionally, find out if the

From the Real World
By far, the biggest problem I experience with students involves too much debt. I am constantly meeting with students concerned about their overall debt load after they finish advanced degree programs. These students often have a case of "buyer's remorse" and almost always say they wish they had planned better before rushing into an advanced degree program. I cannot underscore enough the need to strategize proactively when it comes to the costs associated with advanced degree programs. A large debt burden can follow you for a long time and can really have a negative impact on your financial future.

graduate program sponsors specific networking events like career fairs with prospective employers.

2. Law schools are a little different in terms of the research you should conduct before applying. The first step you should take is accessing the Standard 509 Report for the law schools you will apply to.[5] These are American Bar Association (ABA)–required reports providing full disclosures about important law school statistics such as tuition and fees, living expenses, GPA and LSAT scores for admissions, attrition rates, and bar passage rates. These reports foster transparency in the law school application process.

3. For both graduate and law school programs, you should also do your own extensive research online. Look for sources like *U.S. News and World Report* that provide rankings for advanced degree programs.[6] See how the programs you are thinking about applying to stack up against the competition. And when it comes to law school rankings, do not just look at the overall general ranking, but also rankings of specific specialty areas of law schools as well. For example, if you are specifically interested in studying environmental law, the general list of top-ranked law schools overall would differ greatly from the top list of law school programs specializing in environmental law. Also, look to professional networking sites like LinkedIn to solicit feedback on programs from current students and graduates of these same programs. When visiting these online resources, ask questions like, "What is the overall reputation of the program?" Is it overwhelmingly positive or negative? Conducting this type of online investigation will enable you to form an overall assessment of the quality of the advanced degree program well before you sign on the dotted admission line. Here are some online resources for graduate and law school:

> *College Confidential – collegeconfidential.com* – Large online forum covering admissions, test prep, discussion of different higher education programs, and more.
> *The Grad Café – thegradcafe.com* – Graduate school discussion forum.
> *Top Law Schools – www.Top-Law-Schools.com* – Offers an interactive forum where a lot of information and feedback gets posted about various law school programs.
> *US News and World Report – https://www.usnews.com* – Wide-variety of information on graduate and law school programs including ranking lists.

---

[5] A link to the Standard 509 Information Reports can be found at http://www.abarequireddisclosures.org.
[6] *Source*: https://www.usnews.com/best-graduate-schools.

PREPARING FOR THE GRADUATE RECORD EXAMINATION (GRE) GENERAL TEST

The GRE is a common standardized test required for admission into many graduate school programs. The GRE is administered through the Educational Testing Service (ETS), and according to their own website (*ets.org*) the GRE includes the following sections:

1. **Verbal Reasoning** – This section measures ability to analyze and evaluate written material, and identify relationships between different words and concepts.
2. **Quantitative Reasoning** – This section measures mathematical problem-solving abilities covering areas in geometry, algebra, and analyzing data.
3. **Analytical Writing** – This section measures writing skill ability and requires the writer to be able to articulate and support complex ideas in an effective manner.

The GRE is a computer-adaptive test, meaning it is administered through a computer and as you answer questions correctly, the test questions become more difficult. According to the ETS, the GRE General Test is available at more than 1,000 testing centers across the world, and is available to be taken throughout the entire calendar year. You will want to schedule taking the actual GRE well in advance of your planned test date at the approved testing center most convenient for you. The information regarding scheduling the GRE can be found on ets.org.

According to the ETS, the GRE's Verbal Reasoning section has a score scale of 130–170 in 1-point increments, as does the Quantitative Reasoning section. The Analytical Writing section is scored between 0 and 6 in half-point increments. The global test-prep company Kaplan states an average GRE score on the Verbal Reasoning section is approximately 150–152. This same scoring range of 150–152 holds true for the average score on the Quantitative Reasoning section as well. Kaplan also says the average score on the Analytical Writing section is about a 3.5.

Graduate programs are different in terms of where they establish their minimum GRE cutoff scores for admission into their program. It is a good idea to contact the graduate programs you are interested in applying to before you start fully preparing for the GRE to see what their minimum cutoff score is, what the average GRE score is for accepted applicants, and the average GRE score of applicants receiving funding opportunities within the program is. These scores will be helpful for establishing benchmarks as you begin your test preparation course of study. For graduate programs in the social science field, a score range from 160–170 on either section of the GRE (verbal or quantitative) is generally considered an excellent score. The Analytical Writing section score is generally not viewed so strictly for admission purposes compared to the Verbal and Quantitative section scores. However, you still want to strive to attain a score of 4.0 or higher on the Analytical Writing section, especially for graduate programs that are more writing-intensive.

Two of the best ways to prepare for the GRE General Test are to begin your test preparation early and to take many practice tests along the way. Just remember it is never too early to start preparing for a standardized test, even if your initial preparation involves completing one or two practice problems each day during your first year of higher education. The more time you have to familiarize yourself with the type of problems found on the actual GRE the better. But you should seriously dedicate, at a very minimum, at least three months of intensive test preparation before you take the actual GRE. This means practicing at least one hour per day for that time period to really maximize your scoring potential on the Graduate Record Examination. During this three-month period of intensive test preparation, take one GRE practice test per week. Taking practice tests and familiarizing yourself with the types of questions asked and the time constraints of the GRE will greatly benefit your score. The major test-preparation companies like Kaplan, The Princeton Review, and Barron's all have GRE test preparation material, including computer-adaptive practice tests structured just like the real GRE. Use these practice materials to your advantage, because the more practice and preparation time you put into the equation, the more confident and comfortable you will feel going into the actual exam. The old saying "Practice makes perfect" holds true when preparing for standardized tests. And just think, effectively preparing for the GRE can mean gaining admission into your top program choice and potentially saving a lot of money along the way with various funding opportunities.

According to the ETS, you can take the computer-delivered GRE General Test once every 21 days, and up to five times within any continuous rolling 12-month period of 365 days. ETS also recommends thinking about your application deadlines when selecting a GRE testing date because your score reports will be sent to your designated score recipients (the graduate programs you are applying to) approximately 10 to 15 days after your test date. You will want to have thoroughly researched graduate programs well before you take the actual GRE General Test, so you can select your designated score recipients the day of the test in order to have your scores automatically sent to these graduate programs. Most application deadlines for graduate programs tend to start in December and January. It is a good strategy to take the GRE General Test the summer before your applications are due. Your summer will tend to afford you more preparation time away from the stressors of a regular academic semester, and taking the GRE over the summer will give you plenty of time to take the test again if you get a lower score than desired the first time you take the GRE. However, it is critical to note you should be fully prepared to take the GRE on your first attempt. Do not take the GRE simply to try it out and test the waters. The GRE is $160 per test, so if you want to just test the waters on the GRE, take a computerized unofficial practice test instead. Another reason you do not want to aimlessly take the real GRE test just to see what it is like is because graduate programs will see your entire history of GRE test scores. Most programs take your highest score, but there are some programs out there that will take the average of all your official GRE test scores. This is why it would not be a good idea to simply test the waters on the GRE and possibly get a low score. Be fully committed to achieving your best score possible the very first time you register to take the GRE General Test.

FINDING OUT MORE ABOUT THE GRE SUBJECT TESTS

Some graduate programs require or recommend taking a GRE Subject Test designed to measure knowledge in a specific field of study. According to the ETS, the Subject Test can even help you stand out from other applicants by highlighting your knowledge in your specific field of study. It is important to contact the graduate programs you are interested in to see if they require or even recommend taking the GRE Subject Test. Here are the specific subjects covered on the six separate GRE Subject Tests:

Biology
Chemistry
Literature and English
Mathematics
Physics
Psychology

PREPARING FOR THE LAW SCHOOL ADMISSION TEST (LSAT)

The Law School Admission Test (LSAT) is a standardized test required by 98.5% of law schools.[7] While the LSAT is only one part of an overall admission application, it is an extremely important piece to the admission equation. Obtaining a quality LSAT score is critical to getting into a top law school. Recently a few law schools have announced they will start accepting the GRE as an option for entry, but the vast majority of law schools still require the LSAT. Because of so many issues with grade inflation and the way GPAs are calculated between weighted and unweighted scales, law schools really emphasize the LSAT score since it is the same measure for everyone across the board. Without a good LSAT score you will really limit your admission potential for quality law schools. GPAs are secondary to the importance law schools place on the LSAT score. Even a person with a 4.0 GPA with a lower LSAT score will struggle to get into top-ranked law school programs.

The Law School Admission Council (LSAC) is a nonprofit corporation where you will register to take the LSAT. The easiest means to do this is to go to their website, LSAC.org. This is also where you will request letters of recommendation to send to law schools. LSAC.org includes helpful tips covering testing strategies for the LSAT, picking a testing

From the Real World
The biggest problems I find with students taking the LSAT are lack of preparation time and failure to be familiar with the time constraints on the LSAT. The LSAT is a hard test and you have to know how to manage your time properly during the exam to maximize your scoring potential. Taking multiple practice tests leading up to the real thing is essential. I would recommend at a very minimum 5 months of preparation time before taking the actual LSAT, and to study at least 1 hour per day during this 5-month period of time (a total of about 150 prep hours). I would also recommend taking a practice LSAT test once every 2 weeks during this 5-month preparation time. Of course, the earlier you start preparing for the LSAT the better! Preparing for the LSAT should be viewed as a full-time job because of the significance law schools place on attaining a high LSAT score.

---

[7] "About the LSAT," LSAC.org. https://www.lsac.org/jd/lsat/about-the-lsat.

▲ Law school requires major time and monetary commitments. If you are interested in pursuing law school, make sure you plan ahead. Look at the costs and job placements of any law school before you even apply.

center to take the LSAT, and discussions about fees and fee waivers. Just about all of the major test preparation companies like Kaplan, Barron's and The Princeton Review have LSAT preparation guides and practice tests. The general recommendation is that you take the LSAT in the month of June following the end of your junior year in your undergraduate education. The LSAT score range is from 120 to 180. Law schools vary widely concerning their average applicant's LSAT score. A score of 162 might be considered an excellent score at one school, while a score of 175 might need to be achieved to even receive consideration at another school. The specifics on LSAT score ranges can be found in the 509 Standard Report for each law school. The key to doing well on the LSAT, like any other standardized test, is to prepare early and take plenty of practice tests. The LSAT is considered a difficult test, so proper preparation time is essential to doing well.

The LSAT is broken down into five 35-minute sections of multiple choice questions. According to the LSAC, these sections include one Reading Comprehension section,

▲ Yale Law School is consistently ranked as one of the very top law schools in the country.

one Analytical Reasoning section, and two Logical Reasoning sections. There is also a 35-minute unscored writing sample administered at the end of the test. According to the LSAC, the LSAT measures the following abilities:

1. **Reading comprehension** – Ability to read with understanding and insight of complex information routinely encountered in law school.
2. **Analytical reasoning** – Ability to understand a structure of relationships and to draw logical conclusions about this structure.
3. **Logical reasoning** – Ability to analyze, critically evaluate, and complete arguments.

According to the LSAC's website (lsac.org), the LSAT is offered on specific dates, varying each year, in the months of June, September, December, and February. Make sure to schedule your test date early because seats fill up quickly for the LSAT. Generally, test registration for the LSAT starts on the LSAC's website 10 to 12 months prior to the actual test date. It is important to note that approximately 14 law schools, including top schools like Harvard and Georgetown, have recently started accepting students without an LSAT

▲ The LSAT (Law School Admissions Test) score is a critical factor when it comes to gaining admission into law school. You must plan ahead and prepare well in advance to achieve your best LSAT score.

score, who have taken the GRE instead.[8] Law schools say the rationale for this change has to do with recruiting students from a wide variety of backgrounds, including those studying mathematics and engineering.[9]

GEOGRAPHIC CONNECTIONS AND ADVANCED DEGREE PROGRAMS

One final point to contemplate while planning for advanced degree programs is that the geographical connections and networking for most advanced degree programs is strongest in the general geographical location of the degree program. There are some exceptions to this with top-ranked programs in any discipline. For example, if you attend a top-ranked law school and graduate at the top of your class, you will have employment opportunities in many of the major legal markets across the country. If you attend a top-ranked PhD program in a given academic discipline, you increase your employment chances in academia or an applied clinical setting all over the country. But for many advanced degree programs, employment opportunities will be greater around the

[8]Andrew Nusca, "LSAT No Longer Required for Top Law Schools Including Harvard, Georgetown," *Fortune*, December 6, 2017. http://fortune.com/2017/12/06/lsat-law-school-harvard-georgetown/.
[9]Sara Randazzo, "Law Schools Say: Please Come, No LSAT Required," *Wall Street Journal*, December 7, 2017. https://www.wsj.com/articles/law-schools-say-please-come-no-lsat-required-1512556201.

geographical area of your academic institution because networking and professional connections in that same area will be tied to that advanced degree program. Advanced degree programs offering internship, externship, co-op, and practicum-type work experiences present an excellent opportunity to get hired upon graduation at the same employer where you completed one of these work experiences as a student. Think about where you want to work geographically before you start applying to advanced degree programs, and then tailor your search for advanced degree programs to your personal geographical preferences.

SUMMARY

Researching and applying to advanced degree programs can be a very complex and intimidating process. It is essential that you, the consumer, do as much research as possible about the degree program before actually enrolling in it. Research your job field to find out if you need an advanced degree, and how earning an advanced degree can actually benefit your own career. Put in the time to research if the advanced degree programs are indeed quality academic programs. Ask questions like, "Where are they placing their graduates," and "Does this program have a quality reputation behind it?" Be proactive in your research, instead of reactive, because once you are stuck in a bad situation you have already lost time and money.

Advanced degree programs require a lot of planning in order to maximize your potential success. You need to prepare early for the standardized tests required to gain entry into these competitive programs. A high standardized test score is not only one of the main hurdles to gain admission into a quality program, but that same high test score can also potentially save you thousands of dollars through tuition waivers in the form of graduate teaching and research assistantships, and possibly even scholarships at some schools. Do not minimize the significance of doing well on standardized tests. Focus on taking practice tests and preparing early for your standardized admissions tests.

Three Key Takeaway Points
1. Thoroughly research advanced degree programs before applying to them. This includes visiting the program in person, talking with the directors or admissions staff of the program, researching the program online, and trying to talk with current students and graduates of the program.
2. Start preparing for the standardized test required for entry into your advanced degree program early. Do not procrastinate when it comes to preparing for these tests. Put in full effort and take as many practice tests as possible before you take the official standardized test.

3. Crunch numbers and look at the cost of your program before applying. See if it makes fiscal sense to enroll in the degree program, and look at how an advanced degree can really benefit your career.

ASSESSMENT QUESTIONS

1. Discuss one major misconception mentioned in this chapter regarding advanced degree programs.
2. What is one reason you should thoroughly research advanced degree programs *before* applying to them?
3. What are the main components of the GRE General Test?
4. What are the main components of the LSAT?
5. What is the score range for the LSAT?

CRITICAL THINKING EXERCISE

Why do you think graduate programs and law schools place so much emphasis on standardized test scores?

ACTIVE LEARNING ACTIVITY

Look up three types of specific jobs that interest you utilizing job websites like *Indeed. com*, *Monster.com*, and *USAjobs.gov*. (Examples would include general job titles like "special agent," "police officer," "forensic scientist," "forensic psychologist," etc.). Find two job advertisments for each of these job titles (6 job vacancy announcements total). Examine the educational qualifications and preferred qualification sections for each job advertisement. Do these jobs require or prefer an advanced degree? And if so, what types of advanced degrees are these jobs looking for?

KEY TERMS

Standard 509 Report – Helps to provide transparency with law schools and provides extremely important statistics on law school programs.

Law School Admission Council (LSAC) – Nonprofit corporation providing products and services to help with the law school admission process worldwide.

Juris Doctor degree (JD) – Graduate-entry professional degree in law. Typically takes three years to complete at a law school.

8

Ethics and Professionalism in Criminal Justice Careers

"Real integrity is doing the right thing, knowing that nobody's going to know whether you did it or not."

—Oprah Winfrey

"Whoever is careless with the truth in small matters cannot be trusted with important matters."

—Albert Einstein

INTRODUCTION

Working in the field of criminal justice often puts you directly into the public spotlight, especially in today's digital world. There is always a strong possibility your actions are being recorded, analyzed, and documented for everyone to see. One mistake can cost you your career and even open you up to criminal or civil litigation. Working in a criminal justice profession requires you to be cognizant of these realities at all times. Both maintaining a professional image and performing the job the right way are critical to having a successful career in this field. Criminal justice practitioners frequently interact with the public and need public support in order to perform their jobs to the best of their abilities.

Two sought-after traits of applicants entering the field of criminal justice are compassion and service-orientation.[1] You should want to be in this line of work for the correct reasons, and not simply because you want to be on a power trip or abuse your authority. Researchers have identified five personality characteristics that enable a law enforcement officer to perform well; these include emotional stability, agreeable nature, conscientious, extrovert, and open to experience.[2] Possessing these personality traits and characteristics will help ensure you maintain a strong moral compass throughout your career. A recent report by the U.S. Department of Justice (DOJ) detailed the importance of recruiting and hiring individuals who have a service orientation, high standards of integrity, and the ability to resist temptations that deviate from high moral standards.[3]

Criminal justice professionals always need to strive to maintain a strong moral compass and engage in ethical behaviors. Ethics are defined as basic moral principles that govern individuals' behavior and how individuals go about conducting their daily life. Ethical training is something that should be consistent and continually given to employees. In order to maintain high ethical standards, research has shown that exercises geared toward forming and maintaining good ethical habits and character, exercising value in choices, and rehearsing proper responses to ethical dilemmas need to be covered on a frequent basis by employers.[4] Questionable ethical behavior by criminal justice professionals causes the public to lose confidence in the criminal justice system. A loss of public confidence can foster strained relationships with the public, and also makes the job of criminal justice practitioners even more difficult than it already is. Use of excessive force, abuse of power, and failing to fulfill duties as a criminal justice professional can hurt public trust and reduce credibility of an institution in the eyes of the public.[5] Doing

---

[1] *Building Trust between the Police and the Citizens They Serve* (Washington, DC: Office of Community Oriented Policing Services, U.S Department of Justice, 2009). http://www.theiacp.org/portals/0/pdfs/buildingtrust.pdf.
[2] Ibid.
[3] *Police Integrity—Public Service with Honor: A Partnership Between the National Institute of Justice and the Office of Community Oriented Policing Services* (Washington, DC: U.S. Department of Justice, Office of Community Oriented Policing Services and Office of Justice Programs, National Institute of Justice, January 1997). www.ncjrs.gov/pdffiles/163811.pdf.
[4] E. Delattre, *Character and Cops: Ethics in Policing*, 5th ed. (Washington, DC: American Enterprise Institute Press, 2006). www.aei.org/docLib/9780844742175.pdf.
[5] *Building Trust between the Police and the Citizens They Serve* (Washington, DC: Office of Community Oriented Policing Services, U.S. Department of Justice, 2009). http://www.theiacp.org/portals/0/pdfs/buildingtrust.pdf.

things the right way and maintaining professionalism in the job function will help bridge positive relationships with the communities criminal justice personnel serve. Chapter 8 focuses on the importance of upholding strong ethical standards and engaging in professional behavior when working in the field of criminal justice. There will also be ethical dilemmas presented in this chapter where you, the reader, will need to give thought as to how you would respond should situations like these occur during your career. To learn more about ethics and professionalism in criminal justice careers check out www.oup.com/us/klutz.

IMPORTANCE OF ETHICS

Criminal justice careers come with a great deal of power. Utilizing this power in an ethical way is paramount to meeting your moral responsibilities of your job function. Discretion is a key term that many professionals in this field deal with on a daily basis. Discretion can be defined as going outside of the exact letter of the law and having the ability to decide what should be done in a particular situation with a degree of flexibility. This means there is some amount of flexibility in how you will act and respond to certain situations, but

▲ Criminal justice careers require you to keep your ethical compass intact at all times.

you want to ensure that discretion is only exercised with strong moral and ethical principles in mind. For example, consider a situation in which a police officer pulls over a driver for speeding three miles per hour over the posted speed limit. Under the letter of the law, the driver is in violation of the legal speed limit, and therefore warrants a citation for breaking the law. However, the police officer, utilizing his or her discretion, examines the specific situation, and because the driver is only going three miles per hour over the speed limit, may decide to only give the driver a warning this time. The officer surmises that this is the reasonable thing to do, and giving speeding tickets for such minor offenses may foster discontent with the public's view of law enforcement in the long term. The police officer in this scenario has exercised a prudent amount of discretion.

Another example of discretion in the criminal justice system could involve a probation officer working with one of his or her clients. A probation officer's client is a convicted offender who has been given a probationary sentence by the court. Under the exact letter of the law, if the person on probation violates the terms of his or her probationary sentence, this is known as a technical violation and can result in the court suspending the probationary sentence and incarcerating the offender. However, a probation officer might consider other factors in dealing with their client, such as length of good behavior on the probationary sentence, and the client's attitude and willingness to improve. A client who has almost completed a lengthy probationary sentence who commits a technical violation by failing a drug test near the very end of their sentence might get some leniency by his or her probation officer. The officer may choose not to report this technical violation to the court, and not reporting this to the court is the probation officer utilizing his or her discretion in what that officer deems to be the right decision at the time outside of the exact letter of the law.

In order to utilize discretion effectively, you must always ask yourself if you are acting ethically. Criminal justice practitioners must always seek to avoid abusing their power. Not only is abusing power the wrong thing to do, but in the field of criminal justice abusing power can also come with significant legal consequences. Arbitrary application of power can lead to civil and even criminal liabilities down the road. The key to using discretion effectively in criminal justice professions is consistency. You must be consistent with your application of discretion and always treat everyone equally. For example, if you are a patrol officer and decide to let speeders going less than four miles per hour over the speed limit off with just a warning, it should be for *all* individuals meeting these criteria. An arbitrary and unethical use of discretion would be only letting speeders of a certain gender or race off with a warning, and then ticketing all others. Make sure your use of discretion in the field is always consistent and fair.

ETHICAL DILEMMA #1:

A female police officer decides to not issue speeding tickets for male drivers, and instead lets all male drivers off with only a warning. The same female police officer tickets all female drivers who are speeding. What is the major ethical issue present in this situation?

Criminal justice professionals can face much more serious ethical issues as well. According to the American Civil Liberties Union (ACLU), racial profiling refers to the discriminatory practice by law enforcement officials of targeting people for suspicion of a crime based on a person's race, ethnicity, religion, or national origin.[6] It is important to note that racial profiling, according to the ACLU, does not refer to the act of a law enforcement official pursuing a suspect when the specific description of the suspect in question includes race or ethnicity in combination with other identifying factors pertaining to a crime that has been committed.[7] It is extremely important, when working in the criminal justice field, to treat everyone equally and with respect at all times, regardless of a person's race, ethnicity, gender identity, sexual orientation, or age. The due process clauses found in the 5th and 14th Amendments, and also the equal protection clause found in the 14th Amendment of the U.S. Constitution, ensure that everyone, regardless of race, ethnicity, and gender, receives equal protection in our legal system.

Another serious ethical issue in the criminal justice system involves varying forms of corruption. Corruption can be defined as dishonest or fraudulent conduct by those in positions of power.[8] Working in the criminal justice system creates opportunities to abuse power if moral integrity and ethical standards are not upheld consistently. For example, there are two major forms of police corruption known as "grass-eaters" and "meat-eaters."[9] Grass-eaters are more common, and routinely accept small payoffs and kickbacks through their role as a law enforcement official. A grass-eater might have a system set up with a towing company wherein the officer calls to report a car illegally parked and the towing company then pays the officer a small gratuity for their report. Meat-eaters are involved in much more serious forms of police corruption, including actively seeking situations to misuse their personal power for exploitation and personal gain. An example of "meat-eating" behavior could be looking for and shaking down known drug dealers carrying large amounts of cash. Meat-eaters pocket the large amounts of cash for personal gain because they know a drug dealer is probably not going to report the theft to the police.

ETHICAL DILEMMA #2:

You are a rookie officer and your training officer pulls a car over for speeding. You overhear your training officer tell the driver that she can make it easier for both of them (the training officer and the driver of the car), if she pays your training officer $100 on the spot. Your training officer says he will let the driver out of the speeding citation if she hands over the cash right then and there. What are the major ethical issues present in this scenario?

---

[6] "Racial Profiling: Definition," *ACLU.org.* https://www.aclu.org/other/racial-profiling-definition.
[7] Ibid.
[8] *Oxford Living Dictionary*, s.v. "corruption." https://en.oxforddictionaries.com/definition/corruption.
[9] Michael F. Armstrong, *They Wished They Were Honest: The Knapp Commission and New York City Police Corruption* (New York: Columbia University Press, 2012).

Many forms of corruption are gleaned by new employees seeing established employees engaging in unethical and illegal behaviors. Over time, these new employees begin to normalize these behaviors, and it segues into the concept of "learned criminality." Learned criminality is the idea behind Edwin Sutherland's deferential association theory, which states that an individual who has been exposed to a criminal subculture for long enough begins to adopt the norms of that criminal subculture.[10] The mentality "If others are getting away with unethical and illegal behaviors and reaping perceived benefits from these actions, then I should too!" begins to creep into the equation. However, even if others are doing things that are unethical and illegal, you should always refrain from these behaviors. You do not want your career ruined and to possibly face criminal and civil sanctions just because you were simply going along with the crowd. "Yeah, but they did it too!" is not a valid defense in a court of law. One should always place a great emphasis on upholding strong ethical standards in the field of criminal justice.

ETHICAL DILEMMA #3:

You have been working in a loss prevention role in a large retail store for about six months. You notice some employees stealing store merchandise and when you confront the store manager with this information, the manager tells you not to worry because everybody working in the store takes a little bit here and there. The manager says that if you see anything you want in the store to help yourself right before closing as well. You now have a decision to make in terms of reporting this information to your district loss prevention manager. What are the ethical implications of this scenario?

Another ethical issue frequently encountered in criminal justice professions involves working with confidential and classified information. These types of information are considered privileged communications where only a select few individuals are privy to the information as a whole. Attorney–client relationships and working with a security clearance serve as two common examples of working with these forms of sensitive information. The takeaway is that working in the field of criminal justice means you must be cognizant of the fact that you will routinely deal with sensitive information. You must be very careful with how you handle it and make sure you do not disclose any information to unauthorized parties. Improper disclosure could occur by talking to an unauthorized party over the phone, in-person, or online. Be very careful to only use a work-approved email account and server to access confidential information and to not take classified information from your place of employment unless instructed to do so. Many careers have ended over the mishandling of sensitive information, and in some

---

[10]Sutherland, Edwin Hardin, *Criminology*, 9th ed.. (Philadelphia: Lippincott, 1974).

cases, even criminal and civil charges have been leveled against the wrongdoer over the improper use and dissemination of classified information.

ETHICAL DILEMMA #4:

Your employer is a federal government agency and you have a top-secret security clearance in your job. There is a strict policy in your office that your email account is not to be accessed outside of the office's secure server because there is classified information in this account. There is a tight time deadline to finish a project at work, but you fail to complete the project during work hours. So, you make the decision to take the project home and email it to your work email to open at home, thereby violating agency policy. You finish the project at home, but when you arrive to work the next morning you realize your email account has been compromised. How do you respond to this ethical dilemma?

▲ Working in the field of criminal justice comes with great power. However, you must always utilize this power in an ethical and moral manner. There are many different roads you can go down, but always choose the one with high ethical standards and integrity.

PROFESSIONALISM IN THE CRIMINAL JUSTICE FIELD

Working in the field of criminal justice requires engaging in professionalism at all times. Professionalism can take on many forms, but can be defined as a high level of skills and competency from individuals working in their given field. Some of the most important aspects of professionalism working in the criminal justice system involve maintaining a professional image and always acting in a professional manner. Criminal justice professionals are often the center of media attention and intense scrutiny in the public eye. One misstep in this field and your career can be tarnished forever. There are not many second chances with criminal justice careers, and one must always remain on their toes and aware of their surroundings in order to maintain consistent professionalism.

The Media and Criminal Justice Careers

Criminal justice professionals need to err on the side of caution when dealing with the media. Make sure that you always have approval from your employer before talking with any form of media outlet. Know that the media is not always on your side, and versions of events can be distorted based on inaccurate or incomplete narratives. The media will also sway public opinion with their coverage, and often this is not in favor of criminal justice professions. Keep in mind that media outlets routinely engage in sensationalism, meaning they present information in a manner to garner viewership but usually at the expense of complete accuracy. In order to help thwart the spread of misinformation when dealing with the media, many criminal justice agencies will have prepared statements ready, and a designated public information officer handling media relationships.

Engaging and building relationships with the media is a good mechanism to build positive perceptions from the community.[11] Always maintain professionalism when dealing with the media. Demonstrate positive body language and remain courteous in your interactions. If you are a public information officer in the future, the key is to always be prepared and know what you are going to say when you will face the media. You never want to be caught off-guard, or violate agency protocol talking with the media. When in doubt, consult your supervisor before giving any statements to media outlets. Research has shown that highlighting programs such as community-oriented policing efforts and citizen academies in the media helps to convey a positive image to the public.[12]

---

[11] *Building Trust Between the Police and the Citizens They Serve.* (Washington, DC: Office of Community Oriented Policing Services, U.S Department of Justice, 2009). http://www.theiacp.org/portals/0/pdfs/buildingtrust.pdf.
[12] 12 S. Chermak and A. Weiss, *Marketing Community Policing in the News: A Missed Opportunity?* (Washington, DC: Office of Justice Programs, National Institute of Justice, U.S. Department of Justice, 2003). www.ncjrs.gov/pd les1/nij/200473.pdf.

Social Media and Criminal Justice Careers

Social media has revolutionized the way information is disseminated. Not only is information through social media disseminated outside of the realm of traditional media outlets, but the dissemination of content is also extremely quick. A video uploaded to social media can garner millions of views within minutes. However, social media can serve as a double-edged sword as well. On one hand, social media has been positive in how it has fostered transparency and oversight with cases concerning abuse of power and corruption. In these types of events, had a citizen's video not been taken and uploaded to social media, the truth might never have surfaced surrounding the case. But on the other hand, social media can serve as a negative when content is released that fails to show the whole event in question. This type of piecemeal reporting can lead to the public misconstruing what really happened, and therefore formulate a false narrative surrounding the entire event. Once a false narrative is in place, it is very difficult to walk back and change people's minds.

When you are working with the public in various criminal justice professions, nowadays you should expect to be filmed and recorded on video with all of the new forms of digital recording devices available for mass consumption. Social media enables these recorded instances to immediately be uploaded and disseminated to a massive online audience. This all underscores the need to always engage in professionalism while dealing with the public and performing your job function. Uphold high ethical standards and moral integrity constantly. Maintaining a professional image is vital, and will prevent a lot of potentially negative situations from occurring when interacting with the public.

It is also important to note that citizens are legally allowed to record most interactions with criminal justice personnel as long as the person conducting the recording is not impeding or interfering with law enforcement investigations. Technology has been popularized now that actively video records interactions and live-streams these interactions to the Internet so footage cannot be deleted on the scene. Never attempt to take a recording device away from a law-abiding citizen, delete footage or other evidence on a personal recording device without consent, or lie and say a law-abiding citizen is not allowed to film. Engaging in these behaviors is a bad look for the profession, and it will also put you directly into the "YouTube Hall of Fame" for all of the wrong reasons. Furthermore, failure to understand the public's right to film and record could cost you your job, and possibly open up criminal or civil legal consequences depending on how a situation escalated. Working in the criminal justice system requires you to always be up-to-date on the law, and one area receiving much attention over the past couple of decades has been filming law enforcement professionals pertaining to citizen interactions. Remember that filming is almost always allowed, and is considered a basic 1st Amendment right, as long as the public is not hindering or impeding law enforcement investigations with their filming.

One final very important rule to remember when dealing with social media is to be extremely careful in how you personally use social media while employed in your line of work in the field of criminal justice. Think before you post or share information on these accounts. A great many careers have been terminated due to something an employee said or commented on involving social media. It is not worth losing your job over a tweet or post on any social media outlet. Best practice is to simply avoid posting anything questionable that could be used against you by someone in the future. Think before you act with a social media post, and if you have to question whether or not to post something, you probably should not. Avoid posting about politics, religion, and other potentially controversial subjects on your social media profile while employed in the field of criminal justice. Even if your privacy settings are set to the highest levels, content on social media can still be used against you because it is in a public forum. Keep your social media accounts professional at all times if you choose to have them at all.

Email and Professionalism

Email has become a primary tool of communication, but just like with any tool you must know how to properly use it for it to be effective. Make sure to ask your employer about their rules for using a work email outside of the office, especially if you are dealing with confidential information through your email account. Keep in mind email accounts pertaining to public business are generally considered public record, so anything you send or receive in an email can be available for "outside" consumption through public records requests. The best rule of thumb is to not send anything questionable through your work email, and do not conduct official work business through your personal email accounts. Keep the two accounts separate and you will avoid a lot of potential trouble.

Email etiquette is also very important to use throughout your career. You should always maintain professionalism while conversing through email just as you would in-person. Always address an individual with a greeting and by their full title unless you are on a first-name basis with them. Avoid using slang or short-hand terminology in your emails. Read your drafted email a couple of times before sending it to make sure the tone sounds polite and professional, and the email is free of grammatical and spelling errors. Avoid sending extremely long emails with lots of questions and text. Two paragraphs is about the maximum length you want an email to be before the reader starts losing focus. Anything longer, or with multiple questions, should be addressed in person or over the phone. When sending emails, make sure they are sent at a reasonable time during the day and not late at night or in the early morning hours unless it is extremely urgent. Many people now have emails automatically linked with their phones and might be awakened in the middle of the night over a late email sent past normal business hours.

From the Real World
A U.S. Supreme Court case to read on a recent legal issue regarding filming law enforcement can be found in the 2014 SCOTUS case *Riley v. California*. The SCOTUS held that police generally may not, in the absence of a warrant, conduct a search of digital information on a cell phone seized from an arrested individual.[13]

---

[13]*Riley v. California*, SCOTUSblog. http://www.scotusblog.com/case-files/cases/riley-v-california/.

▲ Exuding professionalism is an important component for a successful career.

Professional Dress and Appearance

Working in most criminal justice jobs requires professional dress. Remember the adage "First impressions are lasting impressions." You want to look professional in your appearance at work. Business-professional dress attire is the way to go until you see what the dress norms and expectations are around the office. Ask your supervisor about dress expectations or requirements before your first day at the job just to be safe. Make sure your clothes or uniform are clean and free of wrinkles. Err on the side of conservative dress when you are unsure about dress expectations. It is always better to be over-dressed than under-dressed in terms of conveying professionalism. Research shows that when workers wear nicer clothes, they actually achieve more in their line of work.[14]

Your personal appearance should also be neat and tidy in this line of work. Maintain good grooming habits, and find out if your employer (especially if you are working in the field of law enforcement or corrections) has a policy on hair length and the style in which hair can be worn. Make sure that you are showing up clean and appropriately

---

[14]Ray Smith, "Why Dressing for Success Leads to Success," *Wall Street Journal*, February 21, 2016. https://www.wsj.com/articles/why-dressing-for-success-leads-to-success-1456110340.

groomed for work. Basic hygiene is underscored here. Personal appearance goes a long way in conveying professionalism. You want to look well put-together instead of appearing disheveled when showing up for work.

Interpersonal Skills

The way you engage interpersonally in a work environment is a very important component of professionalism. Maintaining good-quality professional relationships is key here. You do not want to "burn bridges," so to speak, when it comes to your work relationships. It is far easier to maintain positive relationships than it is to try to repair a broken work relationship. Adhering to quality interpersonal skills will help you avoid trouble and drama in the workplace, and will help pave the way for a successful career. Here is a helpful list of things you can do to foster healthy work relationships and to convey excellent interpersonal skills:

1. Always greet someone the first time you see your colleagues during the workday; be sure to say, "Hello!"
2. Smile at work and remain positive with your thought process and interactions with others.
3. When conversing with your colleagues make sure you are engaged in the conversation and do not make it all about you. Ask them what their thoughts are about the issue at hand. A conversation should be a two-way street and engaging for all parties.
4. Do not interrupt people when they are talking. Let them finish what they are saying before you start speaking.
5. Always remain polite and respectful even if you think a colleague is not acting that way to you personally. Take the moral high ground and avoid engaging in negative behaviors and actions at work.
6. Do not engage in gossip at work. Talking behind people's backs can have many unintended consequences, so just do not do it. Your colleagues might like to gossip, but stay completely out of it in order to maintain professionalism. Research shows that people who gossip are less respected.[15]
7. Maintain a quality professional relationship with your direct supervisor. Communication is key. Sit down with your supervisor to inquire about your performance and what you can do to improve on the job. Solicit feedback when appropriate. This demonstrates that you are a conscientious employee that shows initiative and concern.
8. Always be punctual in work-related matters, and submit assignments when due. Being on time is a great way to convey professionalism. Plan ahead to avoid lateness.

---

[15]Jessica Stillman, "Think Gossip Is Harmless? Research Says Otherwise," CBS News, August 30, 2011. https://www.cbsnews.com/news/think-gossip-is-harmless-research-says-otherwise/.

SUMMARY

Striving to maintain high ethical standards is paramount to enjoying a long, successful career in the field of criminal justice. When it comes to ethics, always think about moral integrity and doing the right thing. Avoid taking advantage and abusing the power that comes with working in the criminal justice profession. Never look to misuse this power and exploit others. You will need public support in your profession to perform the job effectively, just like the public needs you to serve and protect them. Upholding high ethical standards will help avoid potential legal programs from questionable actions and behaviors.

Consistently engaging in professionalism will make a very positive impact on your career as well. Being likeable and well-versed with basic interpersonal skills in the workplace will foster a positive image for your colleagues and other work relationships. Avoid the pitfalls of social media and ensure you always maintain professionalism when using these types of online outlets. Your reputation precedes you, and it is so easy to ruin a career these days based on one social media post. Always be cognizant of maintaining your professional image and reputation. Working in the criminal justice system comes with being subjected to public scrutiny. Look to mitigate this scrutiny and other potential pitfalls by always engaging in professionalism.

Three Key Takeaway Points

1. Maintaining high ethical standards is critical to having a successful career in the criminal justice system. This means always trying to do the right thing, and avoiding abusing one's power to exploit others.
2. Always look to convey professionalism in your work. Professionalism is important when it comes to building your personal brand. Strive to put out a quality work product and to also build positive relationships at work.
3. Avoid potential pitfalls that serve to undermine ethics and professionalism such as social media. Always know working in the field of criminal justice that you are being watched and evaluated by the public. Adhere to strong ethical principles and engage in professionalism, and you will help insulate yourself from being portrayed in the media for all of the wrong reasons.

ASSESSMENT QUESTIONS

1. What does the term "ethics" mean?
2. Why is it so important to adhere to high ethical standards when working in the criminal justice field?
3. What is meant by the term "professionalism?"
4. Why is social media referred to as a "double-edged sword"?
5. When it comes to professionalism, what are two applications of quality interpersonal skills in the workplace?

CRITICAL THINKING EXERCISE

Think about a time you experienced or heard about an ethical dilemma involving another individual or institution. What happened? How did the ethical dilemma impact your perception of that individual or institution?

ACTIVE LEARNING ACTIVITY

Find two cases of misconduct involving abuse of power committed by criminal justice practitioners (could be practitioners working in law enforcement, corrections, the legal field, etc.). What happened in these specific cases, and what were the criminal and/or civil liabilities against the criminal justice personnel in these specific cases?

KEY TERMS

Ethics – Basic moral principles that govern individuals' behavior and how individuals go about conducting their daily lives.

Professionalism – High level of skills and competency from individuals working in their given field.

Discretion – Going outside of the exact letter of the law and having the ability to decide what should be done in a particular situation with a degree of flexibility.

Racial profiling – Discriminatory practice by law enforcement officials of targeting people for suspicion of a crime based on a person's race, ethnicity, religion, or national origin.

Corruption – Dishonest or fraudulent conduct by those in positions of power.

Grass-eater – One who routinely accepts small payoffs and kickbacks through their role as a law enforcement official.

Meat-eater – One who engages in serious forms of police corruption including actively seeking situations to misuse personal power for exploitation and personal gain as a law enforcement official.

9

Working in Law Enforcement— Public and Private Sectors

INTRODUCTION

Law enforcement can be defined as professions within the field of criminal justice that enforce the law, conduct investigations, make arrests, and work with the public on a frequent basis. The most visible form of law enforcement is found at the local government level through police departments and sheriff's offices.[1] Hardly a day goes by in public when we do not see a police officer or deputy sheriff driving around in their patrol vehicles. However, there are many other, lesser-known career options in the field of law enforcement as well. For example, the private sector in itself has numerous career opportunities related to law enforcement jobs. Most private corporations have security and investigation divisions containing intriguing law enforcement-related career options. Chapter 9 will cover a variety of different law enforcement career options, including jobs in the public sector at the local, state, and federal levels, as well as examining law enforcement–related careers in the private sector. All of these different career paths in law enforcement need to be on your radar if you are interested in applying to this field. Chapter 9 also provides real job postings to highlight specific qualifications needed to be competitive for these careers. Additional law enforcement career resources can be found on the companion website to this textbook at www.oup.com/us/klutz.

WORKING IN LOCAL LAW ENFORCEMENT

Police Officer

BASIC JOB DESCRIPTION

Police officers have a wide-ranging job description with primary tasks including enforcing the law, protecting the public, responding to calls for service, making arrests in certain situations, and testifying in court. A police department has many different divisions such as criminal investigations, patrol, K-9, narcotics, homicide, internal affairs, and a fugitive apprehension task force. Because of all these different divisions within a typical police department, there are a variety of career paths available within a police department as well. Police officers, generally speaking, serve a municipality (city) in terms of their jurisdiction. In some cities, police officers will also help provide security for municipal courthouses and city jails. While television shows like *Cops* tend to show police officers constantly involved in foot and high-speed car chases, the actual majority of a police officer's job is spent on routine patrol, filling out paperwork, and testifying in court.

---

[1] George Cole, Christopher Smith, and Christina DeJong, *The American System of Criminal Justice*.13th ed. (Boston, MA: Cengage Learning, 2014).

▲ Becoming a police officer is a great entry point into the field of law enforcement.

MINIMUM QUALIFICATIONS

Minimum qualifications will vary across police departments in the United States, however some common qualifications seen across the board are being at least 21 years of age, being a U.S. citizen, and having no felony convictions on your record. Your entire criminal history will be scrutinized, and some police departments will even view misdemeanor convictions as an automatic hiring disqualification. In order to become a police officer you will also need to successfully complete a physical fitness test, hearing, medical, and sight tests, firearm proficiency test, written police exam, drug test, psychological exam, and a panel interview asking questions about situations likely to be encountered as a police officer. Panel interviews often present prospective hires with situational questions that do not have a clear right or wrong answer, but the purpose of these interviews is to see how well you think on your feet and if you think in an ethical manner. The psychological examinations are generally something similar to the Minnesota Multiphasic Personality Inventory (MMPI) where questions are asked to determine attributes associated with a prospective applicant's personality characteristics. Evaluators in these psychological exams are looking for any major red flags that might prevent an individual from using sound judgment as a police officer.

Police officers are required to successfully pass a pre-hire training academy as well. Police training academies generally average approximately 21 weeks in the United States. In these training academies prospective police officers are trained in state and local laws, arrest procedures, Constitutional law, ethics, self-defense tactics, administering first aid, report writing, and firearm proficiency. Once the training academy is successfully completed the newly minted police officer is converted to full-time work with a supervisory officer overseeing the new hire for a probationary period ranging typically anywhere from 6 to 12 months.

Education requirements for police officers vary widely by police department. According to the Bureau of Labor Statistics, a police officer must have a high school diploma at the very minimum. Many police departments are now requiring the completion of some college coursework, and some departments even require the successful completion of a bachelor's degree. While possessing a bachelor's degree might not specifically be written into the actual job description, police departments frequently have "unwritten" requirements where a minimum of at least an associate's degree is highly desired in order to be considered a competitive applicant in the hiring process. The advent of criminal justice–type curriculums and majors across colleges and universities over the past few decades has made it very popular for students interested in becoming a police officer to pursue these areas of study.

SAMPLE MINIMUM QUALIFICATIONS IN JOB POSTINGS FOR A POLICE OFFICER

The minimum qualifications needed in order to be considered for employment as a police officer vary by location. Two examples are presented in Figures 9.1 and 9.2.

FIGURE 9.1

Job Posting for a Police Officer in Dekalb County, Georgia

- High school diploma or GED.
- Must be 20 years of age, a citizen of the United States and possess and maintain a valid Georgia driver's license.
- The working test period for this classification is 12 months.

FIGURE 9.2

Job posting for a police officer in Longview, Texas

- High School Diploma or equivalent; no experience is required as this is an entry-level position.

- Two years of experience may be required before assignment to specialized function or area of responsibility.
- Basic Texas Peace Officer License is required within 20 weeks of employment. Must possess a valid Texas Driver's License.
- PREFERRED REQUIREMENTS: Ability to speak and understand Spanish.

TIPS FOR GETTING HIRED

One of the best steps you can take to make sure becoming a police officer is right for you is to complete ride-along programs where you shadow a police officer in their patrol function. See if your higher education program offers course credit hours for completing a work experience with a police department. Another helpful step is to apply to complete an internship with a police department while you are full-time student. Internships will enable you to experience a broader array of the different divisions within a police department, and an internship will also enable you to network and make connections within the department. Some police departments offer what they call "cadet programs" where interested future applicants who have not yet turned 21 years of age can complete basic training programs and get involved in the police department.

Obtaining a minimum of an associate's degree will help in getting ahead of your competition during the hiring process to become a police officer. Pursuing a course of study related to the legal field is valuable in this profession. Additionally, if you can become proficient in the Spanish language it will greatly help you in the hiring process. Some police departments even give signing bonuses or extra monthly pay for officers who are proficient in the Spanish language.

▲ Sheriff's departments offer a great opportunity to gain entry-level experience in the field of law enforcement.

Deputy Sheriff

BASIC JOB DESCRIPTION

Deputy sheriffs perform a very similar job function to police officers. The primary difference is that a sheriff's jurisdiction is generally the county. A deputy sheriff is also commonly found providing courtroom security in the county courts, and helping to administer and provide security in the county jails as well. Besides those main differences, a deputy sheriff's job description is almost identical to that of a police officer. The minimum qualifications and tips for getting hired as a deputy sheriff are the same as for a police officer.

SAMPLE MINIMUM QUALIFICATIONS IN JOB POSTINGS FOR A DEPUTY SHERIFF

The minimum qualifications needed in order to be considered for employment as a deputy sheriff vary by location. Two examples are presented in Figures 9.3 and 9.4.

FIGURE 9.3

Job posting for a deputy sheriff in Multnomah County, Oregon

- Must have or receive within 6 months (from application date) a bachelor's degree from an accredited college or university
- Must be 21 years of age within 90 days of application date
- Must be or become a U.S citizen within 90 days of application date
- Must be able to obtain a valid driver's license by time of appointment

FIGURE 9.4

Job posting for a deputy sheriff in Fairfax County, Virginia

Any combination of education, experience and training equivalent to the following: high school diploma or a GED issued by a state department of education.

CERTIFICATES AND LICENSES REQUIRED:

- Possession of a valid motor vehicle driver's license at time of appointment.
- The following must be obtained from the Virginia Department of Criminal Justice Services within one year of appointment:
- Certification as a law enforcement officer;
- Certification as a jailor;
- Certification in court security/civil process;
- Certification in firearms proficiency.

NECESSARY SPECIAL REQUIREMENTS:

- Must be a U.S. citizen;

- Must be twenty-one years old or within 180 days of 21st birthday at time of application;

- Must successfully complete a criminal background investigation, polygraph examination, and a psychological examination;

- Must never have been convicted of a felony or a serious misdemeanor;

- Must be able to obtain a Class "A" medical rating in the assigned medical group before appointment;

- Must be a non-smoker at time of appointment, and be willing to sign a Condition of Employment Agreement to refrain from smoking, both on and off duty.

- Must possess a valid motor vehicle driver's license without a negative point balance at the time of appointment.

- Must successfully complete a field training program (on-the-job training) upon graduation from the Fairfax County Criminal Justice Academy.

SALARY ESTIMATES FOR POLICE AND SHERIFF PATROL OFFICERS

Annual salary estimates for police and sheriff patrol officers are presented in Figure 9.5.

Detective (Local Law Enforcement)

BASIC JOB DESCRIPTION

Detectives conduct investigations in order to solve crimes. Collecting evidence, interviewing witnesses, interrogating suspects, making arrests, testifying in court, and writing reports are all common components of a detective's job description. Shows like *The First 48* tend to focus on the more action-packed aspects of being a detective like apprehending suspects and intense interrogation showdowns; however, the majority of a detective's time is generally spent in the courtroom and writing reports. Detective work

Figure 9.5 Annual salary estimates for police and sheriff patrol officers[2]

Percentile	10%	25%	50% (Median)	75%	90%
Hourly Wage	$16.46	$21.15	$28.69	$37.57	$47.36
Annual Wage	$34,230	$44,000	$59,680	$78,140	$98,510

[2]*Source*: Bureau of Labor Statistics. https://www.bls.gov/oes/current/oes333051.htm#(3).

is often perceived as a glamorous position where the shrewd investigator always catches their suspect, but research shows that detectives solve a surprisingly small percentage of crimes due to the fact much of their time is spent working on cold cases. Witnesses recant their original stories, or become difficult to track down, evidence deteriorates, and once a case starts to go cold it is difficult to solve. This can be one very frustrating aspect of working in the field of investigations. Detectives can work a variety of long hours during both days and nights. Crime does not sleep, so detectives are frequently called out to crime scenes at random times at all hours in various work environments.

MINIMUM QUALIFICATIONS

Working as a detective requires prior experience in policing to be a competitive applicant. Detectives have generally worked in a patrol function on the streets for at least a few years before they are qualified enough to apply to coveted investigative positions. The idea here is that detectives need to learn the basics of law enforcement work before actually beginning to work in an investigatory function. Larger and more competitive local law enforcement agencies might require as much as 5 to 7 years of patrol experience at a minimum to even be considered for an investigatory position, while smaller local law enforcement agencies might require only 3 to 4 years of experience. You have to put time in on the street in order to learn and know the ropes of basic policing. Field experience is key when it comes to becoming a detective. Educational requirements for detectives vary, but earning at least a bachelor's degree will make you more competitive for future openings in addition to work experience. Detectives need strong interpersonal skills in order to communicate with people, and also solid writing skills.

SAMPLE MINIMUM QUALIFICATIONS IN JOB POSTINGS FOR DETECTIVES

The minimum qualifications needed in order to be considered for employment as a detective vary by location. Two examples are presented in Figures 9.6 and 9.7.

TIPS FOR GETTING HIRED

The best tip for getting hired as a detective is to start working as a patrol officer and gain real-world experience in this role. You will want to work hard and receive positive performance evaluations because your supervisors will have a big say when it comes to being nominated or applying for the investigations positions. It is a very competitive field with limited job vacancies. Avoid red flags on your work record like coming to work late, poor writing skills, lack of attention to detail, and questionable uses of force. Strive to be a model patrol officer, and this will help when it comes time to put in your application to become a detective. One final tip to get hired as a detective is to become proficient in the Spanish language. Many local law enforcement departments are actively seeking Spanish-speaking applicants for detective positions. Being proficient

FIGURE 9.6

Job posting for a detective in Philadelphia, Pennsylvania, with the Philadelphia Police Department

The following statement represents the minimum training and experience standards which will be used to admit or reject applicants for tests. Candidates must meet requirements by the written exam date: March 17, 2018.

1. Presently employed by the City of Philadelphia with permanent Civil Service status in the Police Department with a performance rating of Satisfactory or higher;

   AND

2. Experience:

   One year of experience as a Police Officer.

FIGURE 9.7

Job posting for detective position within the Metropolitan Transportation Authority Police (MTA) in New York City

Interested employees must, at a minimum, possess:

- Five (5) years of Police experience (as defined in section 1.20 of the NYS criminal procedure code) with at least three (3) years of service with the MTA Police Department.
- Be able to demonstrate strong communication and multi-tasking skills
- Must be able to show self-initiated activity
- Must show demonstrated writing ability as well as exhibit proficiency in report writing. All candidates will be required to submit their most recent arrest process record prior to October 1, 2017 along with two (2) additional reports dated before October 1, 2017.
- Flexibility to work various tours, various work locations and be willing to be "on call" based on the needs of the Department.
- Ability to access databases from other law enforcement agencies.
- The ability to travel from residence to incidents within the MTA PD service area in a reasonable time will be taken into consideration.
- Must have extensive knowledge of the New York State and Connecticut criminal law statutes
- Successful completion of the panel interview.

Figure 9.8 Annual salary estimates for detectives and criminal investigators[3]

Percentile	10%	25%	50% (Median)	75%	90%
Hourly Wage	$20.30	$26.53	$37.56	$49.68	$63.08
Annual Wage	$42,220	$55,180	$78,120	$103,330	$131,200

[3]*Source*: Bureau of Labor Statistics. https://www.bls.gov/oes/current/oes333021.htm.

in Spanish, along with experience as a patrol officer coupled with a bachelor's degree, will help put your application at the very top of the stack for a detective job vacancy announcement.

SALARY ESTIMATES FOR DETECTIVE AND CRIMINAL INVESTIGATORS

Annual salary estimates for detectives and criminal investigators are presented in Figure 9.8.

Specific Divisions within a Local Law Enforcement Agency

Local law enforcement agencies offer opportunities to specialize working in specific divisions like narcotics, fugitive apprehension, homicide, criminal investigations, crime scene investigations, internal affairs, water patrol divisions where applicable, K-9 units, and mounted units in some cases, and tactical teams. These divisions generally require a minimum of 2 to 3 years of experience as a patrol officer first. Working in these specific job roles within a police department or sheriff's office offers great experience for applicants looking to transition into state or federal law enforcement employment one day down the road.

WORKING IN STATE LAW ENFORCEMENT

State Trooper

BASIC JOB DESCRIPTION

State troopers enforce state vehicular laws and codes at the state level in order to promote public safety and keep roads safe. Troopers frequently patrol interstates and issue citations, render aid to stranded motorists, respond to traffic accidents on interstate highways, conduct searches and seizures during vehicular stops when necessary, and also make arrests when needed. A state trooper's job description requires a lot of time spent in a squad car enforcing traffic laws. State troopers often encounter dangerous situations because motorists are traveling at such a high rate of speed on highways and interstates.

MINIMUM QUALIFICATIONS

A high school degree is required for state trooper job postings, and a minimum of some college coursework is desired in today's job market. There is often an age requirement of 21 years for this career path. Troopers are required to go through an academy very similar to the academy requirements at the local law enforcement level. Through the academy physical fitness standards are tested; Constitutional and state laws are taught; search, seizure, and arrest protocols are taught; and defensive driving techniques are acquired.

SAMPLE MINIMUM QUALIFICATIONS IN JOB POSTINGS FOR STATE TROOPERS

The minimum qualifications needed in order to be considered for employment as a state trooper vary by location. Two examples are presented in Figures 9.9 and 9.10.

TIPS FOR GETTING HIRED

Most state trooper agencies offer internship opportunities for students. Completing an internship is a great way to network and gain experience in the field before you officially apply to become a trooper. A minimum of an associate's degree related to criminal justice will greatly help your application stand out when applying to be a state trooper. Being familiar with the Spanish language will also make an application

---

FIGURE 9.9

Job posting for a state trooper in Florida

- United States citizen
- High School graduate or equivalent
- Minimum of 19 years old at time of application (no maximum age restriction)
- Valid driver's license
- Willing to accept an initial assignment anywhere in Florida.

- **One** of the following–One year of law enforcement experience (sworn or non-sworn); Two years of public contact experience; Two years of active continuous U.S. military service with an honorable discharge; Completed 30 semester or 45-quarter hours of college credit from an accredited college or university.

FIGURE 9.10

Job posting for a state trooper in North Carolina

- Age–Must be 21 years of age by the first day of basic school **to apply** and no more than 39 years of age on the first day of Basic School.
- Must have High School diploma or equivalency (GED)
- Must be a Citizen of the United States or Naturalized Citizen
- No Felony Offenses, no serious misdemeanor convictions, good driving record
- Applicants must be willing to live and work in any area of the state of NC
- Vision–Must have 20/20 vision in each eye; uncorrected vision of no more than 20/200 in each eye corrected to 20/20 in each eye
- Physically fit
- A qualified cadet must meet Medical, Physical, Psychological and Background Requirements: Pass COOPER Fitness Test; Score at or above 10th grade reading level on standardized test; Successfully complete polygraph examination, complete background investigation, review boards, physical exam to include drug screening; and psychological exam.

really stand out when applying to these jobs. As with any career in the criminal justice field, make sure to keep your background clean. Felony convictions are almost always treated as an automatic disqualification, and misdemeanor convictions are treated on a case-by-case basis.

State Bureaus of Investigation

BASIC JOB DESCRIPTION

Almost everyone has heard of the Federal Bureau of Investigation (FBI), but many people are unaware each state has their own investigatory bureau as well. A state bureau of investigation investigates and upholds state laws. Their legal jurisdiction is only retained in one specific state. State bureaus of investigation will have field offices throughout the state, and preside over a wide variety of criminal and civil cases.

MINIMUM QUALIFICATIONS

While specific qualifications for state bureaus vary between states, generally applicants must be a minimum of 21 years old at the time of hire, and possess some completed college coursework. In this line of work, a college degree is preferred and many applicants will even have an advanced degree as well. Field experience is also desired generally in the form of previous work in local law enforcement, or another state law enforcement agency. This is to ensure that applicants are familiar with basic investigatory and arrest procedures. Part of the hiring process for most state bureaus of investigation will require the successful completion of a training academy designed to familiarize trainees with Constitutional and state laws, evidence collection, in-depth investigatory procedures, and use-of-force protocol.

SAMPLE MINIMUM QUALIFICATIONS IN JOB POSTINGS FOR STATE BUREAU OF INVESTIGATION POSITIONS

The minimum qualifications needed in order to be considered for employment in a state bureau of investigation vary by location. Two examples are presented in Figures 9.11 and 9.12.

TIPS FOR GETTING HIRED

Earning a bachelor's degree will help make your application more competitive in this career path in conjunction with field experience. Marketable degrees include accounting and computer science, with criminal justice or legal studies as a supplement. Having 3 to 5 years of law enforcement field experience will go a long way in getting hired in a state bureau of investigation. Most state bureaus of investigation offer internship opportunities for students. Take advantage of these internship opportunities while in school to network and gain state law enforcement experience to make your résumé more competitive when applying to these state jobs in the future.

FIGURE 9.11

Job posting for a special agent position with the Georgia Bureau of Investigation

- Education–Completion of a Bachelor's degree from an accredited four-year college or university
- Must be age 21 or older
- Must be a United States citizen
- Vision Requirements:
- Distant vision–minimum vision of 20/20 in one eye and 20/40 in the other eye, corrected (with glasses or contact lenses), and minimum of 20/200 in each eye, uncorrected (without glasses or contacts).
- Near vision- minimum of 20/40, corrected or uncorrected in each eye.
- Adequate depth perception and the ability to distinguish colors.
- Peripheral vision-at least 70 degrees in each eye.

FIGURE 9.12

Job posting for a special agent position with the
North Carolina State Bureau of Investigation

1. Must be a responsible and law abiding citizen of the United States with high moral character and personal integrity.
2. Must be at least 21 years of age.
3. Must have a four-year degree or an advanced degree from a resident college/university certified by one of the six Regional Accreditation Associations.
4. Must have, or be eligible for, a valid North Carolina Driver's License.
5. Successfully complete a comprehensive background investigation including contacts with references, employers, co-workers, close personal associates, etc., and review of driving record, credit history, criminal history, and service in the military.
6. Successfully complete a pre-employment polygraph, psychological evaluation, medical examination, and urinalysis drug test.
7. Successfully complete pre-screening fitness assessment. Cooper fitness test will be used for assessment. This includes, one minute of sit-ups, 300 meter sprint, one minute push-ups and 1.5 mile run.
8. Accept employment under one (1) year probationary status, which includes successful completion of the SBI Special Agent Academy, approximately six months in duration.
9. Accept permanent assignment anywhere within North Carolina.
10. Accept temporary assignments anywhere or anytime.
11. Accept job responsibility in any area of criminal investigations, homicide, burglary, arson, drugs, etc.
12. Accept assignments requiring irregular hours; day or night, any day of a week or holidays.
13. Accept assignments requiring undercover investigation.
14. Accept assignments requiring overnight travel possibly over extended periods of time.
15. Must be willing to carry and use a firearm.
16. Must be willing to use deadly force, if warranted, to protect his or her life or the life of someone else. (Must be willing to take a person's life should circumstances dictate.)

Alcohol Enforcement Agent

BASIC JOB DESCRIPTION

Alcohol enforcement agents are present in the majority of states, and are tasked with upholding and enforcing state laws encompassing the sale of alcohol. Alcohol enforcement agents retain authority only in the specific state in which they are employed. Agents in this line of work frequently conduct undercover missions, engage in surveillance activities, and check liquor licenses of establishments selling alcohol.

MINIMUM QUALIFICATIONS

Minimum qualifications differ depending on which state you are in, but, generally speaking, applicants must be a minimum age of at least 21 and have no criminal convictions for an alcohol-related offense. A high school diploma is required, and completed college coursework is preferred. All applicants prior to official hire will have to successfully complete a training academy covering the basics of Constitutional law, state laws especially related to the sale of alcohol, arrest procedures, and what constitutes a legal search and seizure.

SAMPLE MINIMUM QUALIFICATIONS IN JOB POSTINGS FOR ALCOHOL ENFORCEMENT AGENTS

The minimum qualifications needed in order to be considered for employment as an alcohol enforcement agent vary by location. Two examples are presented in Figures 9.13 and 9.14.

FIGURE 9.13

Job posting for an agent trainee with the Texas Alcoholic Beverage Commission

*Note, meeting minimum qualifications will not guarantee an invitation to participate in written and physical assessments

- *Current Texas Commission on Law Enforcement (TCOLE) Basic Peace Officer Certification—required at time of application.*

*Note: If you do not possess a minimum Texas Basic Peace Officer Certification you will NOT be considered for this role. *TABC does not currently sponsor or issue TCOLE certification or allow other state peace officer certifications.*

At least 21 years of age.

–AND–

*Current Texas Commission on Law Enforcement (TCOLE) Basic Peace Officer Certification-required at time of application.-**AND**-High school diploma or GED -**AND**- minimum Four years experience in law enforcement.

–OR–

Current Texas Commission on Law Enforcement (TCOLE) Basic Peace Officer Certification-required at time of application.-**AND**- High school diploma or GED -**AND**- Four years of Military experience.

–OR–

continues

continued

*Current Texas Commission on Law Enforcement (TCOLE) Basic Peace Officer Certification-required at time of application. **-AND-** Associate's Degree **-AND-** Two years Military or Law enforcement experience.

–OR–

*Current Texas Commission on Law Enforcement (TCOLE) Basic Peace Officer Certification-required at time of application. **-AND-** Graduation from an accredited four-year college or university with a bachelor's degree.

FIGURE 9.14

Job posting for an Alcohol Law Enforcement (ALE) agent in North Carolina

- A four-year degree from an accredited college or university or an equivalent combination of training and full time experience, with full arrest authority.
- **Necessary Special Qualifications**: Current certification as a law enforcement officer in accordance with the provisions of the North Carolina Criminal Justice Education and Training Standards Commission; Or the ability to achieve certification within one year of employment.

TIPS FOR GETTING HIRED

Most state alcohol enforcement agencies offer internships for current college students. Plan to complete an internship in the state you would like to ultimately work in so you can effectively network within the agency before you officially apply. Successfully completing a minimum of a bachelor's degree related to the field of criminal justice will help your application stand out in this line of work. Two to 3 years of experience in local law enforcement would also help your application stand out when applying to work as a state alcohol enforcement agent.

Park Ranger—State Parks

BASIC JOB DESCRIPTION

Park rangers working at the state level patrol state parks and enforce regulations in these parks. Rangers have frequent interaction with the public, and will sometimes serve as guides and hold informational sessions about the parks where they work. They also make sure parks are secure and well-maintained for public safety. Park rangers spend much of their time outdoors in various weather conditions. Rangers are well versed in first aid training and land conservation. State park rangers only have jurisdiction in the state where they are currently employed.

MINIMUM QUALIFICATIONS

Minimum qualifications for park rangers vary by state, but many states want their park rangers to have educational training in land management and conservation, forestry, biology, ecology, or environmental science. An undergraduate degree in one of these related areas of study will significantly increase an applicant's chances of getting hired.

SAMPLE MINIMUM QUALIFICATIONS IN JOB POSTINGS FOR PARK RANGERS

The minimum qualifications needed in order to be considered for employment in a state park ranger position vary by location. Two examples are presented in Figures 9.15 and 9.16.

FIGURE 9.15

Job posting for a park ranger in the Department of Conservation and Recreation in the state of Virginia

- Preferred qualifications include demonstrated work history or volunteer experience in a parks and recreation or similar environment.
- Education, training, or demonstrated progressive experience related: to nature and the environment, or facilities and grounds maintenance, or retails sales and cash management. Prior experience in the maintenance and upkeep of a historical park and/ or cultural site/facility is highly preferred.

FIGURE 9.16

Job posting for a park ranger in Lake Roland Park in Baltimore, Maryland

- Associates Degree or 60 college credits majoring in recreation, park operations, education, forestry, natural resources, or a related field and/or at least one year successful experience as a recreation leader, teacher or worked in a related field. Additional qualifying experience may be substituted on a year-for-year basis.
- Applicants are required to submit proof of driver's licenses. If applicant possesses an associate's degree or coursework related to the position, applicants are advised to submit proof of degree or transcripts. Unofficial transcripts will be accepted.
- At least 1 year experience working in an environmental field. Degree in Environmental Science or Park/Recreation may be substituted for experience.

TIPS FOR GETTING HIRED

Most state park agencies offer internship opportunities for current college students. For networking and experience, it is important to complete an internship with a park agency if you desire to work there in the future.

Police Officer—State College or University

BASIC JOB DESCRIPTION

Police officers working for state colleges and universities are considered state employees. These jobs offer a unique opportunity to work in state law enforcement. Police officers in these settings ensure campus safety and security for students, staff, and faculty. Officers will regularly provide security details for campus sporting events, graduation ceremonies, and residential student living accommodations. Working on a college or university campus offers a much different work environment than working in a city or county jurisdiction. Campus police offers are generally considered staff, so they also enjoy benefits like using campus facilities and receiving financial discounts on educational courses offered on campus.

MINIMUM QUALIFICATIONS

While minimum qualifications for campus police officers varies between colleges and universities, most of these positions require a minimum age of 21 years and successfully passing a training academy prior to full-time employment. An extensive criminal background investigation will be conducted and must be passed prior to employment. An undergraduate degree is preferred for working at these institutions. Many colleges and universities want their campus police officers to have at least 2 to 3 years of experience working in law enforcement prior to hiring.

SAMPLE MINIMUM QUALIFICATIONS IN JOB POSTINGS FOR COLLEGE AND UNIVERSITY POLICE OFFICERS

The minimum qualifications needed in order to be considered for employment as a college or university police officer vary by location. Two examples are presented in Figures 9.17 and 9.18.

TIPS FOR GETTING HIRED

Gaining work experience with a local law enforcement department is a great way to be competitive for campus police officer positions. Obtaining an undergraduate degree related to the field of criminal justice will also greatly help your application standout. Most campus police departments offer internship opportunities. Take advantage of these while you are a student in order to network and gain work experience while completing your degree.

FIGURE 9.17

Job posting for a police officer at The University
of Alabama in Tuscaloosa, Alabama

- High school degree or equivalent.
- Successfully passing a police officer recruit exam, physical agility and physical ability examinations, review panel and a comprehensive background check. Physical Agility exam includes running the course and completing the following requirements within 90 seconds: push a vehicle on a level surface; climb a six-foot wall; climb through a window-like metal structure; walk a balance beam; drag a 165 lb. dummy. Physical Ability exam includes completing 22 push ups within one minute, 25 sit-ups within one minute and completing a 1.5 mile run within 15 minutes and 28 seconds.
- United States citizen or permanent resident. For those that have been in the Armed Forces, an honorable discharge from military service.
- Must have valid U.S. driver's license. Must be at least 21 years of age at time of hire and have an acceptable Motor Vehicle Report as determined by the insurance carrier.
- Must be able to perform foot patrol and work outside in all weather conditions. Must be able to work day, evening or night shift to include weekends and holidays. Must be able to work various overtime events, both voluntary and mandatory, based on the needs of the department and the university community. Conditional Hire/ Pre-Employment Requirements: Complete a psychological assessment. Drug screen.
- Post-Hire Requirements: Successful completion of the recruit orientation training. Successful completion of the Alabama Peace Officers Standards and Training Commission's academy within six months of employment; or a certificate verifying the successful completion of the Alabama Peace Officers Standards and Training Commission's academy. Successful completion of the University of Alabama Police Department's field training and evaluation program. After completion of these phases, the position has a 1040-hour probationary period of solo field assignment duty.

Additional Required Department Minimum Qualifications: An individual who has had a conviction of a felony crime is not eligible for employment as a police officer per Rule 650-X-2-.05 of the Alabama Peace Officer Standards and Training Commission administrative code.

FIGURE 9.18

Job posting for a police officer at Duke University
in Durham, North Carolina

- Associate's degree, Bachelor's degree preferred.
- Work requires comprehensive and communication skills normally acquired through a high school education. Work requires a North Carolina Basic Law Enforcement certification, as well as a North Carolina Campus Police Certification or certification eligibility.
- Work requires no prior experience. OR AN EQUIVALENT COMBINATION OF RELEVANT EDUCATION AND/OR EXPERIENCE. Work requires a minimum age limit of 20 years. Work also requires a North Carolina driver's license.

Fish and Game Warden (Also Called Conservation Officers in Many States)

BASIC JOB DESCRIPTION

Fish and game wardens are tasked with upholding laws designed to protect wildlife and natural resources. Wardens patrol designated land areas and have the authority to arrest violators of gaming laws. These positions require work outdoors and in a variety of weather conditions. Wardens frequently interact with the public to educate about land and wildlife conservation methods.

MINIMUM QUALIFICATIONS

Qualifications vary between states, but a minimum age requirement of 21 years is generally required along with the successful completion of a training academy prior to employment. An undergraduate degree in land management or conservation is preferred, along with an educational background in criminal justice.

SAMPLE MINIMUM QUALIFICATIONS IN A JOB POSTING FOR A FISH AND GAME WARDEN

A sample of the minimum qualifications needed in order to be considered for employment as a fish and game warden is presented in Figure 9.19.

TIPS FOR GETTING HIRED

Pursuing an undergraduate degree in fields related to land management and conservation studies will help make for a competitive applicant in this job role. An educational background in criminal justice and legal studies will also help. Many gaming agencies offer internships to students. Plan to complete an internship with a game enforcement agency while you are in school if you are interested in this field for a future career.

FIGURE 9.19

Job posting for a fish and game warden in Henderson, Nevada

- Bachelor's degree from an accredited college or university in wildlife management, biology, criminal justice or closely related field and three years of professional experience in enforcing wildlife and/or boating safety laws; OR two years of experience as a Game Warden II in Nevada State service; OR an equivalent combination of education and experience.
- Special Notes–Candidates hired in this series must acquire Peace Officers Standards and Training (POST) certification in Nevada. Special Requirements Pursuant to NRS 284.4066, this position has been identified as affecting public safety. Persons offered employment in this position must first submit to a pre-employment screening test for controlled substances.

SALARY ESTIMATES FOR FISH AND GAME WARDENS

Annual salary estimates for fish and game wardens are presented in Figure 9.20.

WORKING IN FEDERAL LAW ENFORCEMENT

There are approximately 73 federal law enforcement agencies employing full-time officers possessing the authority to carry a firearm and make arrests working in the federal government. Many of these positions are found within the 1811-series (criminal investigative job series) which are criminal investigators working for the federal government. The Criminal Investigation Series 1811 is a highly competitive, highly sought-after career field. Familiarity with foreign languages such as Spanish, Mandarin-Chinese, Arabic, and Russian will help make your application competitive in many of these federal agencies. Computer skills are highly desired in this field given all of the current cyber-security threats in our society. Accounting and math backgrounds are also viewed favorably in many of these careers specializing in combating white-collar crimes. Advanced degrees are commonplace in federal law enforcement largely due to how competitive the applicant field has become in recent years.

Figure 9.20 Annual salary estimates for fish and game wardens[4]

Percentile	10%	25%	50% (Median)	75%	90%
Hourly Wage	$16.52	$20.20	$24.87	$31.55	$37.23
Annual Wage (2)	$34,360	$42,010	$51,730	$65,610	$77,440

[4]*Source*: Bureau of Labor Statistics. https://www.bls.gov/oes/current/oes333031.htm.

Applicants for federal law enforcement positions frequently possess at least a few years of professional work experience in law enforcement or legal professions. It is fairly difficult to get hired into federal law enforcement straight out of an undergraduate or even an advanced degree program. If you are currently in school or have recently graduated, your best bet to attain a federal job is to apply to the federal government's "Pathways" program. This program was created to hire current college students for internship-type opportunities, and to recruit recent college graduates into entry-level federal jobs. Pathways job advertisements, and all other federal vacancy announcements, can be found on the federal government's hiring website, *USAjobs.gov.*

Another good avenue to get hired directly into the federal government out of school is to apply to agencies like the Bureau of Prisons (BOP) and U.S. Customs and Border Protection. Both of these agencies have many vacancy announcements across the country at any given time. The key is to get your foot into the door of the federal system, and generally this requires taking an entry-level position. Once there, build some work experience and after a couple of years you can look to laterally transfer to another federal agency if desired. Applying internally as a current federal employee is much easier than applying from the outside of the federal system as an external applicant. The following section will cover some popular agencies where federal law enforcement jobs are commonly found.

The General Schedule (GS) classification and pay system is how the majority of federal jobs base their salary structure. Sometimes you will see the abbreviation GL, which means this is for a law enforcement officer position. The GL pay structure is very similar to the GS system. Here are the details of the GS system as outlined by the U.S. Office of Personnel Management (OPM) on OPM.gov:[5]

> The General Schedule (GS) classification and pay system covers the majority of civilian white-collar Federal employees (about 1.5 million worldwide) in professional, technical, administrative, and clerical positions. GS classification standards, qualifications, pay structure, and related human resources policies (e.g., general staffing and pay administration policies) are administered by the U.S. Office of Personnel Management (OPM) on a Government-wide basis. Each agency classifies its GS positions and appoints and pays its GS employees filling those positions following statutory and OPM guidelines.
>
> The General Schedule has 15 grades—GS-1 (lowest) to GS-15 (highest). Agencies establish (classify) the grade of each job based on the level of difficulty, responsibility, and qualifications required. Individuals with a high school diploma and no additional experience typically qualify for GS-2 positions; those with a Bachelor's degree for GS-5 positions; and those with a Master's degree for GS-9 positions.
>
> Each grade has 10 step rates (steps 1–10) that are each worth approximately 3 percent of the employee's salary. Within-grade step increases are based on

---

[5]https://www.opm.gov/policy-data-oversight/pay-leave/pay-systems/general-schedule/.

GS Grade	Step 1	Step 2	Step 3	Step 4	Step 5	Step 6	Step 7	Step 8	Step 9	Step 10
Figure 9.21 2017 GS Base Payscale Table[6]										
GS-1	$18,526	$19,146	$19,762	$20,375	$20,991	$21,351	$21,960	$22,575	$22,599	$23,171
GS-2	$20,829	$21,325	$22,015	$22,599	$22,853	$23,525	$24,197	$24,869	$25,541	$26,213
GS-3	$22,727	$23,485	$24,243	$25,001	$25,759	$26,517	$27,275	$28,033	$28,791	$29,547
GS-4	$25,514	$26,364	$27,214	$28,064	$28,914	$29,764	$30,614	$31,464	$32,314	$33,164
GS-5	$28,545	$29,497	$30,449	$31,401	$32,353	$33,305	$34,257	$35,209	$36,161	$37,113
GS-6	$31,819	$32,880	$33,941	$35,002	$36,063	$37,124	$38,185	$39,246	$40,307	$41,368
GS-7	$35,359	$36,538	$37,717	$38,896	$40,075	$41,254	$42,433	$43,612	$44,791	$45,970
GS-8	$39,159	$40,464	$41,769	$43,074	$44,379	$45,684	$46,989	$48,294	$49,599	$50,904
GS-9	$43,251	$44,693	$46,135	$47,577	$49,019	$50,461	$51,903	$53,345	$54,787	$56,229
GS-10	$47,630	$49,218	$50,806	$52,394	$53,982	$55,570	$57,158	$58,746	$60,334	$61,922
GS-11	$52,329	$54,073	$55,817	$57,561	$59,305	$61,049	$62,793	$64,537	$66,281	$68,025
GS-12	$62,722	$64,813	$66,904	$68,995	$71,086	$73,177	$75,268	$77,359	$79,450	$81,541
GS-13	$74,584	$77,070	$79,556	$82,042	$84,528	$87,014	$89,500	$91,986	$94,472	$96,958
GS-14	$88,136	$91,074	$94,012	$96,950	$99,888	$102,826	$105,764	$108,702	$111,640	$114,578
GS-15	$103,672	$107,128	$110,584	$114,040	$117,496	$120,952	$124,408	$127,864	$131,320	$134,776

[6]*Source*: FederalPay.org at https://www.federalpay.org/gs/2017.

an acceptable level of performance and longevity (waiting periods of 1 year at steps 1–3, 2 years at steps 4–6, and 3 years at steps 7–9). It normally takes 18 years to advance from step 1 to step 10 within a single GS grade if an employee remains in that single grade. However, employees with outstanding (or equivalent) performance ratings may be considered for additional, quality step increases (maximum of one per year).

Bureau of Alcohol, Tobacco, Firearms, and Explosives (ATF or ATFE)

ABOUT THE AGENCY

The ATF is a federal law enforcement agency located in the U.S. Department of Justice (DOJ). The ATF's mission is to investigate and attempt to prevent violations of federal laws involving the unlawful use, possession, and manufacturing of firearms and explosives, acts of arson and bombings, and trafficking of alcohol and tobacco products (ATF.gov). The ATF works extensively with local, state, and other federal law enforcement agencies.

SAMPLE MINIMUM QUALIFICATIONS IN A JOB POSTING FOR AN ATF SPECIAL AGENT

The minimum qualifications needed in order to be considered for employment as an ATF special agent are shown in Figure 9.22.

Drug Enforcement Administration (DEA)

ABOUT THE AGENCY

The DEA is a federal law enforcement agency located in the U.S. Department of Justice (DOJ). The DEA's mission is to enforce the controlled substances laws and regulations,

---

FIGURE 9.22

Job posting for an ATF special agent

To qualify at the GL-5 level, you must meet ONE of the following:

- Education: Applicants must have completed a 4-year course of study leading to a bachelor's degree in any field of study. (Must include a copy of unofficial or official transcripts to verify eligibility.)

  OR

- Experience: Applicants must have 3 years of progressively responsible experience, 1 year of which was equivalent to at least the GL-4 that demonstrates the ability to work in criminal investigative or law enforcement fields that require knowledge and application of laws relating to criminal violations.

Note: non-qualifying general experience: Work experience as a uniformed law enforcement officer, where the principle duties consist of arrests involving traffic violations, misdemeanors and comparable offenses.

  OR

- Work experience in which the major duties involve guarding and protecting property; preventing crimes, and/or legal research without the application of investigative techniques.

  OR

- Combination of education and experience: Experience and education can be combined to meet the minimum qualification requirements. Experience and education should be computed as percentages of the overall requirements and must equal 100% when combined. Example: For 3 years of general experience, 18 months general experience (50% of the required experience) plus 2 years of undergraduate course work (50% of the required education) is qualifying for the GL-5 level. (Must include a copy of your unofficial or official transcripts if qualifying based on education.)

and to combat drug smuggling within the United States. Property and drug seizures, along with asset forfeiture over assets derived from illegal drug trafficking are common practices of the Drug Enforcement Administration. The DEA frequently works with local, state and other federal enforcement agencies over cases involving the trafficking and distribution of illegal drugs. The agency also has an international presence, and frequently coordinates efforts with the United Nations and Interpol over international drug control initiatives.

SAMPLE MINIMUM QUALIFICATIONS IN A JOB POSTING FOR A DEA SPECIAL AGENT

The minimum qualifications needed in order to be considered for employment as a DEA special agent are presented in Figure 9.23.

FIGURE 9.23

Job posting for a DEA special agent,

- A bachelor's degree (GPA of 2.95 or higher), a master's or a J.D. or LL.B.;

- **OR** experience assisting in investigations of alleged or suspected violations of the law; participating in multi-agency/organization venues, briefings, meetings, conferences; researching, collecting and analyzing data from a variety of sources relating to investigations; writing reports and conducting briefings of findings, results, or accomplishments for information or action relating to law enforcement activities and/or court cases; assisting court officials and law enforcement personnel with case-related materials; and testifying or presenting evidence for court, legislative, or administrative proceedings;

- **OR** three+ years of substantive work experience and special skills; e.g., pilot/maritime, accounting/auditing, military/technical, mechanical including information systems, telecommunications, engineering, and/or a foreign language fluency (fluency subject to verification); **and** a bachelor's degree or higher (no minimum GPA required) with coursework related to the aforementioned special skills;

- **AND**, possess the following competencies:

    o Written and Oral Communication   o Flexibility

    o Attention to Detail/Memory   o Problem-solving

    o Decision-making/judgment   o Self-management

    o Interpersonal skills   o Teamwork

    o Integrity/Honesty

United States Marshals Service (USMS)

ABOUT THE AGENCY

The U.S. Marshals Service is a federal law enforcement agency located within the U.S. Department of Justice (DOJ) with a very diverse mission statement. The USMS is the nation's oldest and most versatile federal law enforcement agency established all the way back in 1789. U.S. marshals serve as the enforcement arm of the federal court system, provide security details for federal judges, operate the Witness Security Program, transport federal prisoners, help administer the Department of Justice Asset Forfeiture Program, and play a key role in apprehending federal fugitives. The USMS also operates a tactical division known at the Special Operations Group (SOG) for classified missions.

SAMPLE MINIMUM QUALIFICATIONS IN A JOB POSTING FOR A DEPUTY U.S. MARSHAL

An example of the minimum qualifications needed in order to be considered for employment as a deputy U.S. marshal is presented in Figure 9.24.

FIGURE 9.24

Job posting for a deputy U.S. marshal

- Must be a U.S. citizen
- Must be between the ages of 21 and 36 (must be appointed before 37th birthday)
- Must have a bachelor's degree, 1 year of specialized experience, or a combination of education and experience equivalent to the GL-07 level
- Must have a valid driver's license in good standing
- Must successfully complete a structured interview and other assessments
- Must successfully complete a background investigation
- Must meet medical qualifications
- Must be in excellent physical condition
- Must undergo a rigorous 21½ week basic training program at the United States Marshals Service Training Academy in Glynco, GA

Federal Bureau of Investigation (FBI)

▲ The FBI is an extremely competitive federal law enforcement agency. Generally the FBI wants its applicants to have at least a few years of professional work experience in fields like law enforcement, computer science, foreign languages, law, and accounting.

ABOUT THE AGENCY

The Federal Bureau of Investigation is a federal law enforcement agency located within the U.S. Department of Justice (DOJ). The FBI provides a variety of law enforcement and intelligence functions including protecting the United States against acts of terrorism, espionage, cyber security threats, and major criminal threats including child predators and serial killers. The Federal Bureau of Investigation has many specialized divisions including one well-known entity called the Behavioral Analysis Unit (BAU). This specialized unit has been popularized on many television shows and movies concerning FBI special agents who specialize in "criminal profiling." While the job title "Criminal Profiler" does not exist within the FBI, special agents who formulate profiles of criminals do exist. However, entry into specialized units like the BAU within the FBI are highly competitive, and usually require serving as a regular special agent within the Bureau for at least 3 to 5 years to gain entry-level experience within the basic job function. The FBI also has a tactical unit known as the Hostage Rescue Team (HRT) that responds to advanced critical-incident scenarios. Becoming a member of the HRT is an extremely competitive and selective process requiring elite tactical skills and physical abilities.

SAMPLE MINIMUM QUALIFICATIONS IN A JOB POSTING FOR A SPECIAL AGENT IN THE FBI

The minimum qualifications needed in order to be considered for employment as a special agent in the FBI are presented in Figure 9.25.

United States Secret Service (USSS)

ABOUT THE AGENCY

The U.S. Secret Service is a federal law enforcement agency located in the Department of Homeland Security (DHS). The Secret Service was originally created in 1865 strictly to suppress the counterfeiting of U.S. currency and treasury bonds. Now the U.S. Secret Service provides protective details for our nation's political leaders and families, along with still attempting to thwart the counterfeiting of U.S. currency. This 50/50 mandate between physical protection and counterfeiting investigations makes for a varied job description for U.S. Secret Service Special Agents. The USSS tends to conduct large-scale hiring announcements approximately 1 to 2 years before the next presidential election cycle. This is an excellent time to apply if you are thinking about working for the U.S. Secret Service in the future.

FIGURE 9.25

Job posting for an FBI special agent

While the FBI encourages applicants from all backgrounds to become Special Agents, the FBI is currently looking for special agent applicants with skills in the following areas:

- Science, Technology, Engineering and Math (STEM)
- Foreign Languages
- Law
- Emergency Medicine
- Certified Public Accountants (CPAs)
- Detectives
- Military (specifically Special Forces, Explosives, WMD and Intelligence Experts)
- Pilots (helicopter, fixed-wing)
- Be between 23 and 37 years of age
- Have a minimum of a bachelor's degree from a U.S accredited college/university
- Have at least three years of full-time (36+ hours per week) professional work experience
- Possess a valid driver's license and 6 months of driving experience
- Meet the Special Agent physical fitness standards

SAMPLE MINIMUM QUALIFICATIONS IN A JOB POSTING
FOR A SPECIAL AGENT IN THE SECRET SERVICE

The minimum qualifications needed in order to be considered for employment as a special agent in the Secret Service are presented in Figure 9.26.

At least one year of specialized experience equivalent to the GL-5 level. Specialized experience is defined as performing duties such as: assisting in opening and closing case files; conducting criminal name checks through various databases/electronic systems; experience writing non-technical reports, drafting responses to requests for information, and writing brief, informative or routine reports by gathering information, analyzing it and summarizing the results of findings to draw valid conclusions and to make sound recommendations; taking responsibility for own actions to meet deadlines; presenting specific, pre-determined information at meetings, conferences, or seminars as a representative of a work or academic group; OR

A combination of specialized experience, as described above, and related graduate level education.

- The Secret Service prohibits employees from having visible marking (including but not limited to tattoos, body art, and branding) on the head, face, neck, hand and fingers (any area below the wrist bone).

United States Customs and Border Protection (CBP)

ABOUT THE AGENCY

The U.S. Customs and Border Protection (CBP) is located within the Department of Homeland Security. CBP has approximately 60,000 employees, making it one of the world's largest law enforcement agencies. Customs and Border Protection seeks to keep our borders along Mexico and Canada secure. CBP's main mission is to keep terrorists and their weapons out of our country, and at the same time facilitate lawful international travel and trade. Two popular jobs within CBP are the Border Patrol Agent (BPA) and Customs and Border Protection Officer (CBPO). The Border Patrol Agent is tasked with securing international land borders and coastal waters with Mexico and Canada, in order to prevent illegal entry and drug smuggling. Customs and Border Protection Officers work entry

FIGURE 9.26

Job posting for a U.S. Secret Service special agent

- A bachelor's degree from an accredited college or university with superior academic achievement (S.A.A.), which is a based on class standing, grade-point average, or honor society membership.
- At least one full year of graduate-level education (i.e., 18 semester hours).

points into the U.S. in order to help prevent illegal entry and trafficking of substances while enforcing immigration and customs laws. The CBP offers applicants a good entry point into the federal law enforcement community due to the sheer size of the agency.

SAMPLE MINIMUM QUALIFICATIONS IN A JOB POSTING FOR A CBP OFFICER

The minimum qualifications needed in order to be considered for employment as a CBP officer are presented in Figure 9.27.

United States Immigration and Customs Enforcement (ICE)

ABOUT THE AGENCY

ICE is a federal law enforcement agency located in the Department of Homeland Security tasked with enforcing federal laws relating to customs, trade, and immigration to promote security of the homeland. One of ICE's primary responsibilities is enforcement and removal operations (ERO) where illegal aliens are identified, detained, and removed from the United States. ERO upholds U.S. immigration laws in a fair and

FIGURE 9.27

Job posting for a CBP officer at the GS-5 level

Three years of general work experience that demonstrates the ability to:
- Meet and deal with people and
- The ability to learn and apply a body of facts

Note: Qualifications based on work experience will be determined by what is listed on your resume.

OR

A bachelor's degree from an accredited or pre-accredited college or university. You may apply within 9 months of receiving an accredited or pre-accredited college or university.

Note: Transcripts must be provided in your application to verify you meet the education requirement.

OR

A combination of successfully completed post-high school education and general work experience. To determine if you meet the combination of experience and education requirement, you must divide your total number of months of qualifying experience by 12 and divide the number of undergraduate semester hours by 120 or undergraduate quarter hours by 180 and then add the two percentages together—they must equate to at least 100%.

FIGURE 9.28

Job posting for a special agent with ICE as a GL-7

- training in criminal or civil investigative principles and techniques;
- applying laws and rules associated with criminal or civil procedures, searches, seizures, arrests, and rules of evidence; and (or),
- preparing investigative reports using clear and proper written language.

One full year of graduate level education beyond a bachelor's degree or Superior Academic Achievement (S.A.A.) in an undergraduate degree

---

effective manner. Immigration and Customs Enforcement also tracks the illegal movement of people and goods into and out of the United States in an effort to combat acts of terrorism and other criminal activities.

SAMPLE MINIMUM QUALIFICATIONS IN A JOB POSTING FOR A SPECIAL AGENT WITH ICE

The minimum qualifications needed in order to be considered for employment as a special agent with ICE are presented in Figure 9.28.

United States Transportation Security Administration (TSA)

ABOUT THE AGENCY

The Transportation Security Administration (TSA) is a federal law enforcement agency located within the Department of Homeland Security. The TSA's main mission is to protect the nation's transportation infrastructure to provide safe and efficient travel and commerce. The most visible position within the Transportation Security Administration is the Transportation Security Officer (TSO) who commonly screens passengers, baggage, and cargo at airports. A less visible position within the TSA is the Federal Air Marshals (FAMs) who are tasked with thwarting acts of terrorism on domestic and international flights. FAMs help to instill public confidence in the safety and security of our aviation infrastructure. Federal air marshals are often in plain clothes to blend in with other passengers, but they carry a firearm and are highly skilled from a tactical standpoint. There is little room for error when a critical security incident starts to unfold mid-flight.

SAMPLE MINIMUM QUALIFICATIONS IN A JOB POSTING FOR A FEDERAL AIR MARSHAL WITH THE TSA

The minimum qualifications needed in order to be considered for employment as a federal air marshal are presented in Figure 9.29.

FIGURE 9.29

Job posting for a federal air marshal (FAM) with the TSA

- Written application
- Panel interview
- Psychological assessment
- Medical examination
- Polygraph
- Physical training assessment
- Complete background investigation before a final hiring decision is made.

United States Postal Service Office of Inspector General (OIG)

ABOUT THE AGENCY

Special agents working in the Office of Inspector General protect the safety and integrity of the U.S. mail. These agents also conduct investigations in the following areas: contract fraud, financial fraud, internal mail theft, official misconduct, and special inquiries including whistleblower reprisal and workplace environment complaints.

SAMPLE MINIMUM QUALIFICATIONS IN A JOB POSTING FOR A U.S. POSTAL INSPECTOR

The minimum qualifications needed in order to be considered for employment as a U.S. postal inspector are presented in Figure 9.30.

FIGURE 9.30

Job posting for a U.S. postal inspector

- Applicants must be U.S. citizens and at least 21 years of age and less than 37 years of age at the time of appointment, except for preference eligible veterans for whom there is currently no maximum age limit.
- Male applicants born after December 31, 1959, must have registered with the Selective Service prior to applying.
- The applicant must possess a conferred Bachelor's Degree from a college or university that is accredited by a regional or national organization recognized by the U.S. Department of Education, hold a current valid state driver's license issued not less than two years prior to the application, have no felony convictions or a misdemeanor conviction involving domestic violence (felony and misdemeanor charges may also

render the applicant ineligible), pass a comprehensive visual examination and a hearing acuity test, and be in good physical condition, with weight in proportion to height, and possess emotional and mental stability.

- In addition, the applicant must demonstrate the following attributes, as measured by the Assessment Center evaluation: (1) write and speak English clearly, (2) schedule and complete activities in a logical, timely sequence, (3) comprehend and execute instructions written and spoken in English, (4) think clearly and comprehend verbal and nonverbal information, (5) interact with others to obtain or exchange information or services, and (6) perceive or identify relevant details and associate them with other facts.

Naval Criminal Investigative Service (NCIS)

▲ "The NCIS mission is to investigate and defeat criminal, terrorist, and foreign intelligence threats to the United States Navy and Marine Corps—ashore, afloat, and in cyberspace" (http://www.ncis.navy.mil).

ABOUT THE AGENCY

According to the mission statement of NCIS, they are tasked with investigating and defeating criminals, terrorists, and foreign intelligence threats to the U.S. Navy and Marine Corps. NCIS agents investigate a wide variety of cases. One day an NCIS agent could be investigating a traffic accident on a naval base, and the next day the same agent could be assigned to investigate an act of terrorism.

MINIMUM QUALIFICATIONS

The minimum qualifications needed in order to be considered for employment as an NCIS agent are:

- You must not have reached 37 years of age (exceptions are preference eligible veterans and those currently covered under the 6C Federal Law Enforcement retirement system).
- You must have an accredited baccalaureate degree.
- You must have vision correctable to 20/20 with normal color vision.
- You must be a U.S.-born or naturalized U.S. citizen.
- You must pass a background suitability screening.
- You must pass a polygraph examination.
- You must be able to obtain and maintain a Top Secret security clearance.
- You must have a valid driver's license.

U.S. Army Criminal Investigation Command—Army Criminal Investigations (CID) Civilian Special Agent

ABOUT THE AGENCY

Civilian criminal investigators in CID do not investigate general crimes but are specialists in areas such as investigating computer system intrusions, polygraph, operations, sexual assault, investigative policy, and major contract procurement fraud.

MINIMUM QUALIFICATIONS

The minimum qualifications needed in order to be considered for employment as a civilian criminal investigator in the U.S. Army Criminal Investigation Command are as follows:

- Qualification requirements for the entry-level procurement fraud investigator include either a minimum of 3 years felony investigative experience or a master's degree in a related field such as law, business, accounting, contracting, or criminal justice.
- Specialized experience involves obtaining physical and documentary evidence; interviewing witnesses; applying for and serving warrants for arrest; searches and seizures; seizing contraband, equipment, and vehicles; examining files and records; maintaining surveillance; performing undercover assignments; preparing investigative reports; testifying in hearings and trials; and assisting U.S. attorneys in the prosecution of court cases.

Air Force Special Investigations Officer

ABOUT THE AGENCY

According to the U.S. Air Force, these special investigations officers are tasked with focusing on conducting investigations into criminal, fraud, counterintelligence, internal security, and other security concerns related to the United States Air Force.

MINIMUM QUALIFICATIONS

The minimum qualifications needed in order to be considered for employment as an Air Force special investigations officer are:

- Bachelor's degree or graduate degree
- Knowledge of special investigative policy, procedures and techniques concerning criminal, fraud, counterintelligence, personnel background, and technical security services
- Must be an Air Force Officer with less than 12 years total active military service and no more than 6 years total commissioned service
- Favorable interview by an AFOSI detachment commander
- Qualification to bear firearms
- Ability to speak and write English clearly and distinctly
- Must possess or be eligible for a valid state vehicle operator's permit
- Normal color vision
- No record of emotional instability
- Completion of a Single Scope Background Investigation (SSBI)
- Completion of Officer Training School (OTS), Air Force Academy (AFA), or Air Force Reserve Officer Training Corps (AFROTC)
- Must be between the ages of 18 and 34

Other Criminal Investigation Series 1811 Positions

There are many federal agencies with criminal investigative positions in the 1811-series not typically thought of by prospective applicants. For example, the Environmental Protection Agency (EPA) and Social Security Administration (SSA) both have criminal investigators employed through their agencies. These positions are advertised through USAjobs.gov, and can be found by searching for Criminal Investigation Series 1811 openings on the website.

WORKING IN PRIVATE SECTOR LAW ENFORCEMENT CAREERS

Railroad Special Agent

BASIC JOB DESCRIPTION

Special agents working for privately owned railroad companies are broadly referred to as railway police. These agents are typically sworn law enforcement personnel in the state in which the railroad company operates. If the railroad company has railways in multiple states, then some railroad police will have jurisdiction in all states in which the railroad company operates. Railroad police are tasked with keeping passengers and cargo on the railroads safe and secure. These special agents routinely conduct investigations into matters concerning the railroad company's assets, and occasionally make arrests when needed.

MINIMUM QUALIFICATIONS

Minimum qualifications for these positions vary between different railroad companies. Most companies require applicants to have successfully completed an accredited police academy and possess at least three years of law enforcement or military experience. An undergraduate degree in a criminal justice–related major is also a common requirement for these positions.

SAMPLE MINIMUM QUALIFICATIONS IN JOB POSTINGS FOR RAILROAD SPECIAL AGENTS

The minimum qualifications needed in order to be considered for employment as a railroad special agent are presented in Figures 9.31 and 9.32.

FIGURE 9.31

Job posting for a special agent with Kansas City Southern Railway in Louisiana

- College degree in Criminal Justice or related field preferred
- Police certification in State of Louisiana preferred
- Minimum of three years law enforcement experience

FIGURE 9.32

Job posting for a special agent with Canadian National Railway in Michigan

- High School Diploma or GED is required
- The successful candidate MUST be a commissioned and certified police officer in Michigan with a minimum 5 years experience in law enforcement
- Experience working with federal, state, and local agencies in emergency response situations is essential
- Knowledge of state and federal criminal and civil laws
- DOT and FRA regulations are preferred
- Must be able to render credible testimony in a court of law and before railroad disciplinary hearings
- Investigative expertise
- Computer proficiency; Microsoft Excel, Word, and PowerPoint
- Strong interpersonal and communication skills
- Knowledge of railroad operations is a plus
- Operation Lifesaver Authorized Volunteer

TIPS FOR GETTING HIRED

Railroad companies commonly offer internships for current undergraduate students. Completing an internship with one of these companies is an excellent way to network and gain experience in this industry. The following list includes some of the well-known railroad companies in the United States: Union Pacific, Norfolk Southern, CSX Transportation, and BNSF Railway Company.

SALARY ESTIMATES FOR TRANSIT AND RAILROAD POLICE

The annual salary estimates for transit and railroad police are presented in Figure 9.33.

Loss Prevention Officer (LPO)—Asset Protection Specialist

BASIC JOB DESCRIPTION

Loss prevention officers work for private companies to mitigate fiscal losses. Often loss prevention officers work in retail settings where company loss is referred to as shrinkage. This job involves conducting internal investigations of company employees, and external investigations with customers and the public where applicable. Loss prevention officers (LPO) routinely work in plain clothes and attempt to blend in with customers while monitoring store assets. LPOs commonly coordinate with local law enforcement when a suspect is apprehended within the company with which the LPO is employed.

MINIMUM QUALIFICATIONS

Loss prevention officers have to go through a formal training program sanctioned by their employer in order to learn about basic surveillance and investigatory techniques. LPOs may be tasked with also learning first aid procedures and basic arrest principles. Some experience in the law enforcement or private security community is preferred in these jobs, and a minimum of a high school degree is a requirement.

Figure 9.33 Salary Estimates for Transit and Railroad Police[7]

Percentile	10%	25%	50% (Median)	75%	90%
Hourly Wage	$19.97	$26.24	$32.03	$39.39	$46.48
Annual Wage	$41,540	$54,570	$66,610	$81,920	$96,670

[7]*Source*: Bureau of Labor Statistics. https://www.bls.gov/oes/current/oes333052.htm.

SAMPLE MINIMUM QUALIFICATIONS IN JOB POSTINGS FOR LOSS PREVENTION OFFICERS

The minimum qualifications needed in order to be considered for employment as a loss prevention officer are presented in Figures 9.34 and 9.35.

TIPS FOR GETTING HIRED

An undergraduate degree in a criminal justice–related area of study combined with experience in local law enforcement or as a security officer will help make your application stand out. Also, many companies offer loss prevention internships for students

---

FIGURE 9.34

Job posting for a loss prevention officer with ACE Hardware

- Degree in Criminal Justice or 3–5 years of practical experience in Security or Loss Prevention.
- Able to work a varied schedule to include early mornings, swing shifts, nights, weekends and holidays.
- CPR/First Aid certified or able to obtain certification through company provided training.
- Computer skills
- Good communication and problem solving skills
- Interested candidate must be at least 18 year of age, legal to work in the US, and have completed a high school degree or equivalent.

FIGURE 9.35

Job posting for a loss prevention officer with Kohl's Corporation

- Prior experience in Loss Prevention or educational background in Loss Prevention, security, or law enforcement preferred.
- Demonstrated ability to make decisions in stressful situations. Strong verbal and written communication skills; basic math and reading skills, and legible handwriting.
- Ability to spend up to 100% of working time moving around the store, including stock storage areas, office areas, and the selling floor. Physical activities include bending, stooping, lifting, climbing, standing, and reaching on a frequent basis. Associate must be capable of detaining theft suspects.

currently enrolled in a degree-seeking institution. Look to these internship opportunities as an effective means to network and build experience in the field if you are thinking about working in loss prevention in the future.

MEDIAN ANNUAL SALARIES FOR PRIVATE DETECTIVES AND INVESTIGATORS:

The Bureau of Labor Statistics compiled the list of median annual salaries for private detectives and investigators presented in Figure 9.36.

Corporate Investigator

BASIC JOB DESCRIPTION

Corporate investigators help ensure that financial assets, intellectual property, and sensitive documents remain safe and secure for corporations. Investigators perform a wide range of activities to mitigate potential loss for corporations from internal and external threats. Currently special attention in this field is given to cybersecurity risks, enhancing security measures within the corporate world, and the very real threat of data breaches.

MINIMUM QUALIFICATIONS

Corporate investigator positions require extensive fieldwork experience in law enforcement operations. Most corporate investigators have work experience in public-sector law enforcement. An undergraduate degree is generally a requirement, and many graduates in this field will also possess an advanced degree.

SAMPLE MINIMUM QUALIFICATIONS IN JOB POSTINGS FOR CORPORATE INVESTIGATORS

The minimum qualifications needed in order to be considered for employment as a corporate investigator are presented in Figures 9.37 and 9.38.

Figure 9.36 Annual Salaries for Private Detectives and Investigators[8]	
Finance and insurance	$54,850
Government	$49,480
Investigation, guard, and armored car services	$48,250
Retail trade	$34,460

[8]*Source*: Bureau of Labor Statistics, May 2016. https://www.bls.gov/ooh/protective-service/private-detectives-and-investigators.htm#tab-5.

FIGURE 9.37

Job posting for an investigator with the University of Maryland Capital Region Health

- 5–7 years experience conducting complex investigations establishing and maintaining liaison with local, state, federal, and/or military law enforcement entities
- Working knowledge of local, state, and federal statutes
- Possess strong organizational skills
- Ability to obtain a Private Investigators License within the first year of employment
- Associates Degree Diploma or higher in Law Enforcement, Criminology or related field

FIGURE 9.38

Job posting for an investigator with Booz Allen Hamilton in McLean, Virginia

- 7+ years of experience with conducting internal investigations for a corporation or with the government
- Experience with the military or otherwise handling confidential and classified matters
- Experience with drafting interview reports and investigation reports
- Experience with government contracting reporting procedures and data security
- Ability to work with other compliance and investigative professionals
- Top secret clearance
- BA or BS degree

TIPS FOR GETTING HIRED

These positions within corporations are very competitive and are higher-paying than their public-sector counterparts. Gaining prior experience in investigations is key to being competitive for corporate investigator positions. Cybersecurity knowledge and skills are greatly in demand currently in the corporate world. Having a computer science and information technology (IT) background will significantly help your résumé find the top of the stack in these jobs.

SALARY ESTIMATES FOR PRIVATE INVESTIGATORS

The annual salary estimates for private investigators are presented in Figure 9.39.

Figure 9.39 Annual Salary Estimates for Private Investigators[9]					
Percentile	10%	25%	50% (Median)	75%	90%
Hourly Wage	$13.08	$17.17	$23.17	$31.87	$41.86
Annual Wage	$27,210	$35,710	$48,190	$66,300	$87,070

[9] *Source*: Bureau of Labor Statistics. https://www.bls.gov/oes/current/oes339021.htm.

Credit Card Fraud Investigator

BASIC JOB DESCRIPTION

Credit card fraud investigators work for credit card companies and other financial institutions to reduce the likelihood of fraudulent credit and debit card activities regarding consumer accounts. Two of the biggest areas of concern for fraud investigators involve application fraud and account takeover. Application fraud involves an individual fraudulently completing a credit or debit card application with someone else's personal information in an attempt to gain access to that new account for a short period of time. Account takeover is usually much more serious, and occurs when an individual gains complete access to an existing credit or debit card account belonging to another person, and the fraudster begins to make purchases under the existing account for their own personal gain. Savvy fraudsters will make inexpensive purchases at first in hopes that fraud investigators do not catch their actions. Then, after some period of time of having access to the account, the criminal will try to make a bigger ticket purchase, or sell the hacked account to another party. Credit card fraud investigators also stay busy trying to combat online bots generating random credit card numbers until they "hit" on a correct account number and then make the fraudulent purchase.

MINIMUM QUALIFICATIONS

Minimum qualifications will vary between credit card companies and other financial institutions. Field experience with investigations, preferably in the form of financial and fraud investigatory work, is desired for these positions. An undergraduate degree is also generally a requirement in fields like accounting or finance. Most credit card fraud investigators have worked in the field of law enforcement for a minimum of five years prior to employment with the credit card company.

SAMPLE MINIMUM QUALIFICATIONS IN JOB POSTINGS FOR CREDIT CARD FRAUD INVESTIGATORS

The minimum qualifications needed in order to be considered for employment as a credit card fraud investigator are presented in Figures 9.40 and 9.41.

FIGURE 9.40

Job posting for a credit card investigator at KeyBank in Buffalo, New York

- Three years risk analysis, bank operations, bankcard, or security/law enforcement experience.
- Knowledge of bank systems, including Hogan, FACTS, ADH, DAG, TSYS ALS, View Direct
- Knowledge of online investigation tools such as LexisNexis
- PC proficient: Word, Lotus, Excel
- Accuracy and organizational skills
- Ability to multi-task
- Analytical and problem solving skills
- Ability to work effectively with minimal supervision
- Strong verbal and written skills
- Work well under pressure or challenging situations
- Knowledge of laws and regulations pertaining to Card Fraud
- Team building, interpersonal, and relationship building skills

FIGURE 9.41

Job posting for a fraud investigator with Citi in Irving, Texas

- College level education (undergraduate degree) required.
- 3–5 years financial or law enforcement investigative experience.
- Comprehensive understanding of Mortgage Investigations to include the ability to assess allegations of mortgage fraud, including fraud related to the origination, processing and underwriting of loans, servicing or sale of a loan or property.
- Comprehensive understanding of Cyber related Fraud trends and emerging risks that impact Investigative performance.
- Considerable knowledge of, as well as experience with, financial products (ATM, Wire, Cards, etc.), frauds, and trends.
- Demonstrated ability to train and mentor junior Investigative staff in specific functions, methods, and products required of the role.
- Possesses the knowledge, skills, and abilities to conduct interviews (potentially in the field).
- Demonstrated ability to achieve targets and goals with minimal supervision.
- Excellent communication and personal skills needed for marketing case work and obtaining cooperation of other parties.

- Good report writing skills to accurately articulate the circumstances and events of the investigation.
- Good analytical skills needed to assess evidence, identify relationships, and develop leads in an investigation.
- Ability to multi-task, managing a high-volume caseload with quick turnaround.
- Highly motivated with demonstrated ability to prioritize tasks in support of investigations and investigative processes.
- Demonstrated attention to detail with ability to manage caseload and produce accurate, concise analytical reports.
- Solid judgment and decision making skills.
- Willingness to travel both domestically and internationally.
- Pursues learning opportunities and self-development.
- Able to develop and maintain relationships with customers and law enforcement officials, as appropriate.
- Proficiency in Microsoft Office products–Word, Excel, Outlook, PowerPoint, and SharePoint for compiling written reports and spreadsheets on an investigation.

TIPS FOR GETTING HIRED

Field experience is key to gaining a job as a credit card fraud investigator. Employers want to see a background investigating financial frauds, an educational background dealing with finances and the ability to handle numbers, as well as experience in the field of law enforcement investigations.

Insurance Fraud Investigators

BASIC JOB DESCRIPTION

Insurance fraud investigators are tasked with mitigating losses associated with fraudulent claims in the insurance industry. Two common types of insurance fraud are known as soft and hard fraud. Soft fraud is more common than hard fraud, and involves exaggerating the existence or worth of assets when filing insurance claims. For example, a home burns down due to legitimate electrical fire and the homeowner decides to claim they had a valuable gold ring when they really did not. Hard fraud is more serious, and involves the deliberate destruction of property in the attempt to collect an insurance settlement. An example of hard fraud could involve a homeowner who faces expensive home repairs the insurance company will not cover, so the homeowner decides to burn the house down and claim it was a legitimate house fire. Insurance fraud investigators are trained with investigatory skills to detect these forms of fraudulent cases involving insurance claims.

MINIMUM QUALIFICATIONS

Insurance companies generally want their fraud investigators to have previous field experience in law enforcement and possess basic investigatory skills. These positions require an undergraduate degree in a criminal justice–type area of study.

SAMPLE MINIMUM QUALIFICATIONS IN JOB POSTINGS FOR AN INSURANCE FRAUD INVESTIGATOR

The minimum qualifications needed in order to be considered for employment as an insurance fraud investigator are presented in Figure 9.42.

FIGURE 9.42

Job posting for an insurance fraud investigator with AIG

- Must have 3+ years of experience in insurance fraud, law enforcement or intelligence-led investigations. The ideal candidate would have experience in a combination of these disciplines.
    - o   Previous law enforcement experience
    - o   Experience in multiple lines of the insurance business
    - o   IBM iBase and i2 Analyst Notebook experience
    - o   Cognos Reporting Tool Experience
- Understanding of data privacy laws and the ability to adhere to company policies and legislation relating to receiving and sharing intelligence
- Strong written and verbal communication skills: With proficiency for summarizing complex ideas and principles in clear and concise written pros.
- Strong technical skills/experience using claims management systems, case management systems, reporting, and in-depth database interrogation.
- Able to demonstrate experience in the gathering and presentation of intelligence from publicly available internet sources or investigation.
- Ability to evaluate large data sets for critical and pertinent information.
- Demonstrate a high level of proficiency in MS Office, particularly Excel, Access, Word, PowerPoint and Outlook.
- Demonstrate a proficiency in IBM i2 Anlayst Notebook, iBase, MS SQL, Oracle, DB2, COGNOS and/or other Data mining tools.
- Have a technical aptitude, keen intellect and high level of adaptability.

TIPS FOR GETTING HIRED

Internships are commonly available for current undergraduate students with these insurance companies. Plan to complete an internship to get relevant experience and to build your networking base. For insurance fraud investigators, previous experience is highly desired so think about acquiring at least 2 to 3 years of work experience in local law enforcement.

Executive Protection (EP) (Close Personal Protection)

BASIC JOB DESCRIPTION

Executive protection involves protecting high-value targets such as leaders in the business community, CEOs, high-value physical targets, and celebrities who are at a high risk of being a target of potential crime due to their high net worth and celebrity status. Executive protection offers these individuals highly trained and skilled tactical support for enhanced safety measures. These measures could include personal escorts, convoys in armored cars, and personal security at a personal residence. Working in executive protection presents the employee with a variety of protection assignments and tasks.

MINIMUM EXPERIENCE

Executive protection positions require applicants to be highly trained and have personalized knowledge of extensive self-defense and tactical skills. Generally applicants in this field have served on a tactical team in law enforcement or the military. These EP positions require superb marksmanship and physical abilities. An extensive background check will be conducted on serious applicants and no red flags can be found.

SAMPLE MINIMUM QUALIFICATIONS IN JOB POSTINGS FOR AN EXECUTIVE PROTECTION AGENT

The minimum qualifications needed in order to be considered for employment as an executive protection agent are presented in Figure 9.43.

TIPS FOR GETTING HIRED

Gaining experience on a specialized tactical or special forces team in law enforcement or the military is key to being competitive for careers in executive protection. Applicants must be extremely physically fit and have excellent accuracy with a firearm.

FIGURE 9.43

Job posting for an executive protection agent with
Pinkerton in Denver, Colorado

- Must have a High School Diploma or GED.
- Must be willing to participate in the Company's pre-employment screening process including drug testing and background investigation.
- Must be at least 18 years of age.
- Must have a reliable means of communication (i.e., email, cell phone).
- Must have a reliable means of transportation (public or private).
- Must have the legal right to work in the United States.
- Must have the ability to speak, read, and write English.
- Must have applicable state and local license/permits to carry a concealed firearm.
- Bachelor's degree with at least five years of executive protection experience including advance planning, surveillance and counter surveillance operations, and security driving for high net-worth clients.

SUMMARY

There are numerous exciting and very different career paths in the field of law enforcement in both the public and private sectors. The key is to be aware of all the different opportunities out there in the job market. If you are planning to pursue a future career in law enforcement, gaining internship experience while in school is extremely important to help ensure your application is competitive once you start to apply to these actual jobs. Foreign language experience is another important factor in your application package for law enforcement jobs. These days, with the many cybersecurity threats in our society, computer skills are also highly in demand for most career paths in the law enforcement community. Keep in mind many law enforcement jobs are highly sought after, and a prospective applicant always needs to be strategizing ways for their résumé to stand out from the sea of other applicants.

Three Key Takeaway Points

1. When thinking about law enforcement jobs, be familiar with all of your options. Not just the well-known public-sector job titles, but also their lesser-known private-sector counterparts.

2. Experience is key in the field of law enforcement. Many positions require a few years of work experience in local law enforcement or the military in order to be qualified for the position. Look to gain experience while in school by completing internships. The more the better!

3. When applying to law enforcement jobs, always remain geographically flexible. Be willing to start your career or gain a promotion by moving to a new location. Limiting yourself geographically will significantly limit your career opportunities, especially when you are applying to entry-level positions.

ASSESSMENT QUESTIONS

1. What is the difference between a police officer and a deputy sheriff in local law enforcement?
2. What is a state bureau of investigation?
3. Name three functions of the U.S. Marshals Service.
4. What are the two primary job functions of the U.S. Secret Service?
5. Briefly discuss what executive protection is.

CRITICAL THINKING EXERCISE

What do you think some primary differences are working in public-sector law enforcement compared to private-sector law enforcement? (Hint: Think about job security, pay, and benefits.)

ACTIVE LEARNING ACTIVITY

Find five job announcements in law enforcement careers that sound interesting to you, using job websites like *Indeed.com*, *Monster.com*, and *USAjobs.gov*. For these five job announcements, compare the different education requirements, duties, and preferred qualifications. What are the main similarities and differences between each job opening?

From the Real World

One of the biggest limiting factors I see from students wanting to work in the field of law enforcement is lack of geographical flexibility. Since some of these jobs are so competitive, the reality is that you are not likely to get your most desired living location at an entry-level job. You need to take a job in the field where you can get it, underscoring the foot-in-the door approach. After gaining a few years of experience in the system, *then* you can look to transfer to a more desired location. I have had students come to me and say, "I only want to work for the FBI in this specific city," and I tell them they might as well go out and purchase a lottery ticket because they will have similar odds of winning compared to getting that specific job. It is difficult enough to just get into the FBI, let alone have the FBI place you the exact living location you desire. The point is to be very flexible when you are just beginning your career. Go for an entry-level position wherever it takes you, build up work experience, and then make your next move. Limiting yourself geographically is only serving to significantly limit your job opportunities.

KEY TERMS

Criminal Investigation Series 1811 – Criminal investigative series for federal jobs.

Pathways Program – A federal hiring initiative for current college students and recent college graduates. This program offers internship-type opportunities and entry-level job opportunities.

USAjobs.gov – Federal government's hiring website and employment resource.

General Schedule (GS) – Predominant pay scale within the U.S. civil service.

10

Working in the Court System

INTRODUCTION

The court system in the United States offers many different career options. There are numerous types of courts including criminal, civil, appellate, probate, family, small claims, traffic, and bankruptcy, just to name a few. Most people think of judges and attorneys when discussing career options in our court system, but there are many additional job titles in this career field as well. Chapter 10 focuses on highlighting a variety of these career paths and illuminating what each position seeks to accomplish in its job function. Special attention will also be given to discussing minimum qualifications needed for these specific career options, as well as employment tips for being a competitive applicant for the job being advertised. Sample qualification requirements for actual job postings will be included in Chapter 10 as well. For more career resources related to the court system, visit this textbook's companion website at www.oup.com/us/klutz.

▲ The legal field offers many different career options associated with the courtroom.

ATTORNEY (LAWYER)

▲ Legal careers are very competitive in today's job market. You must proactively plan ahead and look at job descriptions in this field in order to understand the necessary qualifications.

BASIC JOB DESCRIPTION

There are many areas of law where an attorney can practice in the legal profession. The job description of an attorney will vary greatly based on their legal specialty area. Some lawyers are general practitioners, meaning they practice with a wide variety of different types of laws, and others are specialized in only one specific area of the law. Attorneys can be solo practitioners, meaning they have their own private firm, or they can be part of a group practice, and some lawyers even work for much larger megafirms.[1] An attorney represents client(s), and counsels and guides them through the various steps of litigation. There are two main types of law in which attorneys can practice: criminal law and civil law.

---

[1] A megafirm is an extremely large law firm that is basically a "one-stop-shop" for legal matters. Megafirms can handle a large variety of different types of legal cases. See Anthony Lin's article "The Rise of the Megafirm" (*ABA Journal*, September 2015) for more reading on the subject.

CRIMINAL LAW

An attorney who represents the government and brings charges against the defendant is known as a prosecutor. A prosecuting attorney can work as part of a state government (including local counties and municipalities as well) or the federal government. The burden of proof is on the government to prove their case beyond a reasonable doubt. A state prosecutor generally works for a district attorney's office or state's attorney's office, while a federal prosecutor, known as an Assistant United States Attorney, works for the U.S. Department of Justice (DOJ).

An attorney who represents a defendant in criminal court is known as a criminal defense attorney. Criminal defense attorneys often specialize in fairly specific areas of criminal law. For example, a defense attorney might specialize in drug and DUI charges, or traffic law cases. For indigent defenders, publicly appointed defense attorneys, generally called public defenders, are appointed by the government to represent clients who cannot afford legal counsel on their own financial accord.

CIVIL LAW

Civil law offers practicing attorneys many different specialty areas. Civil law is much different from criminal law. In our civil legal system, generally speaking, a plaintiff brings a suit against the defendant. These suits are commonly referred to as "lawsuits." The issue at hand over the dispute is often called a tort, meaning a civil wrong or harm alleged to have been committed against the plaintiff by the defendant in the civil case. Torts are not the only issues handled in civil court, though, as contractual agreements and disputes are commonly resolved in civil court as well. The burden of proof in civil court is called preponderance of evidence, and is a much lower legal threshold than the legal threshold in criminal court known as "beyond a reasonable doubt." Preponderance in civil court simply means the winner's side of the proposition is more likely true than not. Another unique facet of civil law is that blame can be divided between the two competing parties. For example, the plaintiff could be found 20% responsible for their actions in the case, while the defendant is found 80% culpable.

MINIMUM QUALIFICATIONS

Most states require prospective attorneys to successfully complete law school by earning a Juris Doctor degree (JD), and then successfully passing the bar exam to practice law in that specific state. Many states have reciprocity with one another when it comes to passing the bar, meaning that if you pass the bar in one state that bar passage is honored in another state where there is a reciprocal relationship. Virginia, Vermont, Washington, and California actually allow people to complete legal apprenticeships in lieu of earning a JD degree, and these individuals can still become practicing attorneys.

SAMPLE MINIMUM QUALIFICATIONS IN JOB POSTINGS FOR ATTORNEYS

The minimum qualifications needed in order to be considered for employment as an attorney are presented in Figures 10.1 and 10.2.

FIGURE 10.1

Job posting for an assistant United States attorney in the Department of Justice

- Applicants must possess a J.D. Degree, be an active member of the bar (any U.S. jurisdiction), and have at least 3 years post-J.D. legal or other relevant experience.
- United States citizenship is required.

FIGURE 10.2

Job posting for a city attorney in Casper, Wyoming

- Membership in the State Bar of Wyoming.
- Minimum of five years in the practice of law.
- Juris Doctorate from an accredited college or university.

TIPS FOR GETTING HIRED

Legal careers are extremely competitive in today's job market. Getting into a good quality law school known for the area of law you are planning to specialize in is very important. You must do your research on ranking lists, and on which areas of law are considered strong suits of the law schools where you will apply. Your time studying at a quality law school will also be extremely competitive. Law school students in the top 10% of their class will get the most desirable employment prospects upon graduation. The farther down the list your grades are and your overall class ranking is, the more difficult it will be for you to obtain desirable employment. Law school graduates these days are not guaranteed employment in any way, shape, or form. The frank reality is there are a lot of JD degrees out there with limited opportunities for desirable employment requiring a legal degree.

Another reason law school students should strive to maintain top grades is because of highly competitive internship-type opportunities that must be taken advantage of while in law school for the best chances of securing desired employment opportunities upon graduation. Legal internship-type opportunities fall under many different names including internship, externship, fellowship, and summer associate. The big takeaway here is not to necessarily get caught up in the title of the position but to strive to gain as much experience through these internship-type opportunities as possible. All of these types of positions offer great networking opportunities and real-world experience on your résumé that you will need in order to be competitive for future legal jobs.

Figure 10.3 Annual percentile salary estimates for attorneys/lawyers from the Bureau of Labor Statistics[2]					
Percentile	10%	25%	50% (Median)	75%	90%
Hourly Wage	$27.36	$37.30	$56.81	$84.89	$100+
Annual Wage	$56,910	$77,580	$118,160	$176,580	$208,000+

[2]*Source*: Bureau of Labor Statistics. https://www.bls.gov/oes/current/oes231011.htm#(5).

JUDGE

▲ Becoming a judge usually requires years of extensive legal experience as a successful and respected attorney.

BASIC JOB DESCRIPTION

A judge is a court official who presides over court proceedings. Judges can be elected or appointed, and are tasked with officiating between the parties who are litigating. Some of the primary tasks of judges involve ruling on the admissibility of evidence, instructing the jury in the courtroom, and providing rulings on motions presented by legal counsel during the trial phase of a case. In criminal cases judges frequently decide whether or not bail will be granted to a defendant awaiting trial, and judges also determine sentencing for a convicted defendant. In civil cases, judges commonly determine liability, and compensatory and possibly punitive damages between the litigating parties.

MINIMUM QUALIFICATIONS

Most judges have earned a law degree (JD) and also have many years of litigation experience as an attorney. Judges are appointed or elected, and after this process takes place, typically judges will be required to complete a training program detailing specifics of the job function. Judges are also required to complete educational legal courses throughout their careers to stay up to date on changes pertaining to the law.

SAMPLE MINIMUM QUALIFICATIONS IN JOB POSTINGS FOR JUDGES

The minimum qualifications needed in order to be considered for employment as a judge are presented in Figures 10.4 and 10.5.

TIPS FOR GETTING HIRED

A prospective judge needs a lot of quality experience in the legal field as an attorney with an impeccable trial record and ethical work history. Becoming a judge often involves politics,

---

FIGURE 10.4

Job posting for a judge in district court in Pierce County, Washington

To be eligible to file a declaration of candidacy for and to serve as a district court judge, a person must:

- Be a registered voter of the district court district and electoral district, if any; and
- Be either:

(a) A lawyer admitted to practice law in the state of Washington; or

(b) In those districts having a population of less than five thousand persons, a person who has taken and passed by January 1, 2003, the qualifying examination for a lay candidate for judicial officer as provided by rule of the supreme court.

FIGURE 10.5

Job posting for a municipal court judge in Beaverton, Oregon

- Juris Doctor law degree and a minimum of seven years' experience in the area of municipal law, trial experience, or as an administrative hearings officer, arbitrator or judge, or any equivalent combination of experience and training that demonstrates possession of the knowledge, skills and abilities described in the classification specification.
- Member in good standing with the Oregon State Bar is required.
- Must receive Oregon Criminal Justice Information Services certification within 30 days of hire.
- Ability to pass reference check, background check, and drug screen.

---

so you must be able to play the political landscape as well. Politicians and the community you will serve need to be able to trust and like your personal character.

SALARY ESTIMATES FOR JUDGES, FROM THE BUREAU OF LABOR STATISTICS

Annual salary estimates for judges are presented in Figure 10.6.

Figure 10.6 Annual Salary Estimates for Judges[3]					
Percentile	10%	25%	50% (Median)	75%	90%
Hourly Wage	$16.95	$30.80	$60.52	$75.61	$88.25
Annual Wage	$35,250	$64,070	$125,880	$157,270	$183,570

[3]*Source*: Bureau of Labor Statistics. https://www.bls.gov/oes/current/oes231023.htm.

MAGISTRATE

BASIC JOB DESCRIPTION

Magistrates are a type of judicial official commonly tasked with issuing criminal search warrants in some legal jurisdictions, and evaluating specific requests for criminal charges in minor criminal cases. Magistrates often perform administrative functions in the courtroom that can include conducting initial appearances for defendants and presiding over minor criminal offenses and small claims court.

MINIMUM QUALIFICATIONS

Federal magistrates assist federal district judges. Minimum qualifications to become a federal magistrate are extensive. These qualifications include: a law degree, a minimum of five years of experience practicing law, strong moral character, and sound judicial temperament and reasoning skills. The person being appointed to the magistrate position must be under the age of 70 at the time of the appointment and cannot be related to any of the judges who make the federal magistrate appointment in order to avoid allegations of nepotism.

For state magistrate positions, qualifications vary greatly. Some states only require a high school diploma, while other states require a law degree and extensive experience practicing law in order to become a magistrate. States set their own specific age requirements and generally require residency within the state and sometimes even within county lines for magistrate positions.

SAMPLE MINIMUM QUALIFICATIONS IN JOB POSTINGS FOR MAGISTRATES

The minimum qualifications needed in order to be considered for employment as a magistrate are presented in Figures 10.7 and 10.8.

TIPS FOR GETTING HIRED

Even in states not requiring a law degree to become a magistrate, earning a JD degree will help move your application to the top of the stack. Experience in the legal field is also very important. Many magistrates have practiced as an attorney for at least a few years. Maintaining a clean background free from questionable ethical practices is also very important when being vetted for magistrate positions.

FIGURE 10.7

Job posting for a magistrate in Chesapeake, Virginia

- Bachelor's degree from an accredited institution of higher education
- Excellent English speaking, listening, and writing skills
- Strong interpersonal skills
- Computer proficiency
- A fundamental knowledge of Virginia civil and criminal law and the judicial system is essential. Therefore, relevant legal experience, training, or education, including membership in the Virginia State Bar, is a plus.

FIGURE 10.8

Job posting for a magistrate in Neligh, Nebraska

- REQUIREMENTS: Bachelor's degree in public/business administration, court administration, or related field PLUS five years of progressively responsible experience in court administration or experience in another law-related setting, including some supervisory experience. With the minimum of a high school degree or equivalent, experience working in a court system may be substituted for higher education on a year-for-year basis.
- PREFERRED: The ability to speak Spanish is desired but not required.
- OTHER: Successful completion of training in JUSTICE (the statewide court computer system) will be required on the job. The ability to travel is required.

COURT CLERK

BASIC JOB DESCRIPTION

Court clerks perform various administrative functions in the courtroom including assisting judges, magistrates and attorneys. These administrative functions involve administering oaths to witnesses and jurors in order to swear them in, maintaining court records and paperwork, notarizing court documents by stamping them with an official seal, and keeping records of the court's monetary transactions and other budgetary issues. Court clerks are often appointed by a judge, or elected through a local election process. These positions help to keep the courtroom running smoothly from an administrative standpoint.

MINIMUM QUALIFICATIONS

Minimum qualifications for court clerks vary widely across different legal jurisdictions. Bachelor's degrees are not always required, but it is beneficial to have an undergraduate degree related to criminal justice or legal studies to fully maximize your chances at being competitive. Previous experience in legal and administrative settings is also desired when applying to court clerk job opportunities.

SAMPLE MINIMUM QUALIFICATIONS IN JOB POSTINGS FOR COURT CLERKS

The minimum qualifications needed in order to be considered for employment as a court clerk are presented in Figures 10.9 and 10.10.

FIGURE 10.9

Job posting for a court clerk in Glendale, Arizona

- Two years of college education or two years of experience in one or more of the following areas: records retention, cashiering, or criminal justice.
- **Knowledge of:**

  City Code, Arizona court system, Arizona Revised Statutes, Arizona Rules of Civil and Criminal Procedures, and legal terminology.

  AZTECH software experience
- **Skill in:**

  Use of personal computer, MS Windows, MS Excel, MS Word, MS Outlook and court-specific software and computer systems

  Effective interpersonal relations

  Word-processing and spreadsheets to create letters, forms and reports

  Mathematics including addition, subtraction, multiplication, division and percentages

---

FIGURE 10.10

Job posting for a court clerk in Weber County, Utah

- Bachelor's degree in Administration, Criminal Justice, other related field, or the internal equivalent of a Bachelors degree.
- Three (3) years of progressively responsible experience in court operations.
- Preference may be given to those applicants with more years of related experience and/ or managerial or supervisory experience.
- Education in supervisory and management practices must be completed prior to or within two (2) years in order to retain the position.
- Considerable knowledge of: management practices and procedures; court processes and procedures, including case management techniques; legal terminology and concepts; accounting practices and procedures; and court information systems.
- Ability to supervise the work of others; apply general management principles to specific organizational and operational problems.
- Communicate effectively, verbally and in writing; establish and maintain effective working relationships with employees, representatives of allied organizations, and members of the public.

TIPS FOR GETTING HIRED

Earning a bachelor's degree related to a criminal justice or legal studies curriculum will greatly aid your chances of becoming a court clerk. Real-world experience is also important. Working at a law firm or in other record-keeping administrative settings provides great work experience for making yourself competitive for these positions. Take advantage of completing internship opportunities within the court system while pursuing your undergraduate degree to gain additional relevant real-world experience in the legal field.

SALARY ESTIMATES FOR COURT CLERKS

Annual salary estimates for court clerks are presented in Figure 10.11.

Figure 10.11 Annual salary estimates for court clerks, from the Bureau of Labor Statistics[4]					
Percentile	10%	25%	50% (Median)	75%	90%
Hourly Wage	$11.48	$14.06	$17.63	$22.38	$27.61
Annual Wage	$23,880	$29,250	$36,670	$46,540	$57,420

[4]*Source*: Bureau of Labor Statistics. https://www.bls.gov/oes/current/oes434031.htm.

VICTIM WITNESS ADVOCATE

BASIC JOB DESCRIPTION

Victim witness advocates working for the courts assist victims of crime and help them with emotional support, legal knowledge, and the administrative aspects of the entire court process. Advocates strive to ease the burden and stress on victims, and to make their process through the court system as seamless as possible. Victim witness advocates often act in a social work function through helping victims connect with social service agencies, connecting victims with employers, and finding secure housing opportunities for victims of crimes. Advocates also inform victims about an inmate's release or escape from a correctional institution.

MINIMUM QUALIFICATIONS

In order to be competitive for a victim witness advocate position, applicants should have a bachelor's degree in a social work–related field. Previous work experience in the legal system or with nonprofit agencies focusing on victim support is also very helpful with being competitive for these positions.

SAMPLE MINIMUM QUALIFICATIONS IN JOB POSTINGS FOR VICTIM WITNESS ADVOCATES

The minimum qualifications needed in order to be considered for employment as a victim witness advocate are presented in Figures 10.12 and 10.13.

FIGURE 10.12

Job posting for a victim witness advocate in Albemarle, Virginia

- Graduation from high school or its equivalency. Additional education, experience or training relevant to victim services or human services is preferred. Clerical experience also preferred.

- Ability to assist clients by providing information, to perform complex clerical tasks, to work effectively with people. Ability to maintain confidentiality of information and security of records; ability to follow complex procedures. Skills in communicating clearly in both oral and written form. Proficiency in using current Windows applications. Must be fluent in the Spanish language. SPECIAL REQUIREMENTS A valid Virginia driver's license may be required.

FIGURE 10.13

Job posting for a victim witness advocate in Napa, California

- Two years' experience performing victim services, peer counseling, crisis intervention and social services work activities for the County of Napa or other victim-witness program.

- Completion of 18 units of college-level coursework from an accredited college or university in behavioral science, psychology, sociology, criminal justice or a closely related field. (Additional victim witness advocacy work experience may be substituted for the required education on a year-for-year basis). An Associate's, Bachelor's and/or Master's degree from an accredited college or university is highly desirable.

TIPS FOR GETTING HIRED

Completing internships with the court system and nonprofit agencies specializing in helping victims of crime will greatly aid the strength of your résumé when applying to work in this profession. Additionally, volunteer experience with nonprofit agencies assisting in this line of work is also viewed very positively.

PARALEGAL

BASIC JOB DESCRIPTION

Paralegals assist attorneys in the day-to-day legal profession. They are legal assistants providing an important administrative function for attorneys. The job description for a paralegal is diverse and includes conducting legal research over cases, interviewing prospective clients for an attorney, filing documents in a law firm, preparing exhibits for trial, and conducting a preliminary investigation pertaining to the facts of a case for an attorney. One of the main goals of a paralegal should be to alleviate the administrative workload for an attorney, so that the attorney has more time to spend in the courtroom if desired.

MINIMUM QUALIFICATIONS

Educational qualifications for paralegal positions vary substantially, but a bachelor's degree in a legal studies–related field along with completion of a paralegal certificate program will open the most doors for prospective applicants. Experience in the legal system also helps applicants be competitive when applying to paralegal jobs.

SAMPLE MINIMUM QUALIFICATIONS IN JOB POSTINGS FOR PARALEGALS

The minimum qualifications needed in order to be considered for employment as a paralegal are presented in Figures 10.14 and 10.15.

FIGURE 10.14

Job posting for a paralegal position in Wisconsin

- Paralegal certificate, related degree or experience working as a paralegal or with legal documents
- Education or experience with using legal research tools and methods
- Education or experience with using investigative and interviewing methods
- Experience using computers and associated office software (MS Office, Outlook, Adobe)
- Experience coordinating and assisting in witness preparation
- Experience preparing written materials for presentation at trial or hearing
- Experience independently researching and analyzing legal issues

FIGURE 10.15

Job posting for a paralegal position in Owatonna, Minnesota

- Four year paralegal degree from an accredited college or university, or a two year paralegal certificate from an accredited business or technical school plus two years of approved experience as a Paralegal, or an equivalent combination of education and experience.

TIPS FOR GETTING HIRED

Complete a bachelor's degree in a legal-related field and a paralegal certificate program. Also, look to gain experience with internships at a law firm, district attorney's office, or public defender's office. Plan on completing at least two legal internships before finishing your undergraduate degree to maximize legal experience while completing your academic program.

Figure 10.16 Annual salary estimates for paralegals/legal assistants[5]

Percentile	10%	25%	50% (Median)	75%	90%
Hourly Wage	$14.94	$18.38	$23.80	$30.60	$38.59
Annual Wage	$31,070	$38,230	$49,500	$63,650	$80,260

[5]*Source:* Bureau of Labor Statistics. https://www.bls.gov/oes/current/oes232011.htm.

SUMMARY

The legal field has many career options for applicants to choose from. Minimum qualifications in these career paths vary greatly, so it is important to conduct careful research before planning a career in one of these jobs related to the courtroom. Research academic programs to ensure you are selecting a program with a quality reputation, and an institution that has successful placement rates in your desired legal career path. Gain work experience in the legal field while enrolled in school through internship-type opportunities. The more directly relevant legal work experience you have after completing your education requirements the better. Networking is also extremely important in these various career options in the court system.

Three Key Takeaways

1. The legal field is very competitive. There are a lot of qualified applicants applying to a limited number of jobs. Education and experience are what will make your résumé stand out.
2. Aspiring attorneys have many options when it comes to practicing law. You should be familiar with the different areas of law including opportunities in the criminal and civil courtrooms.
3. In the legal field, just simply meeting minimum qualifications does not mean you will maximize your chances of employment, because many applicants will exceed these minimum qualifications. For example, if a magistrate job vacancy says that a bachelor's degree is the minimum qualification for the job, there will likely be applicants with a law degree and some experience in the legal field that would easily surpass the applicant with just an undergraduate degree.

ASSESSMENT QUESTIONS

1. In criminal law, which side does the burden of proof reside on?
2. What is a megafirm?
3. What are the main differences between criminal and civil court?
4. What is the burden of proof called in civil court?
5. Is a law degree required to practice law in all states?

CRITICAL THINKING EXERCISE

What are some reasons you can think of for why someone would need experience as an attorney before becoming a judge?

ACTIVE LEARNING ACTIVITY

Find five job announcements in legal careers that sound interesting to you, using job websites like *Indeed.com*, *Monster.com*, and *USAjobs.gov*. For these five job announcements, compare the different educational requirements, duties, and preferred qualifications. What are the main similarities and differences between each job opening?

KEY TERMS

Megafirm – Extremely large law firm that is basically a "one-stop-shop" for legal matters, and can handle a large variety of different types of legal cases.

Beyond a reasonable doubt – Legal standard the prosecution needs to warrant a conviction against a defendant in criminal court. No other logical explanation based on the facts of the case and the evidence is feasible except the defendant is guilty.

Indigent defendant – An individual without fiscal means to afford a defense attorney in criminal court. In this scenario, a public defender is appointed by the state for the indigent defender stemming from the landmark SCOTUS case *Gideon v. Wainwright.*

Tort – A civil harm or wrong in civil law.

Preponderance of evidence – Legal standard of proof required to win a civil case, essentially meaning more likely than not. Much lower standard of proof compared to beyond a reasonable doubt.

11

Working
in the Field
of Corrections

INTRODUCTION

When people hear the term "corrections," they often tend to think about physical incarceration settings like jails and prisons. However, jails and prisons are only two components of our correctional landscape in the United States. Another large component in the field of corrections is known as community corrections. This refers to various forms of corrections taking place outside of physical incarceration settings, and in the community in some capacity. Some prominent examples of community corrections are probation, parole, and halfway houses. Community corrections comprise approximately 70% of the overall correctional landscape, while only 30% of offenders are incarcerated in jails and prisons.[1] There are numerous career opportunities available

▲ The field of corrections offers many different career paths. Prospective applicants need to remember there are opportunities within physical incarceration settings and in community corrections.

---

[1] "Corrections and Reentry," National Institute of Justice (NIJ). https://www.crimesolutions.gov/TopicDetails.aspx?ID=2.

within the entire field of corrections. Students interested in working in criminal justice professions tend to focus on law enforcement and courtroom-related careers, but prospective job applicants should also be cognizant of the many exciting and rewarding career opportunities in the field of corrections as well.

Some basic terminology in the field of corrections needs to be addressed before beginning the discussion on the actual career titles in corrections. In public and media discourse, there is a lot of confusion and misinformation over certain terms related to this field. For example, "jail" and "prison" are often used interchangeably, but these physical incarceration settings are not the same thing. Jails are typically administered by a local government at the county or municipal level and are designed for short-term incarceration for a time period of 1 year or less. Many inmates in jail are awaiting their criminal trial. These inmates have either been denied bail by the court or have been unable to post bail in order to secure their pretrial release. Jails are often thought of as a revolving door because of the frequent inmate turnover. Some offenders might be in a jail for only a few hours until their bail is posted. Prisons, on the other hand, are designed for longer-term incarceration, generally defined by a stay of 1 year or more. Prisons are administered by state governments, the federal government, and the private sector. Prisons are better equipped with treatment and rehabilitation programs than jails because inmates will be in prison for a much longer period of time on average. Prisons also differ greatly in terms of their security levels (minimum, medium, maximum, etc.) and the types of crimes inmates have committed to be incarcerated in a prison. Some prisons are designed to even exceed maximum security standards, and are therefore dubbed supermaxium, or "supermax," facilities.

"Community corrections" refers to methods of corrections taking place in the community outside of physical incarceration settings like jails and prisons. Probation and parole are two of the most prominent applications. These two terms are also frequently confused. Probation is a front-end alternative to physical incarceration. A judge handing down a probationary sentence is letting the criminal offender avoid serving time in jail or prison, provided the offender meet specific stipulations and guidelines to successfully complete the probationary sentence. These stipulations and guidelines can include mandating the criminal offender enroll in educational or vocational training courses, having the offender actively seek employment, submitting to and successfully passing drug tests, and adhering to a curfew. Failure to meet these requirements can result in a technical violation, and this could very well mean the probationary sentence is revoked by the court and the offender will find his or her way into jail or prison to meet a harsher sentence. Parole differs from probation in that it is a back-end solution to prison. Generally speaking, parolees receive early release from prison due to good behavior and indeterminate sentencing guidelines. Parolees must meet parole sentences structured much the same way—and with very similar guidelines and stipulations—as probationary sentences. Parole is a mechanism to encourage good behavior and reform within prison, and to better manage the common problem of prison overcrowding.

Some states attach a parole sentence after a determinate, or fixed, sentence is served. The inmate has no option for early release in this case with determinate sentencing, and the rationale is that a parole sentence after release ensures successful reintegration back into free society.

Chapter 11 will provide a breakdown of various careers found within the field of corrections, including careers in both physical incarceration settings and community corrections. It will also discuss the basic job descriptions, minimum qualifications, and tips for getting hired for these career paths. Sample job descriptions will be included from real job postings in the field of corrections. More career resources pertaining to the field of corrections can be found on this textbook's companion website at www.oup.com/us/klutz.

CORRECTIONAL OFFICER (CO)

BASIC JOB DESCRIPTION

Correctional officers serve in a wide variety of correctional facilities where they strive to maintain order and effectively manage inmates. They also can serve in a counseling

▲ A correctional officer working inside a prison.

function to inmates. The safety and security of staff and inmates in these institutions are a correctional officer's primary concern. COs have a tough job function, but there are many employment opportunities. At the local government level, jails are the primary correctional institution and are administered by a county or city government. This means county jails are generally staffed with deputy sheriffs, and city/municipal jails are staffed with police officers to provide security. There is some variation in the specific job title at jails for those employees acting in a correctional officer function, but generally police officers or deputy sheriffs performing in these security roles in jails are called detention or correctional officers.

COs also work in state, federal, and private prisons. Each state has its own prison system, and the federal government's prison system is administered by the Federal Bureau of Prisons (BOP). There are approximately 1,700 state prisons and 122 federal prisons in the United States.[2] There are also private sector companies that run and operate private prisons. Two of the biggest private prison companies in the United States are CoreCivic (formerly known as Corrections Corporation of America) and the GEO Group, Inc. There are numerous opportunities to work as a correctional officer across the country. This is one job field that is always actively hiring and offers a great mechanism to gain entry-level experience in the field of criminal justice.

MINIMUM QUALIFICATIONS

Minimum qualifications for correctional officers vary widely across different agencies. Most correctional facilities mandate that their COs have a high school diploma and prefer some completed college coursework along with field experience in law enforcement or corrections as well. Priority consideration in hiring will be given to applicants with a bachelor's degree in a criminal justice–related area of study, along with at least some work experience in a job related to policing or corrections. Correctional officers need a clean background history and will be required to complete a basic training academy to work in most correctional institutions.

SAMPLE MINIMUM QUALIFICATIONS IN JOB POSTINGS FOR A CORRECTIONAL OFFICER (CO)

The minimum qualifications needed in order to be considered for employment as a correctional officer are presented in Figures 11.1 and 11.2.

---

[2]James J. Stephan, *National Prisoner Statistics Program: Census of State and Federal Correctional Facilities, 2005* (Washington, DC: Bureau of Justice Statistics, 2008).

FIGURE 11.1

Job posting for a correctional officer with the Federal
Bureau of Prisons (BOP)

Minimum qualifications based on previous work experience of a GL-05 (grade-scale used
within BOP jobs):

EXPERIENCE:

GL-05: At least 3 years of full-time general experience, one year of which was equivalent
to the GL-04 grade level, or one year of specialized experience. This experience must have
demonstrated the aptitude for acquiring the qualifications required for correctional work,
and, in addition, demonstrate the possession of personal attributes important to the effectiveness of correctional officers, such as:

- Ability to meet and deal with people of differing backgrounds and behavioral patterns.
- Ability to be persuasive in selling and influencing ideas.
- Ability to lead, supervise, and instruct others.
- Sympathetic attitude towards the welfare of others.
- Ability to reason soundly and to think out practical solutions to problems.
- Ability to make decisions and act quickly, particularly under stress.
- Poise and self-confidence, and ability to remain calm during emergency situations.

General experience may have been gained in work such as:

- Social case work in a welfare agency or counseling in other types of organizations.
- Classroom teaching or instructing.
- Responsible rehabilitation work, e.g., in an alcoholic rehabilitation program.
- Supervising planned recreational activities or active participation in community action
  programs.
- Management or supervisory work in a business or other organization that included
  directing the work flow and/or direct supervision of others.
- Persuasive sales work or commissioned sales work, other than taking and filling orders
  as in over-the-counter sales.

And if using education as your minimum qualification for this job posting (a combination
of the work experience described above AND education is preferred):

GL-05: Successful completion of a full 4-year course of study in any field leading to a bachelor's degree from an accredited college or university.

FIGURE 11.2

Job posting for a correctional officer in Lincoln, Nebraska, with their Department of Corrections

- Some knowledge of the criminal justice system.
- Some knowledge of correctional facility operations.
- Some knowledge of minority cultures and religions.
- Ability to effectively manage inmate behavior in various custody environments.
- Ability to communicate effectively both orally and in writing.
- Ability to observe and assess inmate behavior for signs of potential suicide, riot, and/or other violent behavior.
- Ability to respond to medical and life threatening emergencies.
- Ability to work with outside agencies, inmates, attorneys, coworkers, and the public in a cooperative and professional manner.
- Ability to perform computer data entry and word processing.
- Graduation from a senior high school or equivalent supplemented by college-level coursework in criminal justice and some experience in the following, or any combination thereof: a correctional setting, as a counselor in a social setting, in law enforcement work, in the military particularly in law enforcement or corrections, or with responsibility for individuals in other institutional settings.

TIPS FOR GETTING HIRED

Obtain a bachelor's degree related to the field of criminal justice, and complete at least two internships with a law enforcement agency while pursuing your undergraduate education. In order to advance to the management and supervisory ranks inside a correctional facility, a master's degree in an academic area related to criminal justice is preferred. Applying to be a correctional officer with the Federal Bureau of Prisons (BOP) is a great way to get into the federal government. The BOP is almost always hiring on *USAjobs.gov*. In fact, some BOP facilities offer recruitment incentives: Under a correctional officer job listing currently posted on *USAjobs.gov*, the BOP states, "A 17% recruitment incentive will be paid to selectee(s) at USP Atwater, FCI Herlong and FCI Mendota who meet the criteria for recruitment bonuses. A 15% recruitment incentive will be paid to selectee(s) at FCI Dublin and FCC Victorville who meet the criteria for recruitment bonuses."

SALARY ESTIMATES FOR CORRECTIONAL OFFICERS

Annual salary estimates for correctional officers are presented in Figure 11.3.

Figure 11.3 Annual salary estimates for correctional officers[3]					
Percentile	10%	25%	50% (Median)	75%	90%
Hourly Wage	$13.70	$16.42	$20.59	$27.29	$35.88
Annual Wage	$28,500	$34,150	$42,820	$56,770	$74,630

[3]*Source*: Bureau of Labor Statistics. https://www.bls.gov/oes/current/oes333012.htm.

CORRECTIONAL TREATMENT SPECIALIST/ CORRECTIONS COUNSELOR

BASIC JOB DESCRIPTION

Correctional treatment specialists provide counseling services in correctional facilities and assist inmates with their rehabilitation process. Treatment specialists prepare reports on inmates' behavior during their prison sentence to submit to parole boards where applicable. This job can also entail working with inmates to strategize what the inmate will do once released from the correctional institution including career planning, enrolling in education or vocational programs, and looking for stable housing and employment opportunities.

MINIMUM QUALIFICATIONS

Treatment specialists need to have an undergraduate degree in a social work or counseling psychology-related field. Preference will be given to applicants who also possess work experience in counseling and working in the field of social services.

SAMPLE MINIMUM QUALIFICATIONS IN JOB POSTINGS FOR CORRECTIONAL TREATMENT SPECIALIST/CORRECTIONS COUNSELOR–TYPE JOBS

The minimum qualifications needed in order to be considered for employment as a correctional treatment specialist/corrections counselor are presented in Figures 11.4 and 11.5.

FIGURE 11.4

Job posting for a correctional counselor with the Federal Bureau of Prisons

You must have at least one year of specialized experience equivalent in difficulty and complexity to the next lower grade level in federal service. To be creditable, this experience must have equipped the applicant with the particular qualifications to perform successfully the duties of the position.

Some examples of this qualifying experience are:

- Experience in work such as police officer, mental health counselor in a residential facility, or detention officer.

- Experience in coordinating matters pertaining to inmate personal property and trust fund activities and involvement in the BOP Intake Screening Process and the Administrative Remedy process.

- Experience in demonstrating the knowledge of institution policies on sanitation and security.

- Experience in conducting individual and group counseling sessions.

FIGURE 11.5

Job posting for a correctional counselor in Davidson County, Tennessee, with the Tennessee Department of Corrections

- **Education and Experience:** Graduation from an accredited college or university with a bachelor's degree and three (3) years of full-time increasingly responsible professional social or psychological counseling work.

- **Substitution of Education for Experience:** Additional graduate coursework in a social or behavioral science may be substituted for the required experience on a year-for-year basis to a maximum of two (2) years.

- **Substitution of Experience for Education:** Full-time social or psychological counseling experience may be substituted for the required education on a year-for-year basis to a maximum of two (2) years; requiring two years of study at an accredited college or university.

OR

- Three (3) years as a Correctional Counselor with the Tennessee Department of Corrections.

TIPS FOR GETTING HIRED

While pursuing a bachelor's degree in a counseling-psychology or social work–related field of study, seek internship opportunities with government or nonprofit organizations whose mission statement includes specialization in treatment and counseling.

Percentile	10%	25%	50% (Median)	75%	90%
Hourly Wage	$16.17	$19.01	$24.12	$32.41	$42.76
Annual Wage	$33,630	$39,530	$50,160	$67,420	$88,930

Figure 11.6 Annual salary estimates for correctional treatment specialists/corrections counselors[4]

[4]*Source*: Bureau of Labor Statistics. https://www.bls.gov/oes/current/oes211092.htm.

WARDEN

BASIC JOB DESCRIPTION

A warden is the chief administrative officer of a prison. As head of the prison, he or she effectively manages both inmates and staff in the prison. A warden must be up to date on all policies and regulations of the prison. This job also includes overseeing and investigating inmate complaints against staff, and making sure prison employees are upholding their ethical and professional responsibilities.

MINIMUM QUALIFICATIONS

To become a warden, you will need extensive experience in the field of corrections and administration. Wardens generally have worked many years in correctional settings such as a correctional office and then moved up the correctional ranks toward more supervisory and management positions. To be competitive for a warden position in today's job market, you will likely need a master's degree in a criminal justice–related area of study.

SAMPLE MINIMUM QUALIFICATIONS IN JOB POSTINGS FOR WARDEN POSITIONS WITHIN A PRISON

The minimum qualifications needed in order to be considered for employment as a warden are presented in Figures 11.7 and 11.8.

FIGURE 11.7

Job posting for a prison warden in Tallahassee, Florida, with the Florida Department of Corrections

- Twelve years of professional correctional experience; two years must be at the department head level.
- College education from an accredited institution can substitute at the rate of 30 semester or 45 quarter hours per year for a maximum of one year of the required experience.

FIGURE 11.8

Job posting for a prison warden with CoreCivic
(formerly Corrections Corporation of America)
in Shelby, Montana

- Graduate from an accredited college or university with a Bachelor's degree is required, preferably in Social or Behavioral Sciences or a related field.
- Ten years of correctional work experience, with increasing responsibility, including two years of experience at the Assistant Warden level or above is required. Additional qualifying full-time correctional supervisory experience may be substituted for the education requirement on a year for year basis.
- Must demonstrate a comprehensive understanding and knowledge of the practices and principles of correctional facility management, pertinent correctional laws, rules and regulations, and the principles and practices of supervision and training.
- Proficiency in Microsoft Office applications is required.
- A valid driver's license is required.

TIPS FOR GETTING HIRED

After earning an undergraduate degree in a criminal justice–related area of study, start off working as a correctional officer in a prison. Look to work your way up the ranks into more supervisory and management roles within the prison. This could require moving to another prison for advancement opportunities, but always remain geographically flexible and open to these advancement opportunities. Work on a master's degree in an area of study related to criminal justice in order to be competitive when applying to become a warden. An advanced degree and years of work experience are crucial for being competitive for these positions.

SALARY ESTIMATES FOR PRISON WARDENS

According to PayScale.com, the median pay for a prison warden in 2017 was $80,278.[5]

PROBATION AND PAROLE OFFICERS

BASIC JOB DESCRIPTION

As discussed earlier in Chapter 11, probation and parole are two separate entities of community corrections. Some states, however, lump them together under the same job title, "probation and parole officer," while other states have separate job

---

[5]"Prison Warden Salary." https://www.payscale.com/research/US/Job=Prison_Warden/Salary.

titles and roles marking a distinction between probation and parole officers. The main focus for both probation and parole officers, though, is to supervise their clients—the convicted offenders—and to ensure that these clients are meeting all of the legal requirements established by the courts for their probation or parole sentence. Often this includes making sure that clients submit and pass drug tests, obey specific curfews and geographical restrictions, actively apply and seek gainful employment opportunities, find stable housing options, and enroll in educational or vocational training courses. Probation and parole officers are both law enforcement officers and social workers. The field of community corrections has been experiencing strong growth because of prison overcrowding. Probation and parole officers want to prevent their clients from becoming recidivists (repeat offenders) and get them back on the right track, successfully reintegrated into society as law-abiding citizens.

MINIMUM QUALIFICATIONS

Minimum qualifications for probation and parole officers vary across state lines; however, an undergraduate degree in a criminal justice or social work–type area of study is generally required. Previous work experience in law enforcement or social work is also preferred. Probation and parole officers must successfully complete a training academy before starting as a full-time officer.

SAMPLE MINIMUM QUALIFICATIONS IN JOB POSTINGS FOR PROBATION AND PAROLE OFFICER POSITIONS

The minimum qualifications required for employment in a probation and parole officer position are presented in Figures 11.9 and 11.10.

FIGURE 11.9

Job posting for a probation and parole officer with the Arkansas Department of Community Corrections

- The formal education equivalent of a bachelor's degree in criminal justice, sociology, psychology, social work or a related field.
- Must be able to be certified as a Specialized Law Enforcement Officer by the Commission on Law Enforcement Standards and Training in accordance with ACA 12-9-106 within one year of hire date, or certified by the Department of Community Corrections as a DCC Parole/Probation Officer.

FIGURE 11.10

Job posting for a probation and parole officer in Natchitoches, Louisiana, with the Louisiana Department of Corrections

- A baccalaureate degree
- Six years of full-time work experience in any field may be substituted for the required baccalaureate degree.
- An applicant who has been convicted of a misdemeanor crime of domestic violence or a felony, or who is under indictment on a felony charge will be disqualified until relief from the disabilities imposed by state and federal laws is granted.

TIPS FOR GETTING HIRED

As part of an undergraduate degree, look to complete internship opportunities at probation and parole offices in order to network and build experience in the field. Completing at least two internships in the field of probation and parole will help your chances of getting hired in this field after graduation.

Figure 11.11 Annual percentile salary estimates for probation and parole officers[6]

Percentile	10%	25%	50% (Median)	75%	90%
Hourly Wage	$16.17	$19.01	$24.12	$32.41	$42.76
Annual Wage	$33,630	$39,530	$50,160	$67,420	$88,930

[6]*Source*: Bureau of Labor Statistics. https://www.bls.gov/oes/current/oes211092.htm.

SUMMARY

The field of corrections offers many different employment settings: local and state governments, the federal government, nonprofit agencies, and the private sector. These jobs range from correctional officers to treatment specialists and also include community corrections positions like probation and parole officers. With additional employment experience in corrections, applicants can apply for administrative-type positions within correctional institutions such as prison warden. The field of corrections offers many employment opportunities in the criminal justice arena that are not necessarily thought of as often as positions within law enforcement or the court systems. Prospective applicants need to be aware of these employment opportunities because they offer a great starting point for a career in the criminal justice system.

▲ There are many employment opportunities within state and federal prisons, as well as in the private prison industry.

Three Key Takeaway Points

1. Remember that the field of corrections includes both physical incarceration settings like jails and prisons, and community corrections, encompassing the administration of corrections taking place outside of physical incarceration settings like probation and parole.

2. Jails and prisons are not the same entity. Jails are used for short-term incarceration situations including inmates awaiting trial who have been denied bail or are unable to post bail. Prisons are correctional institutions designed for longer-term incarceration and are better equipped with treatment and rehabilitation programs because inmates will be in these institutions longer on average than in jails.

3. Probation and parole are two of the most common forms of community corrections. Probation is a front-end alternate to jail or prison, while parole usually means early release from prison. Both probation and parole require the convicted offender to adhere to a strict set of rules and guidelines established by the court, and these court-ordered stipulations must be met for the duration of the probation or parole sentence.

ASSESSMENT QUESTIONS

1. What are the primary differences between jails and prisons?
2. What does the term "community corrections" mean?
3. What is the difference between probation and parole?
4. What are two companies in the private sector that employ correctional officers?
5. What is the primary job description of a prison warden?

CRITICAL THINKING EXERCISE

When discussing the term "corrections," why do you think many people automatically think about physical incarceration settings like prisons and jails, which account for only 30% of the overall correctional landscape? As an experiment, ask your friends to name an example of "corrections." See how many mention physical incarceration settings versus different forms of community corrections.

APPLIED LEARNING ACTIVITY

Find five job announcements in correctional careers that sound interesting to you using websites like *Indeed.com*, *Monster.com*, and *USAjobs.gov*. Compare the different educational requirements, duties, and preferred qualifications for each position. What are the main similarities and differences between each job opening?

KEY TERMS

Community corrections – Form of corrections that takes place outside of physical incarceration settings and in the community.

Jail – Short-term physical incarceration facility. Generally inmates are in jail for 1 year or less.

Prison – Longer-term physical incarceration facility that varies by security level based on the severity of crimes committed by offenders. Generally inmates are in prison for 1 year or more.

Supermax – Nickname given to prisons that exceed maximum security standards.

Probation – Form of community corrections that is a front-end alternative to a physical incarceration setting.

Parole – Form of community corrections that is a back-end solution to prison usually involving early release for good behavior.

Recidivist – A criminal offender who reoffends.

12

Chapter Outline

Other Career Opportunities in the Field of Criminal Justice

INTRODUCTION

The field of criminal justice offers a great variety of jobs and career paths. Not all of these employment opportunities are limited to the main components of the criminal justice system: law enforcement, courts, and corrections. Most of the career paths discussed in Chapter 12, though, do have some overlap in job function with the main components of the CJ system. Prospective applicants, current students, and criminal justice practitioners looking for a career change need to be aware of all career options the criminal justice job market offers. Chapter 12 discusses some very desirable lesser-known career opportunities in the field of criminal justice and provides the minimum qualifications required for these specific career paths found in actual job postings. Additional employment resources concerning these career opportunities can be found on the textbook's companion resource www.oup.com/us/klutz.

FORENSIC PSYCHOLOGIST

BASIC JOB DESCRIPTION

The job of a forensic psychologist has been popularized tremendously because of fictional depictions in TV shows and movies such as *Criminal Minds*, *Silence of the Lambs*, and the new Netflix hit *Mindhunter*. The problem with these portrayals is that they fail to show what a real-life forensic psychologist actually does. These depictions also usually fall short in the specifics: how prospective applicants can actually better prepare themselves to be competitive for forensic psychology job postings, for example. Thus, these fictional representations of forensic psychologists can be seen as a double-edged sword: they get potential applicants interested in the field of forensic psychology, but they fail to inform viewers about what it takes in terms of qualifications and work experience to actually land a job in this line of work. The actual job of the forensic psychologist differs a great deal from what is portrayed on television and the movies, and without the right information and career planning, believing the fiction will produce frustrating results.

Forensic psychologists often work with criminals, conducting evaluations on competency to stand trial (i.e., to determine whether an individual has sufficient factual/rational knowledge about legal proceedings and ability to work with their attorneys) and criminal responsibility/insanity (i.e., to determine an individual's mental state at the time of the alleged offense). Defendants who have either been found not guilty by reason of insanity (NGRI) or are unable to be restored to competency by a forensic psychologist may require a violence risk assessment administered over time to determine if and when the offender can be released from an institution—either to a less restrictive setting or into the community. Forensic psychologists also administer the PCL–R

(Psychopathy Checklist–Revised) to determine if an individual displays psychopathic tendencies and the MMPI–2–RF (Minnesota Multiphasic Personality Inventory–2–Restructured Form) to indentify psychopathology, personality characteristics, and response styles of criminal offenders.

Not all of a forensic psychologist's job description involves working with criminal offenders. Forensic psychologists can also work with law enforcement agencies to screen prospective hires and look for any red flags from these incoming hires. These "police evaluations" often utilize personality inventories like the MMPI–2–RF to examine personality characteristics of the potential law enforcement hires as a prescreening measure. Forensic psychologists can also work on the civil side of the law as well, conducting personal injury psychological evaluations, workman's compensation evaluations, child custody evaluations, and evaluations for insurance companies.

Forensic psychologists are employed in a variety of employment settings including state hospitals, the Federal Bureau of Prisons (BOP), academic medical centers (AMCs), private hospitals, private practices, and university research settings. There are always many gainful employment opportunities available for licensed forensic psychologists in the field of criminal justice.

MINIMUM QUALIFICATIONS

Becoming a forensic psychologist involves a very long and arduous process requiring many years of advanced education and clinical training. In order to be qualified for the majority of jobs as a licensed forensic psychologist, an applicant will need to possess a PhD or PsyD (Doctor of Psychology) in clinical psychology. These advanced degree programs in clinical psychology provide years of clinical training and educational experience in the field. At the end of your tenure in the advanced degree program, there will be a required additional year in an internship placement where you will work in a forensic setting full time in order to receive more training and direct supervision in the field of forensic psychology. After the internship year, some students choose to complete 1 more year in a postdoctoral position to receive additional training and supervised clinical hours to become even more competitive for forensic psychology job options. In all, a clinical psychology PhD or PsyD program will take 5 to 7 years to complete on top of an undergraduate degree in psychology.

SAMPLE MINIMUM QUALIFICATIONS IN JOB POSTINGS FOR FORENSIC PSYCHOLOGISTS

The minimum qualifications needed in order to be considered for employment as a forensic psychologist are presented in Figures 12.1 and 12.2.

FIGURE 12.1

Job posting for a clinical/forensic psychologist position with the NSA (NSA.gov)

- Salary Range: $94,796–$145,629 (Senior)
- *The qualifications listed are the minimum acceptable to be considered for the position. Salary offers are based on candidates' education level and years of experience relevant to the position and also take into account information provided by the hiring manager/ organization regarding the work level for the position.
- Entry is with a Doctoral degree plus 2 years of relevant experience.
- Degree must be in Clinical Psychology.
- Relevant experience must be in clinical psychology, and may also include performing psychology-related work (internships count against this requirement). A valid license to practice psychology in any state or territory is required.

FIGURE 12.2

Job posting for a forensic psychologist with the state of Oklahoma in the Department of Mental Health and Substance Abuse Services

- Completion of the curriculum requirements for a doctorate in clinical or counseling psychology from an APA accredited program (or its equivalent as determined by the Oklahoma State Board of Examiners of Psychologists).
- Completion of a one year pre-doctoral internship, including direct supervision from a psychologist licensed in the state with specialization in clinical or counseling psychology. Current licensure by the Oklahoma State Board of Examiners of Psychologists.
- Minimum of one year of post-doctoral specialized training in the evaluation and/or treatment of forensic clients. Experience with providing expert testimony during at least one legal proceeding (or during a mock trial if no opportunity for actual testimony exists.)

TIPS FOR GETTING HIRED

Since becoming a forensic psychologist involves such a lengthy process, there are many important steps along the way to keep in mind, but the most important is gaining entry into a quality clinical psychology graduate program specializing in the field of forensic psychology. For your undergraduate bachelor's degree, you will need to major in psychology, and look to join an undergraduate research lab with a clinical psychology faculty member whose research area is in forensic psychology. Start conducting undergraduate research in a research lab as soon as possible. Ask the faculty member in charge of the research lab about opportunities to present your undergraduate research at a research conference in the form of a poster presentation, and also look to publish your research with faculty members even if it means you will be second or third author on the publication. The more poster presentations and research publications you have throughout your undergraduate career the better.

While you are pursuing your undergraduate degree you also need to focus on studying for the Graduate Record Examination (GRE) and preparing yourself to get the highest score possible because of how competitive clinical psychology graduate programs are. It goes without saying, but a high GPA is also required to gain admission into these graduate programs. *StudentDoctorNetwork.com* provides a great resource forum for students interested in gaining more information about the field of clinical psychology. There are prospective graduate students, current graduate students, and practicing clinical psychologists posting information on this forum.

SALARY ESTIMATES FOR FORENSIC PSYCHOLOGISTS

The median salary for forensic psychologists is presented in Figure 12.3.

Figure 12.3 Annual salary estimates for forensic psychologists[1]

Percentile	10%	25%	50% (Median)	75%	90%
Hourly Wage	$20.11	$26.47	$35.23	$46.11	$57.85
Annual Wage	$41,830	$55,050	$73,270	$95,910	$120,320

[1]*Source:* Bureau of Labor Statistics. https://www.bls.gov/oes/current/oes193031.htm.

CRIME SCENE INVESTIGATORS

BASIC JOB DESCRIPTION

Crime scene investigations (CSI) is another field that has been heavily impacted by faulty media depictions. The so-called *CSI* effect has been a big problem over the years since the popular television show *CSI* came into existence. Due to the *CSI* effect, the public tends to overemphasize the significance of forensic evidence and inaccurately thinks there is a quick forensic test out there for any crime scene. Crime scene investigators' actual job is much different from the way it is portrayed in these fictional television shows like *CSI*. In real life, crime scene investigators are generally members of law enforcement agencies at the local, state, or federal government level. Their primary job function is to find, gather, and preserve evidence from crime scenes. At the actual crime scene, CSI personnel may be tasked with photographing the scene, gathering

▲ Crime scene investigators generally need an extensive background in chemistry coursework.

fingerprint evidence, collecting DNA evidence, photographing footprints, and collecting evidence from any form of weapon used during the commission of the crime. Most crime scene investigators work the crime scenes, while forensic scientists actually perform the laboratory tests on the evidence collected at the scene of the crime.

MINIMUM QUALIFICATIONS

Although minimum qualifications for these positions vary with employers, most agencies require crime scene investigators to have at least an undergraduate degree in chemistry or forensic science and some work experience in the criminal justice field. Most agencies require their crime scene investigators to successfully complete a pre-hire training academy program as well.

SAMPLE MINIMUM QUALIFICATIONS IN JOB POSTINGS FOR CRIME SCENE INVESTIGATORS

The minimum qualifications needed in order to be considered for employment as a crime scene investigator are presented in Figures 12.4 and 12.5.

FIGURE 12.4

Crime scene investigator position in Carrollton, Texas

- Graduation from an accredited university with a Bachelor's Degree in forensic science or related field.
- One (1) year of crime scene investigator experience;
- IAI certification as a Certified Latent Print Examiner
- Texas Forensic Science Academy, IAI or equivalent certification as a Crime Scene Investigator

FIGURE 12.5

Crime scene investigator position in Denver, Colorado, with the Denver Police Department

- Bachelor's Degree in Criminal Justice, Chemistry, Biology, or a related field and
- One year of experience in crime scene processing that includes the techniques generally used in crime scene documenting and processing.
- Additional appropriate education may be substituted for the minimum experience requirement.
- Additional appropriate experience may be substituted for the minimum education requirement. Volunteer experience and scholastic experience may substitute for up to one year of total experience.
- By position, requires a valid driver's license at the time of application.
- Ability to obtain applicable IAI Certified Crime Scene Investigator, Level 1 or LEVA Certified Forensic Video Technician certification within two years of employment.

TIPS FOR GETTING HIRED

Earning a bachelor's degree with a double major—in either chemistry or forensic science, and then criminal justice as your second major—will greatly help your application in this field. While pursuing an undergraduate degree, applicants interested in CSI careers should look to complete internships with various law enforcement departments within their CSI unit. This will provide direct real-world experience in the field and enable you to network with CSI practitioners.

▲ A crime scene unit working a crime scene and dusting for prints.

SALARY ESTIMATES FOR CRIME SCENE INVESTIGATORS

In 2017, the median salary for crime scene investigators was $43,618, according to Pay-Scale.com.[2]

FORENSIC SCIENTIST/FORENSIC SCIENCE TECHNICIAN

BASIC JOB DESCRIPTION

Forensic scientists generally work in a laboratory setting analyzing evidence collected from crime scenes. They work with law enforcement personnel and also work through the trial phase of a given case. These positions require detailed report writing skills, and forensic scientists are often called to testify as expert witnesses in the courtroom about their findings in the laboratory. Additionally, forensic scientists must have an extensive

---

[2]*Source:* "Crime Scene Investigator (CSI) Salary." https://www.payscale.com/research/US/Job=Crime_Scene_Investigator_(CSI)/Salary.

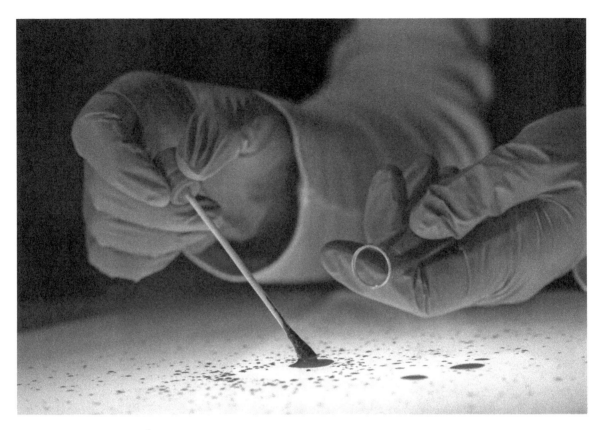

▲ A forensic technician working in a laboratory setting.

background in physical sciences and knowledge concerning advanced scientific principles for testing evidence. There are many specialty areas within the field of forensic science including the following career paths:

Forensic entomology—The study of insects on postmortem human remains.

Forensic toxicology—Analyzing chemicals found in human tissue and bodily remains.

DNA analysis—Obtaining biological data in isolating DNA to a suspect or between victims.

Ballistics analysis—Analyzing firearms, ammunition, and shell casings from a physics standpoint looking at things like trajectory and angles used during a commission of a crime.

Forensic sketch artist—Commonly referred to only as a "sketch artist," draws free-hand or produces computerized drawings of suspects.

Forensic botany—The study of plant materials found at crime scenes. Different plant materials can help formulate a picture of if a body was moved from a certain area, and when a crime actually occurred from the types of plant material found at the crime scene.

MINIMUM QUALIFICATIONS

Minimum qualifications for forensic scientists vary greatly because there are so many subdisciplines in this field of work. Generally speaking, forensic scientists will need a very strong educational background in fields like biology, chemistry, and physics. For subfields like forensic entomology, an applicant would likely need a PhD in entomology. However, for general forensic scientist positions, an advanced degree in chemistry is usually desired. It is very important to note that degrees in these hard sciences are a requirement for most coveted jobs in the broad field of forensic science.

SAMPLE MINIMUM QUALIFICATIONS IN JOB POSTINGS FOR FORENSIC SCIENTISTS

The minimum qualifications needed in order to be considered for employment as a forensic scientist are presented in Figures 12.6 and 12.7.

FIGURE 12.6

Job posting for a forensic scientist with the Kansas Bureau of Investigation

- Hourly Compensation Rate: $22.16
- Duties of this position include, but are not limited to: training in the area of latent print examination by means of an intensive two-year training program to include analysis of latent print evidence, comparison and evaluation of latent prints and known prints, physical and chemical development, report writing and court testimony.
- Bachelor's degree relevant to the field of work. Experience may be substituted for education as determined relevant by the agency.
- Graduation from an accredited four-year college or university with a degree in Forensic Science, Biology, Chemistry or a related scientific field.

FIGURE 12.7

Job posting for a forensic scientist in Jefferson County, Kentucky

- Graduate of a college or university with a bachelor's degree in chemistry, forensic science, biology, microbiology, biochemistry, medical technology, engineering, mathematics, criminal justice or a closely related field.
- Must have three years of professional laboratory experience performing work in a specialty area of forensic science.

TIPS FOR GETTING HIRED

For most of these careers, a bachelor's degree in chemistry, biology, or physics will be needed. From there, depending on which specific field in the study of forensic sciences you are pursuing, an advanced degree in one of these areas of study will also be needed. A PhD specializing in the specific area of forensic science you plan on working in will distinguish you from the competition and make you competitive for the most desirable positions in your given specialty area.

SALARY ESTIMATES FOR FORENSIC SCIENCE TECHNICIANS

The median salary for forensic science technicians is presented in Figure 12.8.

Figure 12.8 Annual salary estimates for forensic science technicians[3]					
Percentile	10%	25%	50% (Median)	75%	90%
Hourly Wage	$16.28	$20.54	$27.29	$35.68	$46.83
Annual Wage	$33,860	$42,710	$56,750	$74,220	$97,400

[3]*Source*: Bureau of Labor Statistics. https://www.bls.gov/oes/current/oes194092.htm.

BOND AGENTS AND BOUNTY HUNTERS

BASIC JOB DESCRIPTION

Individuals who are charged with a crime and are unable to post bail in order to secure their pretrial release have the option of contacting a bail-bond business, who in return will post the individual's bail for a fee. The fee a bonds business charges an individual to secure their pretrial release is usually around 10% of the original bail amount. This is the cost of doing business with a bonds agent. The bonds industry represents a great entrepreneurial opportunity in the field of criminal justice. Bond firms can choose which potential customers they want to do business with. If the firm perceives a potential customer to be a flight risk, it might think twice before taking on this individual as a client. However, if a potential customer is a first-time offender with a pretty clean record, the firm is likely to take on this individual as a client because he or she is much less likely to be a flight risk.

The individual charged with a crime must show up to all of the court dates, and if the offender skips out of town and attempts to evade justice, the bond agents generally have approximately 60 to 90 days to return the fugitive to the court. Some bonds businesses will track down fugitives themselves, but some will contract out with a third-party entity known as a bounty hunter. A bounty hunter's goal is to locate fugitives and then return them to the courtroom. Bounty hunters earn their income by collecting a fee from the bonds business they are assisting, or sometimes directly from the court itself. Bounty hunting is another entrepreneurial opportunity within the criminal justice system, but it requires a great deal of coverage in liability insurance to protect against civil claims. Bonds businesses and bounty hunters operate outside of sworn law enforcement jurisdiction, and authority for these third-party entities essentially stems from citizen arrest powers. That is, if an individual is committing a felony—in this case, becoming a fugitive of the law by skipping out on the court—citizens, including bond agents and bounty hunters, can make a legal and lawful citizen's arrest.

MINIMUM QUALIFICATIONS

Qualifications for individual bonds businesses and bounty hunting services vary greatly. There are usually no formal education requirements for these positions, but field experience in law enforcement or the military is preferred. Working in these positions requires extensive knowledge of the rules and regulations surrounding these trades.

SAMPLE MINIMUM QUALIFICATIONS IN JOB POSTINGS FOR A BOND AGENT POSITION AND A BOUNTY HUNTER POSITION

The minimum qualifications needed in order to be considered for employment as a bond agent and a bounty hunter are presented in Figures 12.9 and 12.10, respectively.

FIGURE 12.9

Job posting for a bond agent in Seattle, Washington, with All City Bail Bonds

- A friendly and outgoing personality that seeks to interact and work with people of varied backgrounds and cultures.
- Previous work or experience with the insurance industry or surety company is preferred but not required.
- Basic proficiency with standard office software (e.g. Word and Excel)
- A valid driver's license and operating vehicle to travel to offices, courts, and detention centers.
- Passing surety exam and county justification before working as an active agent.
- Detailed written and oral communication skills.

FIGURE 12.10

Job posting for a bounty hunter (this firm calls this position a "fugitive recovery agent") position in Tacoma, Washington, with Aladdin Bail Bonds

- Good investigative and research skills.
- Requires a concealed weapons permit.
- Recovery License preferred.
- Tactical training and experience (arrests, searches, detentions).
- Physically fit and able to arrest and transport uncooperative subjects.
- Strong command presence and a professional demeanor.
- Ability to defuse situations and resolve conflict.
- Ability to follow instructions and commands.
- Good report writing and interview skills.
- Thoroughness and attention to detail.
- Excellent time management and organizational skills.
- Accurate typing, filing, computer and data entry skills.
- Proficient at MS Office, Word, Excel and other basic computer programs.
- Ability to multi-task, prioritize and follow up on projects.
- Ability to work independently or as a team.

TIPS FOR GETTING HIRED

Just starting out in this line of work, you will not have the experience, expertise, or capital necessary to open your own business. For both the bond and bounty-hunting industries, contact firms in your local area to see if you can work as an apprentice to learn the ropes of the industry. Look to build experience, knowledge, and capital over the course of 5 to 8 years, after which you can start thinking about starting your own business.

SALARY ESTIMATES FOR BOND AGENTS AND BOUNTY HUNTERS

Salary can vary widely in this career field. Ultimately, pay will depend on how high up in the business you rank. According to PayScale.com, the median salary for bond agents and bounty hunters is $36,410.[4]

---

[4]*Source:* "Bail Bonding Agent Salary." https://www.payscale.com/research/US/Job=Bail_Bonding_Agent/Salary.

▲ The infamous fictional bounty hunter Boba Fett in the *Star Wars* universe.

JUVENILE JUSTICE CAREERS

BASIC JOB DESCRIPTIONS

The field of juvenile justice careers offers many opportunities to work with at-risk youth: as juvenile probation officers, juvenile detention officers, and juvenile counselors. There are also positions working within the juvenile court system and opportunities in the nonprofit sector to work with troubled youth as well.

Juvenile probation officers, who work directly with juveniles who have received a probationary sentence by a juvenile court, oversee the juveniles throughout this probationary period. Requirements of the job can include administering drug tests, verifying that the juvenile is attending school, and conducting regular home visits. Juvenile probation officers work closely with law enforcement, the juvenile court system, and social service agencies.

MINIMUM QUALIFICATIONS

Minimum qualifications for a juvenile probation officer vary across state lines, but most of these positions in today's job market require a minimum of a bachelor's degree. Field experience working in social service agencies with juveniles is also preferred.

SAMPLE MINIMUM QUALIFICATIONS IN JOB POSTING
FOR A JUVENILE PROBATION OFFICER

The minimum qualifications needed in order to be considered for employment as a juvenile probation officer are presented in Figure 12.11.

FIGURE 12.11

Job posting for a juvenile probation officer in Marathon, Florida

- A Bachelor's degree from an accredited college or university is required at the time of submission of application.
- A valid driver's license is required.
- Preference will be given to candidates who have worked with juveniles previously.

TIPS FOR GETTING HIRED

Complete a bachelor's degree in a criminal justice or social work–related field of study. While pursuing your undergraduate degree, complete at least two internships in the field of juvenile probation or with a nonprofit agency whose mission statement involves working with juveniles.

SALARY ESTIMATES FOR JUVENILE PROBATION OFFICERS

The median salary for juvenile probation officers is presented in Figure 12.12.

Figure 12.12 Annual percentile salary estimates for probation officers[5]				
Hourly Wage	$16.17	$19.01	$24.12	$32.41	$42.76
Annual Wage	$33,630	$39,530	$50,160	$67,420	$88,930

[5]*Source*: Bureau of Labor Statistics. https://www.bls.gov/oes/current/oes211092.htm.

JUVENILE COUNSELORS AND BEHAVIORAL DISORDER COUNSELORS

BASIC JOB DESCRIPTION

Juvenile counselors and behavioral disorder counselors focus on working one-on-one with juvenile offenders to assess their overall well-being and areas needing improvement. Counselors work with the court system and social service agencies to improve these areas to continue to build greater stability in the juvenile's life.

MINIMUM QUALIFICATIONS

Most juvenile counselor positions require at least a bachelor's degree in social work or a counseling psychology undergraduate degree. In order to be among the most competitive applicants in this field, a master's degree in social work (MSW) or counseling psychology is preferred. Field experience working directly with juveniles is also desired.

SAMPLE MINIMUM QUALIFICATIONS IN JOB POSTING FOR A JUVENILE COUNSELOR

The minimum qualifications needed in order to be considered for employment as a juvenile counselor are presented in Figure 12.13.

FIGURE 12.13

Job Posting for a juvenile counselor in Lansing, New York, with the Office of Children and Family Services

Bachelor's degree and two years of direct counseling, educational, clinical, or supervisory experience in prevention, protection, or rehabilitative programs for individuals between the ages of 10 and 21 years of age who are generally considered to be "juvenile delinquents," "youthful offenders," or youth residing in a residential setting which may include, youth who are diagnosed with mental or developmental disabilities, mental illness, or addictions who could potentially become involved in the juvenile justice system.

TIPS FOR GETTING HIRED

Completing internships with juvenile service agencies will help. Completing a PhD in clinical psychology or counseling psychology will make you very competitive in this field for the widest range of job opportunities.

JUVENILE COUNSELORS AND BEHAVIORAL DISORDER COUNSELORS.

The median salary for substance abuse and behavioral disorder counselors is presented in Figure 12.14.

Figure 12.14 Annual percentile salary estimates for substance abuse and behavioral disorder counselors[6]

Percentile	10%	25%	50% (Median)	75%	90%
Hourly Wage	$12.60	$15.61	$19.75	$25.33	$31.29
Annual Wage	$26,210	$32,470	$41,070	$52,690	$65,080

[6]*Source*: Bureau of Labor Statistics. https://www.bls.gov/oes/current/oes211011.htm.

CYBERSECURITY ANALYST/INFORMATION SECURITY ANALYST

BASIC JOB DESCRIPTION

Cybersecurity threats have made the headlines over the past few years with the Target, Home Depot, and, most recently, Equifax data breaches. There are growing cyber threats in the financial industry, at nuclear and water plants, in the electrical grids, and overall with vulnerable consumer data. These increasing threats also mean there is a lot of hiring going on in this field. Cybersecurity is still somewhat in its infancy phase. Just about all major companies are advertising cybersecurity jobs now, including financial firms, retail companies, online businesses, and defense contractors. Many of these cybersecurity job vacancies are going unfilled because of the lack of qualified applicants. These jobs require advanced computer skills in computer programming, database management, algorithms, and various programming languages.

Cybersecurity analysts monitor potential threats and look to indentify holes hackers can exploit to gain entry into a network or information system. Often cybersecurity analysts must think like hackers to indentify weaknesses in the system. Growth in this career path is very strong, as evidenced by the Bureau of Labor Statistics forecasting a 37% growth by the year 2022.[7]

MINIMUM QUALIFICATIONS

Minimum qualifications for cybersecurity positions generally include an undergraduate degree in a computer science–related field of study. Preference for these jobs will be given to applicants who have experience working with network and information security and those possessing a master's degree in a computer science–related field.

SAMPLE MINIMUM QUALIFICATIONS IN JOB POSTINGS FOR CYBERSECURITY ANALYSTS

The minimum qualifications needed in order to be considered for employment in a cybersecurity position are presented in Figures 12.15 and 12.16.

FIGURE 12.15

Job Posting for a cyber threat analyst with Booz Allen Hamilton

- 3+ years of experience with IT
- Experience with performing incident handling
- Experience with incident response and vulnerability management
- Experience with ArcSight, HBSS, Retina, Websense, Cyber Forensics, Cloud Computing, ICS/SCADA security, malware analysis, or Command Cyber Readiness Inspections
- Ability to leverage CND–related toolsets to detect and respond to IT security incidents

---

[7]"FAQ—Cybersecurity Jobs 'Heat Map' Initiative," National Institute of Standards and Technology. https://www.nist.gov/sites/default/files/documents/2017/03/14/faq_-_cybersecurity_jobs_heat_map_initiative.pdf.

- Active Top Secret clearance
- BA or BS degree
- IAT Level III Certification, including CISA, CISSP, or CASP
- CND–IR Certification, including GCIH, CSIH, or CEH
- Additional Qualifications:
- TS/ SCI clearance within 6 months of contract start date
- Computing Environment (CE) Certification within 6 months of start date

FIGURE 12.16

Job posting for a cyber threat intelligence analyst with NIKE, Inc.

- Bachelor's Degree in Information Technology, Information Security/Assurance, Engineering, or related field of study; or at least four years of related experience and/or training; or equivalent combination of education and experience preferred.
- Minimum 2 years of general IT experience required.
- Minimum 1 year of Information Security experience required.
- Minimum 1 year of corporate threat intelligence knowledge preferred.
- Excellent written and verbal communication skills required. Must be able to communicate technical details effectively across different audiences.
- Customer-oriented focus required, with a strong interest in a satisfied client.
- Solid understanding of Information Security and Networking required.
- The ability to learn and utilize new technology or concepts very quickly.
- Candidates must be legally authorized to work in the U.S. without sponsorship.

TIPS FOR GETTING HIRED

Complete cybersecurity internships while pursuing a bachelor's degree in a computer science–related field of study. Look at actual job descriptions for cybersecurity-related positions and master specific desired skill sets found in the duties and qualifications sections of these job advertisements. Generally these specific skill sets involve being proficient in specific computer programming languages.

SALARY ESTIMATES FOR INFORMATION SECURITY ANALYSTS

The median salary for information security analysts is presented in Figure 12.17.

Figure 12.17 Annual percentile salary estimates for information security analysts[8]

Percentile	10%	25%	50% (Median)	75%	90%
Hourly Wage	$25.85	$33.58	$44.52	$57.22	$70.81
Annual Wage	$53,760	$69,840	$92,600	$119,020	$147,290

[8]*Source*: Bureau of Labor Statistics. https://www.bls.gov/oes/current/oes151122.htm.

PRIVATE INVESTIGATORS (PIs)

BASIC JOB DESCRIPTION

Private investigators represent one of the great entrepreneurial opportunities within the criminal justice system. One day, with enough experience and capital, you can possibly open up your own PI firm. Private investigators conduct surveillance and investigations for customers regarding scenarios involving marital disputes and divorce proceedings, workman's compensation claims and disputes, location of missing persons, and assistance in preparing evidence to testify in court. Working as a PI can require long and irregular working hours, and often requires undercover work. Initially starting out in this field will require you to gain experience working in an established PI firm. This field requires substantial liability insurance, as well as licensures and accreditation standards varying by state.

MINIMUM QUALIFICATIONS

Minimum qualifications vary across different PI firms, but most require an associate's degree with preference given to applicants who have experience in law enforcement or the military. A clean background record is also required for pre-employment screening purposes.

SAMPLE MINIMUM QUALIFICATIONS IN JOB POSTINGS FOR PRIVATE INVESTIGATORS

The minimum qualifications needed in order to be considered for employment as a private investigator are presented in Figures 12.18 and 12.19.

FIGURE 12.18

Job posting for a private investigator position in Berclair, Tennessee

- A reliable vehicle.
- TN Private Investigator License required.
- A cell phone; to be in contact with a case manager while on surveillance.
- A digital video camera, date and time stamp software with the ability to upload video.

- Be proficient using Word and ability to write detailed reports.
- Worker's Compensation, Auto Accident, or similar surveillance / SIU experience required.
- Cases will be assigned on a Part Time / Per Diem basis.
- Ability and willingness to travel as necessary.

FIGURE 12.19

Job posting for a private investigator position in New Orleans, Louisiana

- PI License – Or able to obtain one.
- 1 – 2 years experience in human surveillance.
- A reliable vehicle.
- A cell phone; to be in contact with a case manager while on surveillance.
- A video camera and capturing device with the ability to upload video with the date and time stamp to our server.
- A covert camcorder, able to discreetly record subjects.
- Computer with video editing software: i.e. (iMovie, Final Cut Pro, pinnacle, adobe premier, or any other suitable software).
- Must be proficient using Microsoft Word and ability to write detailed reports.

TIPS FOR GETTING HIRED

Obtain an associate's degree in a criminal justice–related field. Field experience is preferred for these jobs. Two to three years of experience as a law enforcement officer or working in loss prevention will help in getting hired for private investigator job openings.

SALARY ESTIMATES FOR PRIVATE INVESTIGATORS

The median salary for private investigators is presented in Figure 12.20.

Figure 12.20 Annual percentile salary estimates for private investigators[9]

Percentile	10%	25%	50% (Median)	75%	90%
Hourly Wage	$13.08	$17.17	$23.17	$31.87	$41.86
Annual Wage	$27,210	$35,710	$48,190	$66,300	$87,070

[9]*Source*: Bureau of Labor Statistics. https://www.bls.gov/oes/current/oes339021.htm.

CRIME ANALYST

BASIC JOB DESCRIPTION

Crime analysts work with law enforcement departments acting as researchers to help identify crime trends in order to best effectively utilize departmental resources to reduce crime. Analysts work with statistical programs, GIS mapping technologies (for modeling crime rates), and other technologies to seek out patterns in criminal activity. They create reports and briefing law enforcement administrators on their research findings.

MINIMUM QUALIFICATIONS

Most crime analyst positions require a minimum of a bachelor's degree in a criminal justice or criminology-related field. Preference is given to applicants who also have a background in statistics, and previous scholarly research experience with data entry and statistical modeling as well.

SAMPLE MINIMUM QUALIFICATIONS IN JOB POSTINGS FOR CRIME ANALYSTS

The minimum qualifications needed in order to be considered for employment as a crime analyst are presented in Figures 12.21 and 12.22.

FIGURE 12.21

Job posting for a crime analyst with the Fort Myers Police Department in Florida

- Associates of Science degree with an emphasis in Criminal Justice, computer programming, statistical analysis or closely related field.
- One year experience that demonstrates the ability to analyze collected data and/or statistical reports from various sources and incorporate this information into pertinent reports to be utilized by sworn personnel to structure and incorporate this information into pertinent reports to be utilized by sworn personnel to structure use of patrol time and support investigations as well as crime prevention activities; or an equivalent combination of education, experience, and/or training that provides the required knowledge, skills, and abilities.
- Must possess a valid Florida Driver's License with an acceptable driving record.
- Ability to handle a multitude of diverse tasks simultaneously while maintaining an attention to detail for the purpose of ensuring accuracy in task performance.
- Knowledge of report writing techniques.

- Knowledge of research and analysis techniques.
- Knowledge of laboratory techniques. fingerprinting techniques, and classification systems.
- Knowledge of evidence and lost/found property maintenance and disposition practices.
- Ability to communicate effectively, both verbal and in writing.

FIGURE 12.22

Job posting for a crime analyst with the Sugar Land Police Department in Texas

Minimum requirements include but not limited to: excellent computer skills with knowledge of applications/software; Microsoft Office Suite, Excel and Access experience are essential. A working knowledge of Crystal Reports, Adobe professional, 12 Analyst Notebook, SPSS/SAS are preferred. Excellent communication skills, ability to multi-task, including excellent organizational skills with little or no direct supervision.

Qualified candidate must meet appropriate background standards.

Minimum Qualifications:

- A Bachelor's degree in Business Administration, Accounting, Public Administration, or a related field from an accredited school or university. Additional relevant work experience resulting in acceptable proficiency levels in the above knowledge; skills and education requirements may be substituted in lieu of specific education requirements.
- Three years of progressively responsible experience in a business discipline such as accounting, technical analysis, finance, or the like.
- Valid Texas Driver License
- Municipal government experience is a plus.

TIPS FOR GETTING HIRED

In addition to a bachelor's degree in criminal justice or criminology, look to obtain a double-major in statistics. Complete undergraduate research opportunities in the field of criminal justice. Complete at least two internships with law enforcement agencies before you finish your undergraduate degree. Completing a GIS certificate program is desired for many of these jobs as well.

SALARY ESTIMATES FOR CRIME ANALYSTS

In 2017, according to PayScale.com the median salary for a crime analyst is $45,963.[10]

---

[10]Crime Analyst Salary." https://www.payscale.com/research/US/Job=Crime_Analyst/Salary.

ACADEMIC CAREERS IN CRIMINAL JUSTICE

BASIC JOB DESCRIPTION
Working in academia involves conducting scholarly research, teaching, and advising students. Academic careers are available at two- and four-year higher education institutions. Teaching load and research expectations vary widely between different academic institutions.

MINIMUM QUALIFICATIONS
A master's degree related to the academic discipline you are teaching in is required. Often a PhD in the field you are teaching and conducting research in is preferred. A record of publishing scholarly research is also required for many academic jobs.

SAMPLE MINIMUM QUALIFICATIONS IN JOB POSTINGS FOR FACULTY JOBS IN CRIMINAL JUSTICE
The minimum qualifications needed in order to be considered for an academic position in criminal justice are presented in Figures 12.23 and 12.24.

FIGURE 12.23

Job posting for a criminal justice and criminology professor at UNC–Charlotte

- UNC Charlotte gives primary consideration to the earned doctorate or terminal degree in the teaching discipline or a related discipline.
- Preferred qualifications include strong methodological skills, an active research agenda, and the potential (or track record) for securing extramural funding.

FIGURE 12.24

Job posting for a criminal justice instructor at Florida Technical College

- Master's degree or higher with 18 credits in **Criminal Justice** among undergraduate and/or graduate courses
- Minimum of 2 years of industry experience
- Ability to engage a diverse student population in active learning to meet required course and program outcomes.

TIPS FOR GETTING HIRED

Research highly ranked advanced education programs in your field of study, and plan to obtain your advanced degree from one of these institutions. Name recognition from an advanced degree program, as well as name recognition from your graduate program's faculty base, goes a long way when applying to the academic job market. Conduct as much scholarly research in your field of study as possible. Look to publish this research with faculty members and present your research at research conferences. This is a great way to network for future academic jobs.

SALARY ESTIMATES FOR FACULTY JOBS IN CRIMINAL JUSTICE

The median salary for criminal justice faculty members is presented in Figure 12.3.

Figure 12.25 Annual salary estimates for criminal justice and law enforcement teachers, postsecondary[11]

Percentile	10%	25%	50% (Median)	75%	90%
Annual Wage	$34,650	$45,610	$59,590	$79,320	$105,210

[11]*Source*: Bureau of Labor Statistics. https://www.bls.gov/oes/current/oes251111.htm.

SUMMARY

The criminal justice system affords prospective applicants with many possible career paths outside the traditional focus of the most well-known job titles in law enforcement, courts, and corrections. These "miscellaneous" job titles covered in Chapter 12 offer great job opportunities in terms of pay and career advancement. Many of these jobs also offer entrepreneurial opportunity down the road. For example, with enough experience as a forensic psychologist, you can open up your own private practice one day. With enough training and knowledge in PI work, you might decide to open up your own private investigations firm. Or maybe after having worked for a bonds business for years, you feel one day that opening your own business in the bonds industry will best fit your career goals. These are unique personal business opportunities that are unavailable in most of the traditional criminal justice career paths. Students need to be aware of all of the numerous jobs our criminal justice system has to offer so they can keep all of their options open for a more expansive job search.

Three Key Takeaway Points

1. When planning your future career in the criminal justice system and looking at different job options, do not forget about some of the lesser-known career opportunities covered in Chapter 12.
2. Forensic psychology is a very popular career field these days due to the popularity of shows like *Mindhunter* and *Criminal Minds*. However, attaining a career in this field generally requires a PhD in clinical psychology with an academic program specializing in forensic psychology. There are very few job opportunities within the FBI's Behavioral Analysis Unit (BAU), and it is extremely competitive to get into these limited positions. The more likely career path for a forensic psychologist will be working in a state secure medical facility, at a federal prison, or in a private forensic practice.
3. Working in entrepreneurial opportunities within the criminal justice system like a bonds business or a private investigation firm requires specific licensures and accreditation standards that vary between states. Make sure to check into these requirements in your state well before planning to work in these types of private enterprises.

ASSESSMENT QUESTIONS

1. What are the minimum qualifications to become a forensic psychologist?
2. What are some fields of science to pursue in your educational career if you are interested in working in forensic science?
3. What does a forensic entomologist analyze?
4. What is the basic job description of a crime analyst?
5. What are the primary differences in the job description of a bonds agent and a bounty hunter?

CRITICAL THINKING EXERCISE

What are some specific reasons that the cybersecurity field has such intense hiring demand going into the future?

ACTIVE LEARNING ACTIVITY

Find one job announcement for each of the job titles listed in Chapter 12 using job websites like *Indeed.com*, *Monster.com*, and *USAjobs.gov*. For these various job announcements, compare the different education requirements, duties, and preferred qualifications for each job. What are main similarities and differences between each job opening?

KEY TERMS

PCL-R – The Psychopathy Checklist–Revised is a psychological assessment tool used to assess psychopathy in individuals.

Bail – Sum of money paid directly to the court to secure a defendant's pretrial release.

Bond firm – An independent business that will post bail for a defendant for a fee.

Quick Guide: Building Your Professional Online Brand

The following social media sites offer an excellent opportunity to network and build a positive and professional online presence:

1. LINKEDIN (linkedin.com)

Create a professional profile on LinkedIn by including the following elements on this user-friendly professional networking site:

- Upload a professional headshot. In it, wear professional dress clothes and use a soft color backdrop. Many college and university career centers offer professional headshots to their students for free or at a reduced cost.
- Be sure to specify in your profile the field in which you are seeking a job. For example, you could list law enforcement, cybersecurity, forensic psychology, and so forth.
- Include a summary of your most important professional achievements. This could include specific work product that you have produced, awards and honors, and professional achievements related to your field of study.
- List professional work experience related to your field of study. Include dates and at least one bullet point per work experience explaining what you did on the job. Professional work experience can include internships as well.
- Include your higher education credentials. List your degree(s), name of academic institution(s), graduation dates, and anticipated graduation date if applicable.
- List your specific skills and areas of expertise. If you possess a specific skill set that is desirable to employers, such as proficiency in a foreign language or advanced computer skills, include this in your LinkedIn public profile.

Finally, look to connect with industry professionals in your desired career field on LinkedIn.

2. FACEBOOK (facebook.com) AND TWITTER (twitter.com)

Even though Facebook and Twitter are not exclusively professional networking sites liked LinkedIn is, these two social media sites can still be used as professional networking sites. Just be sure that if you use these forms of social media, you keep them professional at all times. Here are some tips when using Facebook and Twitter for networking:

- Look for networking opportunities with industry professionals, companies, and agencies that use these same sites in your given field of study.
- Engage in Twitter chats around a specific hashtag of interest or relevance to your career field. Similarly, look for Facebook discussion boards with similar topics.
- Follow employers in your career field. Often internship and employment opportunities are posted through these social media outlets.
- Post only images and messages that are appropriate in a professional setting.
- Avoid using profanity in your message posts and image captions.
- Avoid discussing controversial subjects like politics and religion on these social media sites.
- Avoid images or posts related to alcohol consumption.
- Include a video that can serve as your "elevator pitch" to prospective employers. Make it about 1 minute long. Wear professional dress clothes in the video, make sure there is no background noise, and practice until the video is flawless.

3. PINTEREST (pinterest.com) AND INSTAGRAM (instagram.com)

Pinterest and Instagram enable you to provide a visual appeal to building your professional online brand. Think about the following tips when using these visual social media sites:

- Post a résumé. Both Pinterest and Instagram offer a user-friendly medium to get an image of your professional résumé out for public consumption.
- Follow prospective employers and industry professionals who use these same social media sites.
- Post images from professional events you attend, such as conferences and career fairs.
- Include a professional headshot of yourself as one of your images.
- Avoid posting any images that would not convey professionalism. Avoid images with alcohol or individuals engaged in questionable behaviors.

QUICK GUIDE: HOW TO DRESS AS A BUSINESS PROFESSIONAL

When interviewing in the field of criminal justice, you should always assume the dress code is business professional unless you are told differently. The way you dress makes a big impression for prospective internships and employment opportunities. Keep in mind the following tips when you hear the term "business professional dress":

- Purchase a black or navy suit. You do not want suit colors that are loud and will draw negative attention.
- Choose dress shirts and blouses that are a solid color and match well with your suit.
- If wearing a tie, make sure it is a solid neutral color that matches well with your professional dress attire. Avoid ties with intricate designs or images.

- Match your dress socks and stockings well with your overall professional dress outfit. Avoid wearing loud colors and designs that will draw negative attention.
- Wear professional dress shoes that are closed-toed and match well with your overall outfit.
- Make sure that all clothes are clean and neatly pressed.

QUICK GUIDE: BUSINESS PROFESSIONAL GROOMING AND ACCESSORIES

When interviewing in the field of criminal justice, always pay attention to your grooming habits and the types of accessories you wear to the interview. Keep in mind the following tips:

- Do not wear cologne or perfume because it can overpower and other people might find the smell offensive.
- Keep your hair neat and clean. If you have long hair, pull it back in a professional style.
- Maintain neat and clean nails. Forgo any loud nail polish colors and designs that could draw negative attention.
- If you wear jewelry, make sure it is a conservative style. You do not want to wear oversized jewelry or jewelry that can be perceived as being gaudy. Limit your rings to a maximum of one per hand as well.

QUICK GUIDE: PROFESSIONAL VERSUS UNPROFESSIONAL EMAIL

Proper email etiquette is a must for your professional career. Take a look at the following two fictional sample emails to a professor.

Unprofessional Email Example:

From: HotStuff@******.com
To: Dr. Green
Subject: What's up??

hey so I had a flat tire today didnt make it to class so i need the notes from todays lecture

FROM THE REAL WORLD

I actually receive numerous emails such as this unprofessional fictional example each year. One of the fastest ways to burn your professional reputation is through an unprofessional email like the one just shown. There are many common mistakes in this particular email:

1. Unprofessional email address.
2. Unprofessional subject line or no subject line at all.
3. No proper formal address to start the email.
4. No sentence structure or punctuation.

5. No specific information in the email in terms of which class, section number, and so on.

6. Not saying thank you in some capacity, but levying some form of request or demand in the email.

Professional Email Example

From: [student's name]@universityof[name].com
To: Dr. Green
Subject: Missed Class in CJ 100 on February 10

Hello Dr. Green,

I am sorry to inform you, but I missed class today in the 9:30am section of CJ 100 on February 10 due to a flat tire that was completely out of my control. I always attend class lectures and do not want to fall behind on the class lecture material. At your convenience, or during your office hours, can I sit down with you and discuss a few specific points from the missed lecture? Thank you for your time and consideration.

Sincerely,

[Student's Name]

QUICK GUIDE: PROFESSIONAL VERSUS UNPROFESSIONAL REFERENCE/LETTER OF RECOMMENDATION REQUEST

You will eventually need to ask former professors, advisors, and supervisors for reference and/or letter of recommendation requests. In making these requests, you want to always make sure you adhere to professional standards. Take a look at the following two fictional examples for a letter of recommendation request:

Unprofessional Letter of Recommendation Request

Subject: Letter

Dear Dr. Green,

I am writing this email because I need a letter of recommendation from you. I am going to be applying to graduate programs and just found out about application deadlines. The deadline is this Friday. Sorry for the short notice, but I just found out and really need you to write a letter for me because I haven't received a response from other professors yet, and I always did well in your classes. Thank you for doing this for me.

Sincerely,

Desperate Student

FROM THE REAL WORLD

Unfortunately, I receive a lot of recommendation requests just like the unprofessional example just shown. These types of requests do not convey professionalism at all, and they will sometimes even elicit a very curt response back from a faculty member or former supervisor. Here is a breakdown of all that is wrong with this unprofessional letter of recommendation request:

1. Does not include specificity in the subject line. The subject line should include the student's full name followed by "letter of recommendation request."
2. Presumptuous and demanding. When emailing someone for a letter of recommendation, you should never presume or demand that your potential recommender will write the letter. Instead, start by asking something like, "I am writing to ask if you would be comfortable writing a letter of recommendation for me."
3. Lack of specific details. What specific program(s) is the applicant applying to? What are the applicant's career goals, and how will this graduate program benefit him or her?
4. Not enough notice/too last minute. You should ideally give your letter of recommendation writer a minimum of a few weeks to complete the letter. Not days or hours. It is very unprofessional to give someone last-minute notice and pressure like in this example.
5. Desperation. Never sound desperate in a letter of recommendation request. It cheapens your brand, and no one especially wants to be told they are your last hope for a letter.
6. Lacking specifics on how the recommendation requester knows the potential letter of recommendation writer. You should give specifics on classes taken with this professor, grades received, projects completed, and so on. Also, including an attachment of a résumé is helpful.

Professional Letter of Recommendation Request

Subject: [Student's Name]—Letter of Recommendation Request

Dear Dr. Green,

I am writing this email to inquire if you would be comfortable writing me a letter of recommendation for graduate school. I am applying to University of X's graduate program in clinical psychology in hopes of entering in fall 2020. This program would fulfill my ultimate career goal of becoming a forensic psychologist. The deadline for the letter of recommendation is in four weeks, on March 15, 2018.

I have taken three of your classes over the past four years at the University of Y. I earned an A+ in all three of these courses, and in your Research Methods course I won an undergraduate research competition for my paper on psychopathy in fall 2018. For your convenience, I have attached a copy of my résumé as well.

Thank you for your time and consideration. I look forward to your response.

Sincerely,

[Student's Name]

Should your prospective letter of recommendation writer agree to complete your letter of recommendation, you need to then send this person all of the specific details needed to complete the letter: how it will be submitted, email address or account where it is to be submitted, specific details needed in the letter, and the due date. If a physical letter is to be mailed, you need to provide an envelope with the physical mailing address and the adequate postage required to send the letter. Best practice is to send a handwritten thank-you note after he or she completes your letter of recommendation.

Credits

Chapter 1
1.1: Kathy Hutchins/Shutterstock.com; 1.2: Kathy Hutchins/Shutterstock.com; 1.3: Stuart Monk/Shutterstock.com

Chapter 2
2.1: Brian A Jackson/Shutterstock.com; 2.2: © Weerapat1003 | Megapixl.com; 2.3: Monkey Business Images/Shutterstock.com

Chapter 3
3.1: © Janis Smits | Dreamstime.com; 3.2: © Rvlsoft | Megapixl.com; 3.3: © Nito100 | Megapixl.com

Chapter 4
4.1: Andrey_Popov/Shutterstock.com

Chapter 5
5.1: optimarc/Shutterstock.com; 5.2: tongcom photographer/Shutterstock.com

Chapter 6
6.1: © Chelsdo | Megapixl.com; 6.2: © Ibrakovic | Megapixl.com

Chapter 7
7.1: Beth Swanson/Shutterstock.com; 7.2: f11photo/Shutterstock.com; 7.3: Karen Roach/Shutterstock.com

Chapter 8
8.1: © Olivier26 | Megapixl.com; 8.2: 3D_creation/Shutterstock.com; 8.3: Pessmaster/Shutterstock.com

Chapter 9
9.1: Sean Locke Photography/Shutterstock.com; 9.2: Kolidzei/Shutterstock.com; 9.3:Dzelat/Shutterstock.com; 9.4: pixabay.com

Chapter 10
10.1: © Tomloel | Megapixl.com; 10.2: Belenos/Shutterstock.com; 10.3: Sebastian Duda/Shutterstock.com

Chapter 11
11.1: © Txking | Megapixl.com; 11.2: © Lucidwaters | Megapixl.com; 11.3: Sherry Saye/Shutterstock.com

Chapter 12
12.1: Prath/Shutterstock.com; 12.2: Zoka74/Shutterstock.com; 12.3: igorstevanovic/Shutterstock.com; 12.4: Willrow Hood/Shutterstock.com

Index